W9-DJJ-456

# IRISH PLAYS AND PLAYWRIGHTS

From a photograph by Alice Boughton

W. B. YEATS

WITHDRAWN

13-2333

News Bookstore May 29.17 $1.75

# IRISH PLAYS
# AND PLAYWRIGHTS

BY

CORNELIUS WEYGANDT

WITH ILLUSTRATIONS

TOVT
BIEN OV
RIEN

88

Costien College, Students Library Association,

BOSTON AND NEW YORK
HOUGHTON MIFFLIN COMPANY
The Riverside Press Cambridge

Irish literature (English)
Dramatists

PR
8789
W4

5224

COPYRIGHT, 1913, BY CORNELIUS WEYGANDT

ALL RIGHTS RESERVED

*Published February 1913*

5224

822

W54

# PREFACE

THERE are so many who have helped me with this book that I cannot begin to thank them one by one. If I name any, however, there are four I would name together. There is my old friend, long since dead, Lawrence Kelly, of County Wexford, who first told me Irish folk-stories, adding to the wonderment of my boyhood with his tales of Finn McCool, Dean Swift, and "The Red-haired Man." There is Dr. Robert Ellis Thompson, of Philadelphia, who quickened, by his enthusiasm, over "twenty golden years ago," my interest in all things Irish. There is Dr. Clarence Griffin Child, my colleague, who recognized the power of these men I write of in "Irish Plays and Playwrights" when there were fewer to recognize their power than there are to-day. There is Mr. John Quinn, of New York, without whose aid ten years ago the current Irish dramatic movement would not have progressed as it has. He has lent for reproduction here the sketches by Mr. J. B. Yeats of Synge, Mr. George Moore, and Mr. Padraic Colum. All but all of the writers I mention particularly in these chapters have put me under obligation by cheerful response to many letters full of questions as to their work. Mr. James H. Cousins and Mr. S. Lennox Robinson have taken especial trouble in my behalf, and Lady Gregory, Mr. W. B. Yeats, and Mr. George W. Russell have put themselves out in many ways that I might learn of Irish Letters.

UNIVERSITY OF PENNSYLVANIA, December 28, 1912.

# CONTENTS

# ILLUSTRATIONS

# IRISH PLAYS AND PLAYWRIGHTS

## CHAPTER I

### THE CELTIC RENAISSANCE

To the general reader the Celtic Renaissance was a surprise, and even to Irish writers deeply interested in their country the phenomenon or movement, call it which you will, was not appreciated as of much significance at its beginning. Writing in 1892, Miss Jane Barlow was not hopeful for the immediate future of English literature in Ireland; — it seemed to her "difficult to point out any quarter of the horizon as a probable source of rising light." Yet Mr. Yeats had published his "Wanderings of Oisin" three years before; Mr. Russell had already gathered about him a group of eager young writers; and Dr. Hyde was organizing the Gaelic League, to give back to Ireland her language and civilization, and translating from the Gaelic "The Love Songs of Connacht" (1894) into an English of so new and masterful a rhythm, that it was to dominate the style of many of the writers of the movement, as the burden of the verse was to confirm them in the feelings and attitudes of mind, centuries old and of to-day, that are basic to the Irish Gael. Even in 1894, when Mrs. Katherine Tynan Hinkson wrote the

article that for the first time brought before America so
many of the younger English poets, all that she said
of the Renaissance was, "A very large proportion of the
Bodley Head poets are Celts, — Irish, Welsh, Cornish."
She had scarcely so spoken when there appeared the little
volume, "The Revival of Irish Literature," whose chapters, reprinted addresses delivered before she had spoken
by Sir Charles Gavan Duffy and Dr. George Sigerson and
Dr. Douglas Hyde, turned the attention of the younger
men to literature, the fall of Parnell and the ensuing decline of political agitation having given them a chance to
think of something else than politics. In 1895 all the English-speaking world that heeds letters was talking of the
Celtic Renaissance, so quickly did news of it find its way to
men, when it was once more than whispered of abroad. It
was as frequently referred to then as "The Irish Renaissance," because Ireland contributed most to it and because it was in Ireland that it acquired its most definite
purpose. This purpose was to retell in English the old Irish
legends and the still current Irish folk - songs, and to
catch and preserve the moods of Irish men and women of
to-day, especially those moods which came to them out
of their brooding over Ireland, its history, its landscape,
the temper of its people. It would be absurd, of course,
to regard all of the writing of the movement as a result of
a definite literary propaganda, but the very fact that we
instinctively speak of the Celtic Renaissance as a movement rather than as a phenomenon proves that it was
that in part. But even that part of it that was a result
of propaganda came not from an intention to realize the

tenets of the propaganda, but from the kindling of Irish
hearts by thoughts that came of the propaganda, thoughts
of the great past of Ireland, of its romance of yesterday
and to-day, of its spirituality.

It is not so easy to account for the less quickening
of the other Celtic countries by the forces that brought
about the Renaissance. Renan, in his " Poetry of the
Celtic Races" (1859), and Arnold, in his "On the Study
of Celtic Literature" (1867), had roused all the Celtic
countries to an interest in their old literature, an interest
that extended much further than discussion of the authenticity of Macpherson's "Ossian " or of the proper treatment of Arthurian stories, until then the Ultima Thule of
talk on things Celtic. Frenchman and Englishman both
had spoken to Wales and Brittany, the Highlands of Scotland and the Isle of Man, as well as to Ireland, and it
does not altogether explain to say that Ireland listened
best because in Ireland there was a greater sense of nationality than in these other lands. Ireland did listen, it is
true, and, listening, developed popularizers of the old tales
such as Mr. Standish James O'Grady and Dr. P. W.
Joyce, to pass knowledge of them along to the men of letters. It is hardly true, indeed, to say that Ireland had a
greater sense of nationality than Brittany or Wales. Brittany, of course, since her tongue other than her native
Breton was French, gave what was given to the movement in other than Breton in French. Cornwall may
hardly be called a Celtic country, but if it may it is easy
to account for its slight interest in the movement by the
little that was preserved of its old literature and by the

little it had of distinctive oral tradition to draw upon. And yet, I think, had Sir Arthur T. Quiller-Couch been born ten years later Cornwall had not wanted a shanachie. Wales, too, gave little to English literature as the result of the Renaissance, because, perhaps, her chiefest literary energy is in her native language. Wales was proud of George Meredith, whose Welsh ancestry is more evident in his work than is his Irish ancestry, but not only is his writing representative of Great Britain rather than of any one part of Great Britain, but his say had been said before the movement began. The writing of Mr. Ernest Rhys underwent a change because of his interest in the Celtic Renaissance, but Wales has little writing outside of his to point to as a result of the awakening. In Scotland, William Sharp, whose "Lyra Celtica" (1896) was a prominent agent in bringing the Renaissance before the world, was transformed into another writer by it. His work as "Fiona Macleod," both prose and verse, was very different from his earlier work in prose and verse. Mr. Neil Munro, too, was affected by the Renaissance, and in the tales of "The Lost Pibroch" (1896) and in the novels of "John Splendid" (1898) and "Gillian the Dreamer" (1899) and "The Children of Tempest" (1903) he reveals an intimacy with Highland life such as informs the writing of no other novelist of our day. Of recent years Mr. Munro has wandered farther afield than his native Argyll, and, I feel, to the lessening of the beauty of his writing. In the Isle of Man, T. E. Brown had been striving for years to put into his stories in verse the fast-decaying Celtic life of his country, but even with his example and with all that has been done since the Renaissance began, in the preservation of Manx folk-lore and in the recording of vanishing Manx customs, no writer of Brown's power has been developed, or in fact any writer of powers equal to those of the best men of the younger generation in the other Celtic lands. It is with the Celtic Renaissance as it appears in Ireland, then, that I have to deal chiefly in this book, as it is only in Ireland, of the countries that retain a Celtic culture, that the movement is the dominating influence in writing in English; and it is with the drama only that I have now to deal, though when a playwright is a poet or a story-teller, too, I have written of his attainment in verse and tale also. Had I been writing five years ago, I should have said that it was in poetry that the Celtic Renaissance had attained most nobly, but since then the drama has had more recruits of power than has poetry, and it is a question as to which of the two is greater as art. There is no doubt, however, but that the drama has made a stronger and wider appeal, whatever its excellence, than has the verse, and it is therefore of greater significance for its time than is the poetry, whatever the ultimate appraisement will be. Of the men I have written of here, Mr. Yeats and Mr. Russell are to me poets before they are dramatists, and Lionel Johnson, whose only direct connection with the dramatic movement was his beautiful prologue in verse to the first performances of "The Irish Literary Theatre" in 1899, is to me a poet of a power as great as theirs.

One wonders, at first thought, that Ireland had never until our day given to English literature a novelist of first rank. The Irishman is famous the world over as a story-teller, but neither in romance nor in the story of character had he reached first power, reached a position where he might be put alongside of other Europeans as novelist. No Irishman from the time of Scott on, until Mr. George Moore wrote "Esther Waters" (1894), had written a story that might stand the inevitable comparison with the work of Thackeray and Dickens, Meredith and Mr. Hardy. Of Mr. George Moore I have written in detail below.

Miss Edgeworth may have taught Scott his manner of delineating peasant character, but her comparatively little power is revealed when you put her beside Miss Austen, and so it is all the way down the list to our own day. There are many contemporary story-tellers who have managed well the tale, but what Irish novelist of to-day other than Mr. Moore bulks big, can be compared to even lesser men, like Scotland's Mr. Neil Munro or Dartmoor's Mr. Phillpotts?

Lady Gilbert (Rosa Mulholland) has written many pleasant stories of Irish life, and Mrs. Katherine Tynan Hinkson has followed worthily in her footsteps. Equally pleasant, but lighter and more superficial, is the writing of the two ladies who subscribe their names "E. Œ. Somerville and Martin Ross." Their "Some Experiences of an Irish R. M." (1899) and their "All on the Irish Shore" (1903) are like so much of the Irish writing of a generation ago, — Irish stories by Irish people for English people to laugh at.

The Hon. Emily Lawless has written many kinds of

stories about the West Coast, reaching almost to greatness in her "Grania" (1892). In the short story, Miss Jane Barlow, accused of superficiality by many Irish critics and as eagerly declared to get the very quality of Connemara peasant life by others, has sure power and a charm all her own. No one who reads "Irish Idylls" (1892) will stop at that collection. Mr. Seumas MacManus is as truly a shanachie as the old story-tellers that yet tell the old tales about peat fires in Donegal. "Through the Turf Smoke" (1899) and "In Chimney Corners" (1899) and "Donegal Fairy Stories" (1900) are alike in having the accent of the spoken story, but when the last word is said you cannot admit their author to be more than a clever entertainer. The Rev. Dr. Sheehan, although you will find him writing about the effect of the Irish Renaissance in remote parishes in the South, has not subscribed to its ideals, but continues the fashion of story-writing of an earlier generation. "Luke Delmege" (1900) is, however, an interesting character study, and "My New Curate" (1899) very illuminative of the conservatism of the peasantry.

Mr. Shan Bullock, writing of the farmers and farm laborers of the North, has not unwisely gone to Mr. Hardy to learn his art. "Irish Pastorals" (1901) is racy of Fermanagh as "Tess" is of Wessex. "The Squireen" (1903) is a strong and gloomy story. From "By Thrasna River" (1895) to "Dan the Dollar" (1905), Mr. Bullock did no story without power in it. Ireland still looks to him as it looked to Mr. William Buckley, ten years ago, for better work. "Croppies Lie Down" brought Mr. Buckley before the public in 1903, but his writing since then has fallen far short of this his best book. Now, however, the young man with a future, in the estimation of many, is Mr. James Stephens. There is more hope in him, in his twenties, than there is now in "George A. Birmingham" (Rev. J. O. Hannay), another man who ten years ago was, like Mr. Buckley, a young man of promise. "The Seething Pot" (1904) was a serious study of conditions in Ireland, but since its author conceived of the character of the Rev. Joseph John Meldon, he has found it more discreet to continue the adventures of that clergyman than to write seriously out of his own varied experience of West-Country Irish life.

It is perhaps because the energy that in many countries goes into the writing of the essay is absorbed in controversy in Ireland that in the past Ireland has produced few essayists. In the battles of the dramatic movement with the patriotic societies and with the official class, Mr. Yeats and Mr. Moore have dealt good blows, and Mr. Russell and "John Eglinton" (Mr. W. K. Magee) have led the disputants out of their confusion. Among these men, "John Eglinton" is the one who has thrown his greatest energy into the essay, almost all his energy, and in it, in the chapters of "Two Essays on the Remnant" (1896), "Pebbles from a Brook" (1901), and "Bards and Saints" (1906), he has written with subtlety and illumination.

In the collection and clarification and retelling of folk-literature William Larminie and Lady Gregory and Dr. Hyde stand out as the leading workers. Mr. Larminie's

"West Irish Folk-Tales" (1895) are model work of their kind, as are Lady Gregory's several books, of which I speak in detail later. The work of Dr. Hyde is the most important work of this sort, however, and it is not too much to say, as I intimated at the outset, that, without his translation of "The Love Songs of Connacht" (1894) and "The Religious Songs of Connacht" (1906), the prose of the movement would never have attained that distinction of rhythm which reveals English almost as a new language. I would gladly have written at length of Dr. Hyde, but he has chosen to write his plays in Irish as well as most of his verses. Yet so winning are the plays as translated by Lady Gregory, and so greatly have they influenced the folk-plays in English of the Abbey Theatre, that there is almost warrant for including him. I cannot, of course, but I must at least bear testimony to the many powers of these plays. Dr. Hyde can be trenchant, when satire is his object, as in "The Bursting of the Bubble" (1903); or alive with merriment when merriment is his desire, as in "The Poorhouse" (1903); or full of quiet beauty when he writes of holy things, as in the "Lost Saint" (1902). There are many other playwrights in Irish than Dr. Hyde, but as no other plays in Irish than his have reacted to any extent on the plays in English of the movement, I do not consider them, my object in this book being to consider the dramatic writing in English of the Celtic Renaissance, with relation to its value as a contribution to the art of English letters. That there is a great deal else in the Celtic Renaissance than its drama, I would, however, emphasize, though it is true that every man of first literary power in the movement, except Lionel Johnson and "John Eglinton," has tried his hand on at least one Irish play. That Johnson would have come to write drama I firmly believe, for in drama he could have reconciled two of the four loves that were his life. He could not have put his love of Winchester, his school, or his love of the classics into plays, but his love of Ireland and his love of the Catholic Church would have blended, I believe, into plays, still with the cloistered life of the seventh century, that would have rivaled "The Hour-Glass," and plays about the "Ninety-Eight" that would have rivaled "Cathleen ni Houlihan."

There are many other poets, though, of the Celtic Renaissance that are of powers only short of greatness, Nora Hopper Chesson chief among them. Only Mr. Yeats of them all has more "natural falterings" in his verse than she. Mrs. Hinkson, too, whose name has come inevitably into these pages from time to time, is a poet with as sure a place in English literature to-day as has Mrs. Meynell. Beginning, like Mr. Yeats, as an imitator of the Pre-Raphaelites, Mrs. Hinkson found herself in little poems on moods of her own and moods of landscape. She writes also of her love of God, of St. Francis, and of Ireland. "Moira O'Neill" (Mrs. Skrine), too, has a sure place, her verses crying out her homesickness for Ireland, and redolent, every line of them, of the countryside. "The Passing of the Gael" is known wherever there are Irish emigrants, but there are other verses of "Ethna Carberry" (Mrs. Anna Johnstone MacManus) that are

DOUGLAS HYDE

as fine as this. Mrs. Dora Sigerson Shorter is a balladist of stark power, and Miss Eva Gore-Booth a lyric poet whose natural lilt no preoccupation with mysticism can for more than a moment obscure.

Mr. Herbert Trench has of recent years surrendered to theatrical management, but there is to his credit a substantial accomplishment of lyrical verse that George Meredith would have approved. Mr. Colum's verse I have spoken of below, incidentally, in considering his plays. A distinct talent, too, is Mr. Seumas O'Sullivan's, whose "Twilight People" (1905) indicates by its title the quality of his verse.

I have mentioned all these writers, some known in America, but others utterly unknown, not only to indicate the relation of the drama to the other literary forms of the Renaissance, but to account, perhaps in some measure, for the literary quality of the plays themselves. They are written, as plays in English during the past century have too seldom been written, by writers who have read widely in all forms of literature and to whom words are, if not "the only good," at least a chief good. Mr. Russell and Mr. Yeats have sent all the younger men who would write to the masterpieces of the world, telling them to get what they need of the technique of the centre, to know the best in the world, but to write of the ground under their feet. The plays are, as I have said, written, many of them, by men who are widely read, and by men whose friends are writers of some other form of literature, by men who wish their work in drama to be of as high intention as the work of their friends who are poets or essayists or writers of stories. All the other writing of the Renaissance has, then, contributed to make the drama what it is, and one must, if one would see the drama in relation to the Ireland of our day, know what is the accomplishment of the other sorts of writing of the Renaissance.

# CHAPTER II

## THE PLAYERS AND THEIR PLAYS, THEIR AUDI-ENCE AND THEIR ART

THE drama of the Celtic Renaissance is of an ancestry as mixed as is that of the people of Ireland themselves. There is less in it perhaps of the Gael than in them, for Gaelic literature, until to-day, never approached nearer to the drama than the dialogue, the racy give-and-take of two characters, alike of lively imagination, whether gentle or simple. But even had the colloquies of St. Patrick and Oisin, of Dean Swift and his man Jack, of the Lout and his Mother, been developed, by 1890, to a drama as finished as that of Congreve or Goldsmith, Sheridan or Wilde, those who would have their plays abreast of our time would have gone, just as, with the conditions as they are, the dramatists of the Renaissance did go, to Ibsen and M. Maeterlinck, like all the rest of the world. It is a matter of reproach, in the estimation of many patriotic Irishmen, that Mr. Martyn learned his art of Ibsen, and Mr. Yeats a part of his of M. Maeterlinck, but that attitude is as unreasonable as that which would reproach the Irish Industries Organization Society for studying Danish dairy farms or Belgian chickeries. It is only the technique of the foreigners, modern or ancient, Scandinavian or Greek, that the Abbey dramatists have acquired or have adapted to Irish usage. Stories are world-wide, of course, the folk-tale told by the Derry hearthside being told also in the tent in Turkestan — Cuchulain kills his son as Rustum does, and the Queen of Fairy lures Bran oversea as Venus lures Tannhäuser to the Hörselberg. It is in character, in ideals, in atmosphere, in color, that drama must be native, and in color and in atmosphere, in ideals and in character the Abbey Theatre drama is Irish. Reading of life and style are personal qualities, qualities of the artist himself, though they, too, may take tone and color from national life, as in the drama of many of the Abbey dramatists they do. These dramatists have been more resolutely native, in fact, many of them, than the national dramatists of other countries have been, of France and Germany to-day, of the Spain or the England of the Renaissance. It would seem idle to be saying this were not the contention being raised all the time by certain patriotic groups of Irishmen in America as well as in Ireland that the new drama is not a native drama. It is, as a matter of fact, no less natively Irish than the Elizabethan drama is natively English; it is really more native, for no part of it of moment veils its nationality under even so slight a disguise as "the Italian convention" of that drama. The new Irish drama is more native in its stories than is the Elizabethan drama, as these stories, even when they are stories found in variant forms in other countries, are given the tones of Irish life. The structural forms and the symbolic presentation of ideas of which the Abbey dramatists have availed themselves have no more denationalized their plays than has the Church, a Church from oversea, to

which most of them belong, denationalized the Irish
people.

Synge, the master dramatist of the new movement,
while he does not reproduce the average Irishman, is just
as natively Irish in his extravagance and irony as the old
folk-tale of the "Two Hags"; Lady Gregory in her farces
is in a similar way representative of the riot of West-
Country imagination; and Mr. Yeats, if further removed
from the Irishmen of to-day, is very like, in many of his
moods, to the riddling bards of long ago. The later
men, many of them, are altogether Irish, representative
of the folk of one or another section of the country, Mr.
Murray and Mr. Robinson of Cork, Mr. Mayne and
Mr. Ervine of Down, Mr. Colum and Mr. Boyle of the
Midlands.

One need not say that the Irishman is a born actor; all
the Celts are famed for "the beautiful speaking"; for eloquence; for powers of impersonation; for quick changes of
mood; for ease in running the gamut of the emotions. Of
these things come art of the stage, and these things are
the Irishman's in fullest measure. The Abbey Players
have, however, gone abroad for some elements of their
art, perhaps for their repose of manner, a quietude that is
not the quietude of moodiness, a condition not unusual in
the Irishman; and in addition to this repose of manner,
which is fundamental and common to their presentation
of realistic modern plays and of poetic plays of legendary
times, for a slowness and dignity of gesture in the plays
of legend, which is perhaps a borrowing from the classic
stage. Their repose of manner may come from modern

France; at least so held Mr. Yeats, pointing to such a source in "Samhain" of 1902.

The other day [he writes] I saw Sara Bernhardt and DeMax in "Phèdre," and understood where Mr. Fay, who stage-manages the National Theatrical Company, had gone for his model. For long periods the performers would merely stand and pose, and I once counted twenty-seven quite slowly before anybody on a fairly well-filled stage moved, as it seemed, so much as an eyelash. The periods of stillness were generally shorter, but I frequently counted seventeen, eighteen, or twenty before there was a movement. I noticed, too, that the gestures had a rhythmic progression. Sara Bernhardt would keep her hands clasped over, let us say, her right breast for some time, and then move them to the other side, perhaps, lowering her chin till it touched her hands, and then, after another long stillness, she would unclasp them and hold one out, and so on, not lowering them till she had exhausted all the gestures of uplifted hands. Through one long scene DeMax, who was quite as fine, never lifted his hand above his elbow, and it was only when the emotion came to its climax that he raised it to his breast. Beyond them stood a crowd of white-robed men who never moved at all, and the whole scene had the nobility of Greek sculpture, and an extraordinary reality and intensity. It was the most beautiful thing I had ever seen upon the stage, and made me understand, in a new way, that saying of Goethe's which is understood everywhere but in England, "Art is art because it is not nature." Of course, our amateurs were poor and crude beside those great actors, perhaps the greatest in Europe, but they followed them as well as they could, and got an audience of artisans, for the most part, to admire them for doing it.

With these words of Mr. Yeats, written ten years ago, in my memory, it was arresting to hear ten years later a somewhat similar comparison of the acting of the Irish Players to the acting of yesterday on the French stage.

A man who in the late eighties and early nineties had spent seven years as an art student in Paris saw the Abbey Players in Boston. In Paris he had gone frequently to the Théâtre Français, and only there, he said, before he saw the Irish Players, had he seen acting so full of dignity, but never at all before acting so natural.

There is possible, too, however, a native origin for this repose of manner, or perhaps it would be truest to say that it is a blending, like the dramas themselves, of native and foreign elements. Speaking of "Cathleen ni Houlihan" in the notes to his "Collected Works" of 1908, Mr. Yeats says, "I cannot imagine this play, or any folk-play of our school, acted by players with no knowledge of the peasant, and of the awkwardness and stillness of bodies that have followed the plow, or too lacking in humility to copy these things without convention or caricature." Here, too, he refers to the "quiet movement and careful speech which has given our players some little fame" as "arising partly out of deliberate opinion and partly out of the ignorance of the players."

Undoubtedly Mr. Fay knew the still ways of the peasant, and I do not doubt that he was influenced by such knowledge and did in some degree train his actors to bring their movements on the stage in accord with the "awkwardness and stillness of bodies that have followed the plow." But since there are ways of the peasant that are far from still, it is likely, too, that he was led to select such movements, instead of the vehement gesture and lively facial expression that are just as characteristic of the peasant, by a memory of the restrained acting of the

French stage. It is likely, too, that the very inexperience
and lack of knowledge of artifice to which Mr. Yeats refers was an element in making the art of the company
what it became. But it is not altogether impossible that
certain traditions of the English stage — of the statuesque
acting of the Kembles, for instance — had come down
into the time of Mr. Fay's stage experience, to those days
before he became stage manager of the performances of
"The Daughters of Erin" in 1900, and that these traditions influenced his training of the company that was to
attain to a new art of the stage.

Before this there had been two series of performances
in Dublin, each of a week's duration, by "The Irish Liter-
ary Theatre," one in 1899, and the other in 1900, with
English actors gathered together in London by Mr.
George Moore; and another week's series followed in
1901 by the Benson Company and some amateurs of the
Gaelic League under the leadership of Dr. Douglas Hyde.
It was the performances of "The Countess Cathleen" of
Mr. Yeats and of "The Heather Field" of Mr. Martyn
at the Antient Concert Rooms in Dublin, respectively
May 8 and 9, 1899, by "The Irish Literary Theatre,"
that inaugurated the drama of the Celtic Renaissance,
fully a year before there came into being the group of amateurs that were to bring that drama home to Ireland as no
players who inherited the standards and conventions of
the English stage could possibly have brought it home.

It is Mr. Fay's distinction to have been, as I have intimated, the leader who started these players on the long
way to their new art. Such leadership his record hardly

augured. It was in the very lowest forms of vaudeville, in what is the analogue abroad of our negro minstrelsy, that Mr. Fay had his stage experience, a stage experience that had made him well enough known in burlesque rôles to make it difficult for him to assume with success serious rôles in the early years of the National Dramatic Company. Because of this old association, Dublin audiences insisted in 1902 in seeing humor in his Peter Gillane in "Cathleen ni Houlihan." For all this past, however, Mr. Fay was intent on serious drama, and, with the precept and example of Mr. Russell and Mr. Yeats always present to him in the early days of the National Theatre Company, and with what he had gathered from the experimental performance of Irish plays by "The Irish Literary Theatre," he advanced surely in his art until his withdrawal from the company in January, 1908. His loss was compensated for only by the results of his training of other actors, such as Miss Sara Allgood and Mr. Arthur Sinclair, who on certain roads have outrun their master. When I saw Mr. Fay in 1902, in the little hall in Camden Street, Dublin, with no knowledge of what his stage experience had been, I accepted him at once for what he was, a finished "character" actor of poise and confidence, a dignified figure for all his stature and his predilection for comedy, and the possessor of a speaking voice whose natural pleasantness he had made into something higher than pleasantness by his art in the use of it, if it never attained the resonance and nobility of phrasing of that of his brother, Mr. Frank J. Fay. It was a memorable experience to me, that of that August evening in 1902 on

which I was taken to Camden Street to a rehearsal of the
Irish National Dramatic Company. Our guide was Mr.
James H. Cousins, whose "Racing Lug" and "Connla"
were among the plays produced in the following autumn
and which that night were in rehearsal. He piloted us
to an entranceway by the side of a produce shop. We
knocked on the door and waited, and waited. We knocked
again, and at last heard steps coming nearer and nearer.
The door opened and revealed a young man in work-a-
day black suit and derby, with a candle in one hand and
a property spear in the other. He conducted us down a
narrow, drafty hallway, into a hall in which were wooden
benches as rude as those in the bandstand of a backwoods
country fair in the States, and a slightly raised platform
at the farther end. We were soon in eager conversation
with young store clerks and typists and artisans who were
about to set to work at that in which their hearts lay, the
interpreting of plays out of Ireland's heart. It was good
talk we listened to from those young men and women,
boys and girls all of them in their fervor and zest and high
aim. Their enthusiasm carried through "Connla,"
"The Racing Lug," and "Deirdre" with real impressiveness. Of Mr. Cousins's two plays one was realistic of
the north of Ireland shore life of to-day, and the other,
"Connla," like Mr. Russell's "Deirdre," made out of
Ireland's heroic age.

Of the actors we met that night, but Miss Walker
(Maire ni Shiubhlaigh) was with the Irish Players on their
American tour of 1911–12, and even she has not been con-
tinuously with them since 1902. The amateurs had then

but begun, under the direction of Mr. Fay, on the slow fashioning of themselves into the finished folk-actors they proved themselves in America. But even this acting, so little removed from that of amateurs at these rehearsals, had distinction, the distinction of fidelity to life in "The Racing Lug," the distinction of possession by dream in "Deirdre"; and let it be remembered, too, that it was a rehearsal without costume, and that one had to be carried away from the conventional dress of the Dublin streets, and had to be made to feel that the characters in "The Racing Lug" were primitive fishermen, and the people of "Connla" and "Deirdre" the people of Ireland's Homeric age.

Miss Maire T. Quinn, Mr. T. Dudley Digges, Mr. P. J. Kelly, with Miss Walker and the brothers Fay, — Mr. W. G. Fay and Mr. Frank J. Fay, — were then the leading actors of the company. The playwrights, too, took part in their own or their fellows' plays in the lesser rôles, Mr. Russell sometimes playing the druid in his "Deirdre" and Mr. Colum carrying a spear or wearing a pea-jacket as need was. One circumstance or another, politics or need, gradually lost the company every one of these actors that took part in its first performances in 1902. There were comparatively few changes, though, until 1904, the year in which Miss Horniman, "a generous English friend," took for them the old Mechanic Institute Theatre and, rebuilding it in part, turned it over to the Irish National Dramatic Company for six years. Up to this time the actors had received no pay, giving their services for love of country and of art, but with the more frequent performances and their attendant rehearsals it became necessary to take a large part of the time of the leading men and women, and then, of course, they had to be paid. Before the opening of the Abbey Theatre, three of the chief actors, Miss Quinn and Mr. Digges and Mr. Kelly, came to this country to appear in Irish plays in the Irish Section of the St. Louis Fair. The public that gathered in St. Louis was not prepared for the new drama, being more used to the musical play of the type Mr. Olcott has made familiar in America, or to the Bowery Irishman of the Harrigan plays, or to the gross caricatures, Galwayed and ape-accoutred, of the before-curtain interlude of the variety show. As a result the former National Players protested against the policy of the Irish Section and returned to New York. Miss Walker was the principal actress of the company after Miss Quinn's departure to America, and upon Miss Walker's withdrawal in 1905 the burden of the chief women's rôles fell upon Miss Allgood.

Mr. W. G. Fay and Mr. Frank J. Fay were still the leading men of the company, creating the principal characters of all the plays of Synge and of those of Mr. Yeats and Lady Gregory that were produced before 1908. Early in this year, as I have said, Mr. and Mrs. W. G. Fay and Mr. F. J. Fay left the company, and, coming to America in the spring, played "The Rising of the Moon" and "A Pot of Broth" in New York. They made, unfortunately, no great success in their appearances, as their plays were not presented in bills devoted solely to Irish plays, but as curtain-raisers to the usual conventional farce. Almost all the

actors whom I have mentioned as leaving the National
Players eventually found their way into the conventional
plays, but almost none of them made successes there
comparable in any degree to their successes in folk-drama
or in plays out of old Irish legend. Nor can it be said
that actors trained in the dominant forms of present-day
English drama, even when so skilled as Mrs. Patrick
Campbell, were wholly satisfying in their assumption of
rôles in the plays of the Renaissance. It was Miss Allgood,
as chief musician in the London performances of Mr.
Yeats's "Deirdre" in 1908, who won the greatest approval from the London critics, and not Mrs. Campbell
as Deirdre herself.

Miss Allgood had played principal parts with the Abbey
Company from 1904 on. In 1906, her sister, who plays
under the name of Miss Maire O'Neill, came into the
company, assuming the more romantic rôles with a success as great as that of Miss Allgood in character parts and
comedy. From 1906 they have shared the principal women's rôles, but, owing to Miss O'Neill's inability to come
to America in the fall of 1911, Miss McGee fell heir to
many of her rôles. After the departure of the Messrs.
Fay, Mr. Sinclair, Mr. O'Donovan, and Mr. Kerrigan
became the leading men. It is not altogether accurate,
however, to speak of any actor or actress of the company
as leading man or leading woman, for not only is one "a
leading lady" one night, as was Miss McGee as Pegeen
Mike in "The Playboy of the Western World" on the
American tour, and one of the village girls in "The Well
of the Saints" the next night, but the men and women

alternate in the same parts on different nights, as, for instance, on the American tour Cathleen ni Houlihan was played now by Miss Allgood and now by Miss Walker.

The fact that few of the actors who have learned their art with the Irish National Dramatic Society have achieved greatly in other drama is perhaps a proof that their powers are limited to the folk-drama and the legendary drama that comprises almost the entire repertoire of the company. Miss Allgood was, it is true, lent to Mr. Poel for the performances of "Measure for Measure" in the spring of 1908, and won an unquestioned success as Isabella, but actors so skilled as the Messrs. Fay have attained no notable success in other than Irish plays. During the American tour of 1911–12 both Mr. Sinclair and Miss Allgood were much importuned by the managers to accept American engagements, and it is hardly to be doubted but that both could win success in conventional comedy. And yet one feels it was the part of wisdom as well as of loyalty for them to withstand the lure.

The distinguishing characteristic of the art of the Abbey Players is naturalness. It is not that their personalities happen to coincide with certain types of Irish character, but that they know so well the types of the folk-plays, and even the characters who are not types that appear in the folk-plays, that they are able to portray them to the life. The Abbey Players have discarded most of the tricks of the stage, or perhaps it would be truer to say they do not inherit the tricks of the stage or any traditional characterizations of parts. They are taught to allow their demeanor and gesture and expression to rise

SARA ALLGOOD

out of the situation, to "get up" their parts from their
own ideas; and these ideas are interfered with only if they
run definitely counter to the ideas of stage-manager or
author. The smallness of the Abbey Theatre has saved
them from the necessity of heightening effects that they
may carry to the farthest corners of a large house, a necessity that leads so often to over-emphasis by our own
actors. There are less than six hundred seats in the Abbey Theatre (five hundred and sixty-two by actual count),
and it is so arranged that the words uttered on the stage
carry easily without emphasis all over the house.

It is an old saying that the English of Dublin is the
most beautiful English in the world. However that may
be, there can be no doubt whatsoever but that the English that is spoken in Dublin falls on the ear with a mel-
lowness of sound that is a joy to all who cherish proper
speech. In the earlier years of the company Mr. Yeats
was very desirous of having his dramatic verse spoken
with "the half chant men spoke it [poetry] with in old
times." It was in some such way that Mr. Yeats had
tried to have his lines in "The Land of Heart's Desire"
spoken when it was put on at the Avenue Theatre, London, in 1894; and thirteen years later Miss Florence Farr,
whom he believes to speak English more beautifully than
anybody in the world, spoke his dramatic verses in a
"half chant," and his lyrical verses, many of them, to a
definite musical notation, on her American tour of 1907.
It was noticeable, however, when she played one of the
musicians in his "Deirdre" on its later presentations, that
her method of intoning the verses differed a great deal from

their delivery by the regular members of the company. If Mr. Yeats has not changed his views somewhat in regard to the speaking of dramatic verse, he no longer insists on the half chant as it was practiced by Miss Farr, but is content if the actors reproduce its rhythm in "the beautiful speaking" that is characteristic of their art. The most beautiful English that I have ever listened to is the English of Synge as spoken by Mr. O'Donovan in Christy's "romancin'" to Pegeen Mike in the third act of "The Playboy of the Western World." His voice, full and mellow by nature, and in perfect control, responds to all the many changes of emotion that the part demands, the unmatched rhythm of the prose rendered as he renders it carrying one clean out of one's self as one listens. It is only when one comes to one's self on the curtain-fall that one finds one's self wondering, Can this be prose? Surely, never before was prose, English prose, as beautiful to the ear as English verse.

As Miss O'Neill did not come with the Abbey Players to America, we did not have a chance to hear Pegeen Mike's lines spoken with a beauty comparable to Christy's. The part is not one to which Miss Allgood is physically adapted, and Miss McGee is as yet too new to the stage to speak with the confident abandon the lines demand. We did, however, have a chance to hear Miss Allgood's very beautiful musical utterance of the verses given to Cathleen ni Houlihan in this first of the movement's folk-plays, and her equally beautiful speaking of the prose lines of the play. This part of Cathleen ni Houlihan is sufficiently removed from the other parts of the play,

folk-parts, and from the parts of the other folk-plays, to
give us an insight into the versatility of Miss Allgood;
and we saw enough of Mr. Sinclair and Mr. O'Donovan
and Mr. Kerrigan to realize that they, too, could worthily
bear parts in heroic romance.

The rendering of the songs in the plays — it is chiefly
in the plays of Mr. Yeats that they appear — is a distinguishing characteristic of their production. Mr. Yeats
will not have them rendered by what, in the ordinary
sense, is singing. Writing in the notes to volume III of his
"Collected Works "[1] he says: —

No vowel must ever be prolonged unnaturally, no word of
mine must ever change into a mere musical note, no singer
of my words must ever cease to be a man and become an
instrument.

The degree of approach to ordinary singing depends on the
context, for one desires a greater or lesser amount of contrast
between the lyrics and the dialogue according to situation and
emotion and the qualities of players. The words of Cathleen ni
Houlihan about the "white-scarfed riders" must be little more
than regulated declamation; the little song of Leagerie when
he seizes the "Golden Helmet" should in its opening words be
indistinguishable from the dialogue itself. Upon the other hand
Cathleen's verses by the fire, and those of the pupils in "The
Hour-Glass," and those of the beggars in "The Unicorn," are
sung as the country people understand song. Modern singing
would spoil them for dramatic purposes by taking the keenness
and the salt out of the words. The songs in "Deirdre," in Miss
Farr's and in Miss Allgood's setting, need fine speakers of verse
more than good singers; and in these, and still more in the song
of the Three Women in "Baile's Strand," the singers must
remember the natural speed of words. If the lyric in "Baile's

[1] Shakespeare Head Press, Stratford-on-Avon, 1908.

Strand" is sung slowly it is like church-singing, but if sung quickly and with the right expression it becomes an incantation so old that nobody can quite understand it. That it may give this sense of something half-forgotten, it must be sung with a certain lack of minute feeling for the meaning of the words, which, however, must always remain words. The songs in "Deirdre," especially the last dirge, which is supposed to be the creation of the moment, must upon the other hand, at any rate when Miss Farr's or Miss Allgood's music is used, be sung or spoken with minute passionate understanding. I have rehearsed the part of the Angel in "The Hour-Glass" with recorded notes throughout, and believe this is the right way; but in practice, owing to the difficulty of finding a player who did not sing too much the moment the notes were written down, have left it to the player's own unrecorded inspiration, except at the "exit," where it is well for the player to go nearer to ordinary song.

At times Irish actresses who have not come to the stage through the Abbey Company, as has every one of its regular actresses, and every one of its men save Mr. W. G. Fay, have lent it their assistance, as in the instance of Mrs. Patrick Campbell referred to above, and as Miss Darragh did in productions of "The Shadowy Waters" and of "Deirdre" in 1906. It was four years earlier than this, however, that an Irishwoman, better known in her country than either Miss Darragh or Mrs. Patrick Campbell, lent her art to the performance of Cathleen ni Houlihan. "Miss Maud Gonne played very finely," writes Mr. Yeats in recording the incident, "and her great height made Cathleen seem a divine being fallen into our mortal infirmity." With these three exceptions, so far as I have been able to find out, no actors or actresses outside of the company have, since 1902, essayed any other than a subordinate' part. Yet such is the versatility of the company, men and women both, within the range of plays the company feels called upon to present, — folk-drama of to-day and of yesterday in Ireland, folk-history plays, morality plays, and plays in verse out of old legends, — that though there have never been as many as twenty actors in the company there has very seldom been much difficulty in casting a part. Molly Byrne in "The Well of the Saints" and the Wandering Friar of the same play have given the most trouble to the stage directors.

From the very beginning of the Irish National Dramatic Company, Mr. Yeats has been an advocate of scenery that is background chiefly, and in no way divertive of attention from the play itself, its thought, its words, its acting. He would have it, in a way, decorative, but subdued and in harmony with the subject of the play. A very few simple sets suffice for the plays of peasant life, a cottage interior, a village street, a crossroads in a gap of the hills, all to serve the action and the words as background, and to be no more obtrusive than the background of a portrait. It may be that this attitude of Mr. Yeats is in a measure due to his talks with Mr. Gordon Craig, but it is equally true, I think, that some of Mr. Gordon Craig's ideas are due in part to his talks with Mr. Yeats. Equally simple, though of another sort of simplicity, would Mr. Yeats have the scenery for plays out of old legend. "I would like to see," writes Mr. Yeats in "Samhain" of 1902, "poetic drama, which tries to keep at a distance from daily life, that it may keep its emotion untroubled, staged with but two or three colors." Old reds, misty blues, imperial purples, greens that have about them the dimness of haunted woods, and dulled golds have been among the colors used in the legendary plays of Mr. Yeats and in the folk-histories of Lady Gregory, the color schemes being generally either those of Mr. Yeats or of Mr. Robert Gregory, Lady Gregory's son. Scenery and costumes alike are simple. No audience at the Abbey has ever marveled at cycloramic landscape, and no audience and no actress has ever been able to take the joy of the dressmaker and the dressed, of the milliner and the millinered, in gown or hat.

The National Theatre Society, Limited, which is the legal name of the organization that controls the Abbey Theatre Company, may not play what plays it will at the Abbey; the two leading theatres of commerce in Dublin, the Gaiety and the Theatre Royal, having, as Mr. Yeats records, "vigorously opposed" the Abbey being given "a patent as little restricted" as their own. "The Solicitor-General," Mr. Yeats continues, "to meet them halfway, has restricted our patent to plays written by Irishmen or on Irish subjects or to foreign masterpieces, provided these masterpieces are not English." This restriction has not interfered with any feature of the work of the Abbey Theatre, Mr. Yeats believes, save in the building-up of an audience, some people remaining away, perhaps, who might have been attracted had "such bodies as the Elizabethan Stage Society, which brought 'Everyman' to Dublin some years ago, been able to hire the theatre."

No phase of the dramatic movement has been more

interesting and none has been more important than this
building - up of an audience to appreciate the plays.
Whether with the poetic plays of Mr. Yeats and the ironic
extravaganzas of Synge alone, such an audience as has
been built up — an audience estimated by Mr. Yeats in
1906 to consist of four thousand young men and women
— could have been won is problematical; that is, it may
be doubted that the very best the movement has produced would have attracted a sufficient audience to en-
able the company to keep together after the expiration in
1910 of Miss Horniman's guarantee. Certain it is, however, that Lady Gregory's farces were a great help, both
in building up and in holding the Abbey audience. It
was for the purpose of affording comic relief to the plays
of Mr. Yeats and to the first plays of Synge that Lady
Gregory started to create them. They attracted all who
loved laughter and merriness and a loving caricature of
country-folk, — and who do not? — and one of them,
"The Rising of the Moon" (1907), had a distinct patriotic
appeal, as had Mr. Yeats's "Cathleen ni Houlihan,"
which brought some who would not otherwise have come
to the Abbey Theatre. The third most definitely "national" play of the movement, "The Piper" (1908) of
Mr. O'Riordan, may have also drawn some who would
not otherwise have come to the theatre, but if it did so
it brought them there, as did "The Playboy of the Western World " (1907), to object.

The first appeal of the Irish Players, in April, 1902, was
through the "Deirdre" of "A. E.," a play out of old legend, national legend, and "Cathleen ni Houlihan," a

symbolic national play of '98.   Then followed Mr. Cousins's two little plays above referred to; "The Laying of the
Foundations," by Mr. Frederick Ryan, — a realistic satire of Dublin life; and Mr. Yeats's incursion into farce,
"A Pot of Broth." The appeal of the repertoire was
widened in 1903 by the inclusion of plays by Lady Gregory, Mr. Colum, and Synge. "Twenty-five" could give
offense to none in its story of self-sacrificing love, and Mr.
Colum's "Broken Soil," coming as it did after "In the
Shadow of the Glen," would have escaped hostile criticism in such a situation even had it been much more severe
in its portrayal of peasant life in the Midlands than it was.

From the time of "The Countess Cathleen" (1899) to
the time of "In the Shadow of the Glen" (1903), no one
of the plays in the movement had seriously offended any
large section of the public, and the younger generation of
all classes was contributing largely of its intellectual members to the audience of the National Dramatic Company.
The West Britons, the Dublin Castle set, the Trinity College group, were not much interested, and, indeed, that
portion of the theatrical audience that fills the stalls in
the average theatre the English-speaking world over has
never taken very much interest in the plays of the movement, save to protest against "The Rising of the Moon"
as disloyal to England, and to approve, misunderstand-
ing its purpose, "The Playboy of the Western World" as
a savage satire of the Irish Irishman.  The audience that
the movement has built up is an audience of free intelli-
gences, largely from the poorer elements of the public, an
audience that fills the cheaper places in the house.  "The

Pit" of the Abbey Theatre is the envy of all the theatrical managers of Dublin. It is a pit of people young in years or young in heart and mind, who are interested in intellectual things, a group of people largely self-taught, or taught by the Celtic Renaissance, to appreciate fine things. With these has come that element of the intellectuals among the Trinity College set that is interested above all things in Ireland, but this element is not large.

This play and that have attracted, either for purposes of approval or for purposes of disapproval, groups of people outside of the faithful pit that is interested in every sincere portrayal of Irish life. Such a group, from the patriotic societies, prevented the rest of the house from hearing "The Playboy of the Western World," after its first performance on January 26, 1907, for four performances more; and such a group similarly protested against "The Piper," a little more than a year later, because it seemed to the members of the group to be an unpatriotic revelation of the lack of cohesion among Irish political and patriotic factions.

Despite opposition, however, and with new dramatists one by one gaining a place in the repertoire of the company, Mr. Boyle in 1905 and Mr. Robinson in 1908, Mr. Murray in 1910 and Mr. Ervine in 1911, more and more people continued to become interested in the new drama, and by the time Miss Horniman's support, promised in 1904 for six years, was withdrawn at the expiration of that period, the Abbey Theatre was apparently a fixture in the artistic life of Ireland.

It has been the custom, of recent years, for the Abbey

Theatre to begin its Dublin season in October and to continue it on until May, when the company goes to London for a month. In the earlier years, before the company had a home at the Abbey, and even for a year or two after that, performances were not so continuous. Nor are they now given every week or always on every night of the week, the theatre being turned over to the Theatre of Ireland or some other dramatic organization occasionally, and being let, now and then, for lectures or concerts or the like. The London season in May is followed, or preceded sometimes, by visits to other English cities, Manchester and Leeds, Oxford and Cambridge among them; and at home in Ireland, in the intervals between weeks at the Abbey, the company goes to Cork or Belfast for a few performances.

In this country the audiences that attended the performances of the plays of the Abbey Theatre Players were of a very different composition. At their average they included a certain proportion of the younger intellectuals among the Irish-Americans, but very many of these were kept away from the performances, as many, indeed, in Ireland and in England, too, are kept away from the performances, by the opposition in the patriotic societies. In America, as in London and in Manchester, and in the English university towns, it has been largely from among those who are seriously interested in a literary drama that the audiences have been drawn. It was such people as do not habitually go to the theatre, but that are to be found at revivals of old English comedy and Ibsen plays and symphony concerts, that made up the audiences of the Irish Players in America, whether in Boston or in Philadelphia or Chicago. These audiences approximated to the Dublin audiences only in the fact that they were constant in attendance at all the plays of the repertoire. There were, of course, some who came out of curiosity and the love of ruction, but these after all were few. The plays appealed on their merits and won the success that they did win because of their art and their reading of life, and not because of the sensational incidents that had occurred at some of the productions of the company.

The Abbey Theatre has been able to maintain itself successfully in the years that have elapsed since the arrangement between Miss Horniman and the National Theatre Society came to an end. It has begotten many other companies, the Ulster Literary Theatre, best of them all; the Theatre of Ireland; the National Players; the Cork Dramatic Society. It has brought into being a kind of folk-drama that, despite its avowed and evident Scandinavian origin, is a new folk-drama, and it has brought into being, too, a school of dramatists. It has done much more than Mr. Yeats claimed it had done in 1908 when he wrote, "We know that we have already created a taste for sincere and original drama and for sincere, quiet, simple acting. Ireland possesses something which has come out of its own life, and the many failures of dramatic societies which have imitated our work, without our discipline and our independence, show that it could not have been made in any other way." But even were this all it had done, it had done much. What it has done I have attempted to put down in some detail, and to put values upon, in the following pages. Here I wish further to say but this: that I think the dramatic movement the most significant part of the Celtic Renaissance, a movement to me the most original movement in letters the world has known since that movement in Norway which so definitely stimulated it, a movement that gave Björnson and Ibsen to the world.

# CHAPTER III

## MR. WILLIAM BUTLER YEATS

THERE has never been a poet who used better the gifts his country gave him than Mr. Yeats. The heroic legends of Ireland are in his poetry, Irish folk-lore is there, and the look of the country; and a man moulded as only Irish conditions, of old time and of to-day, could mould him, Irish conditions spiritual, intellectual, and physical; a man with eyes on a bare countryside in the gray of twilight, thinking of the stories the peasants tell and of the old legends whose setting this is before him. At this hour, with such surroundings, and in such thought, the Other World is as near to all men as their natures will let it come, and to Mr. Yeats it is very near. Waking dreams come to him at such hours, and he puts them into his verse, waking dreams of his country's legendary past and of its fairy present, and waking dreams born of books of old magic he has read indoors. Now it will be one sort of dream is present, now the other, and now the third, and often two or even all three sorts of dream are intermingled. His volume of prose sketches, "The Celtic Twilight" (1893), gives the title some of his countrymen have fastened on his verse, and the verse of others that take his attitude and use like material, "The Twilight School of Poetry." It is not inapt as giving the quality of most of his writing; but some of his verses have warm sunlight in them, which, strangely, since it is sunlight as it visits Irish shore and mountain, he has deplored. The explanation may be that Mr. Yeats is of those who do not live intensely until the oncoming of night, and so holds out of harmony with his genius the coloring of its moments of lesser energy.

Legends and folk-tales and landscapes and books of mysticism and magic not only give Mr. Yeats the material of his poetry, but suggest its images, its color, and in part its rhythms; but before he found the "faint and nervous" rhythms best fitted to his poetry, and put in it the gray-greens and browns and soft purples and bright whites of Irish landscape, and the symbols from fairy-lore and mythology, he had paid patient heed to certain of the great poets of his language, to Spenser and Blake, to Shelley and William Morris. And in learning the art of drama, which he began to study very carefully after his early plays were tested in "The Irish Literary Theatre," Mr. Yeats has very evidently pondered a good deal on the English morality and taken into account the effects of Greek tragedy as he had before explored M. Maeterlinck and the earlier Ibsen.

As a boy Mr. Yeats wrote in the "Dublin University Review" that the "greatest of the earth" often owned but two aims, "two linked and ardorous thoughts — fatherland and song." Twenty-six years have gone since then and Mr. Yeats is still devoted to poetry and to his country, for all that the Nationalists deplore that his greater interest is now in his art. His art, indeed, he cherishes with an ardor that is akin to the ardor of patriotism; to him, as to Spenser, the master of his youth, poetry is a divine enthusiasm. At first eager to paint, as did and does his father, Mr. J. B. Yeats, he studied in Dublin Arts Schools, but as Nature "wanted a few verses" from him, she sent him "into a library to read bad translations from the Irish, and at last down into Connaught to sit by turf fires." He read, too, Sir Samuel Ferguson, the poet who had done most with Irish legend, and Allingham, who wrote of Irish fairies, and the patriotic poets of the young Ireland group, Davis chief among them. His father, an admirer of Whitman, preached to him the doctrine embodied in the text —

> "Will you seek afar off? You surely come back at last,
> In things best known to you finding the best."

Many influences thus conspired to make Mr. Yeats find his inspiration in Ireland, overcoming, for the time, the denationalizing influences that the art of the centre must always exert. Not only were the national legends and folk-lore constantly with him in these years, but the interest in magic and all things that are hidden. He was one of the Hermetic Society, of which Mr. George W. Russell was the high priest, as early as 1886, but this interest, which has dominated so often in his later poetry, is not to the forefront in "The Wanderings of Oisin" of 1889. The material of the title poem of this volume Mr. Yeats found in the libraries. It recounts the Fenian poet's three hundred years of "dalliance with a demon thing" oversea in three wondrous lands, where were severally pleasure and fighting and forgetfulness, and in each of which Oisin spent a century. It has a half-dramatic frame-work of question and answer between St. Patrick, who appears as upbraider, and the poet, who laments joys gone and the Christian present of Ireland and his own feeble age. Although it is a story Mr. Yeats is telling, the beauties of the poems are lyrical beauties. In exuberance and richness of color it is Mr. Yeats's most typically Irish poem based on legend, and nowhere do his lines go with more lilt, or fall oftener into inevitability of phrase, or more fully diffuse a glamour of otherworldliness. "The Wanderings of Oisin" revealed poetry as unmistakably new to his day as was Poe's to the earliest Victorian days. Beside the title poem another from legend had this new quality, "The Madness of King Goll," with its refrain that will not out of memory, "They will not hush, the leaves a-flutter round me, the beech leaves old." "Down by the Salley Gardens" and "The Medi-tation of the Old Fisherman" bear witness to talks before turf fires, or in herring boats off Knocknarea, and other developments of folk-song or tale have the place-names of his home county of Sligo; but this dis-tinctive quality is theirs in less measure, and few others in the little volume have it at all.

In the years just before "The Wanderings of Oisin," Mr. Yeats had been eager to unite the young writers of Ireland in a movement to give the country a national literature in English. This project developed side by side with Dr. Hyde's to give Ireland its own language again and a modern literature in it. Neither leader was the first to advance either idea, but each was the first to establish the movement in which he was most interested; Mr. Yeats's "Wanderings of Oisin" (1889) is the starting-point of the Celtic Renaissance, and Dr. Hyde's "Leabhar Sgeuluigheachta" (1889), the starting-point of the Gaelic League, though this was not organized until 1893. From that day to this these two men and Mr. George W. Russell ("A. E.") have been the great forces in the literature of the Renaissance. Mr. Yeats was busy in those early days with editing fairy and folk-tales and short stories from the Irish novelists, and in reading these it was but natural that he should be led to write stories. First came "John Sherman" and "Dhoya" in 1891, the one a condensed novel with the slightest of plots about a slow-pulsed young man's troubles with love and laziness in Sligo and London, and the other a sketch of Irish faery in old time. Some of the sketches of "The Celtic Twilight" (1893) approach the tale, but such narrations are not told for their own sake, but as illustrations of fairy-lore, or they have too little body to win for themselves the title of tale. In "The Secret Rose" (1897) there are true tales, some out of Ireland's legendary past, some out of her fairy present, and, akin to both, the Hanrahan series. These last Mr. Yeats so rewrote in 1904 as to be "nearer to the mind of the country places where Hanrahan and his like wandered and are remembered." As they stand now they are his best prose, rid almost entirely of preciousness, and simple and full of mystery as the countryside they reflect. In "The Secret Rose" are two "alchemical" tales and in "The Tables of the Law" (1904), two others of like subject. To me, for all the qualities they share with poetry of his of similar inspiration, they do not seem to be mastered by him. Alone among his writings they are incomplete.

Mr. Yeats was unable until the last few years to give himself up to the writing nearest his heart, drama. He continued to edit Irish literature, to write on literature and fairy-lore for the magazines. The articles about fairies he has published, and a great mass of belief collected but as yet unprinted, he will gather some day into a great book. Known now in the Irish countryside as a man with a power to exorcise spirits, he will then no doubt attain a reputation that will put him well above that of the Irish-American archbishop who was his only rival in that practice in the belief of many Irish peasants. Other of his magazine writing Mr. Yeats has gathered into "The Celtic Twilight" and more of it into the later edition (1900) of this book. Still other of these articles are to be found in "Ideas of Good and Evil" (1903), some of them stating his philosophy, never too definitely formulated. These two collections are very interesting in themselves, but both, like his "Discoveries" (1907), are more interesting as commentary on his powers. Mr. Yeats has used many notes to explain obscure allusions in his poems, though the most obscure he, perhaps with premeditation, fails to explain. Yet the reader unacquainted with his use of symbols will find much interpretation in these essays, especially those in "Ideas of Good and Evil."

Up to 1899, when Mr. Yeats's serious efforts to build up an Irish national drama began with "The Irish Literary Theatre," he devoted his happiest moments to lyric poetry, though the play of "The Countess Cathleen" made half of his second volume of verse, and the third was wholly given to the little play, "The Land of Heart's Desire." Since 1899, in which year "The Wind among the Reeds" appeared, Mr. Yeats has published, of other than dramatic verse, only the little volume of "In the Seven Woods," the little series on Flamel, and a few snatches, in all about a thousand lines. Some of this verse Mr. Yeats wrote for the psaltery, and in 1902 he was determined to write all his shorter poems for recitation to this instrument and "all his longer poems for the stage."

Mr. Yeats was thirty-four when he practically gave up lyrical poetry for dramatic poetry. From the beginning he had written plays, but they were lyrical plays, dramatic only in form, and they were, as soon as he had mastered the technique of verse, great lyrical poems. In the plays he has written since he has striven at that hardest of literary tasks, to make true dramatic speech high poetry, he has written nothing more beautiful than "The Countess Cathleen" and "The Land of Heart's Desire." He has rewritten and rewritten these later plays, and in almost every rewriting made them more dramatic, but sometimes the later versions have lost as poetry, not in the mere decorative features and "lyrical interbreathings," but in the accent of the play and in the sheer poetical qualities. To me it seems a pity, inevitable though it be, that the poet who has struck the most distinctly new note of all the English poets since Swinburne should, at thirty-four, have changed from an art he knew to an art he did not know. That is a ripe age

Associated Students Library Goshen College

for a poet to begin to learn to write in a form barely
essayed before. Unlike so many of the English poets, who
as public school boys were bred up to write verse, Mr.
Yeats had to teach himself to write verse. Overcoming
triumphantly this handicap, though losing by it years
usually fullest of impulse to write, Mr. Yeats greatly attained, and for the ten years from 1889 to 1899 devoted
himself to the writing of lyrics. For the past thirteen
years he has been busiest with dramas, in none of which
has he more than approximated to a dramatic quality
that is as great as the quality of his lyrics. He has owned
himself one reason of such shortcoming, in the notes to
"Deirdre." [1] "The principal difficulty with the form of
dramatic literature I have adopted is that, unlike the
loose Elizabethan form, it continually forces one by its
rigour of logic away from one's capacities, experiences,
and desires, until, if one have not patience to wait for the
mood, or to rewrite again and again till it comes, there
is rhetoric and logic and dry circumstance where there
should be life."

It may be that Mr. Yeats will one day overcome the
difficulties that he alludes to here, but he is now forty-
seven, and I, for one, doubt if, at his age, he can overcome
them. As they are, his plays are beautiful in ideas and
words, and striking in a lyric and decorative way, if not
all of them in a dramatic way, though in some he has in
vain sacrificed poetry to attain true dramatic speech,
attaining instead only "rhetoric and logic and dry circumstance." One values the plays of Mr. Yeats highest

[1] *Collected Works.* Stratford-on-Avon, 1908, vol. II, p. 251.

when one thinks of them as a new kind of drama, as a redevelopment of epic and lyric poetry into drama, an epic and lyric poetry illustrated by tableaux against backgrounds out of faery. Let us not forget that there is one effect which is of "The Tempest," and another effect which is of "Lear," and that it is after all something of a convention to call the latter a success of drama and the former a success of something other than drama. Yet it is just as necessary to remember that drama does mean a definite sort of literature, and the success of a new sort of drama, whether it be a "static" drama, as M. Maeterlinck has called his early drama, or whether it be the kind of drama that Mr. Yeats has created, is the success of something other than what we conventionally term drama. It is curious that no matter how great may be the success of an author in a form he has invented, he will almost invariably attempt also the accepted form from which he has diverged. Impelled by a desire to see his wife in a drama of his own but of the old dramatic sort, M. Maeterlinck made "Monna Vanna" in accord with the usual rules of the theatre, but to find it fall far short of the strange new beauty of his earlier plays. As yet Mr. Yeats has not compromised with the current taste in drama, but it may be that a desire to see some such actress as Mrs. Patrick Campbell in a part of his may lead to such compromise, as the thought of her acting his Deirdre inspired him to rewrite that part for Mrs. Campbell.

Mr. Yeats has not yet passed beyond the danger of falling between two stools. If it prove that he has really attained in a drama in which the verse is true dramatic speech and not lyric ecstasy or decoration, the success of such drama will be worth the sacrifice of the lyric poetry that he has not written because of the absorption of all of his energy in his dramatic writing. If it prove he has not so attained, we shall have no adequate compensation for the lost lyrics that he is now too old to write. I say no "adequate compensation," for compensation there is in the lyrical passages that no play of his is without, lyrical passages that arrest us as do his poems of the nineties; but, after all, these are but passages, not poems with unity and finality of form.

Another question altogether, a question outside of the question of the value as art of the writing of Mr. Yeats, which is what I am considering, is the question as to whether there would have been a dramatic movement at all comparable to what has been, if Mr. Yeats had not devoted so large a portion of his time to drama. I believe there would have been a dramatic movement, but I am sure, from what I know of the other dramatic organizations in Dublin, that they would not have amounted to much unless some other great writer as loyal to art as Mr. Yeats had played for them the beneficent tyrant. And other such great writers, as loyal to art, and as devoted to drama, are far to seek in Ireland as in other countries. It is not in Mr. Russell's nature so to act; it is not in Dr. Hyde's plan of life to foster in others other than propagandist literature; it is more than likely that had Mr. Martyn attempted it it had come to the end to which he has come as playwright. Without Mr. Yeats as moving

power, Synge had not been, without Mr. Yeats to interest
her in the movement, Lady Gregory had not written her
farces and folk-histories; and without the Abbey Theatre's
plays as standard, the younger playwrights of Cork and
Belfast would have written plays very other than those
they have written.

No wonder Mr. Yeats wants to see his dreams take
on bodily reality upon the stage, and to hear beautifully
spoken the words in which he has caught them. There
can be no greater pleasures than these to a writer when
he is past the imaginative intensity of youth. In youth
his imaginings are so real to him he needs no objective
embodiment to see them, and the roll and sing of their
lines are always sounding to his inner ear, but as he passes
"out of a red flare of dreams," such as is youth's, "into a
common light of common hours" in middle age, his imaginative life grows less intense and needs the satisfaction
of seeing itself concretely represented.

Mr. Yeats leaves out of his collected poems the plays
of his boyhood, "The Island of Statues" (1885) and "Mo-
sada" (1886). They were not of Ireland, but the Arcady
of the one and the mediæval Spain of the other he could
easily have paralleled in Irish legend, where anything
wonderful and tragic is possible. Nor is "The Countess
Cathleen" (1892–99), in its presentation of the drama of
a woman that sells her soul that the souls of her tenantry
may be saved, essentially Irish. It is curious that among
English poets of Mr. Yeats's generation it should be Mr.
Kipling that has happened upon the same legend, which
he adapts to his ends in "The Sacrifice of Er-Heb." The

background of "The Countess Cathleen" in the earlier
versions was not more essentially Irish than the story.
"The great castle in malevolent woods" and the country
about it is very like the part of fairyland that M. Maeterlinck refound by following the charts of early discoverers
in Arthurian legend.  In its later versions "The Countess
Cathleen" is more Irish and perhaps more dramatic,
though its greatnesses, after that of atmosphere, the great
lines we may no more forget than those about "the angel
Israfel"

> "Whose heart-strings are a lute";

or about

> "magic casements, opening on the foam
> Of perilous seas, in fairy lands forlorn";

or about

> "old, unhappy, far-off things
> And battles long ago";

or about hearing

> "the far-off curfew sound
> Over some wide-watered shore
> Swinging slow with sullen roar,"

were most of them in the earlier versions. There were
those lines of Maire's denouncement of the two demons
and her prophecy to them: —

> "You shall at last dry like dry leaves, and hang
> Nailed like dead vermin to the doors of God";

and those wonderful lines of Cathleen dying: —

> "Bend down your faces, Oona and Aleel:
> I gaze upon them as the swallow gazes
> Upon the nest under the eave, before
> He wander the loud waters";

and those last lines of all, great as only the greatest lines
are great, —

> "The years like great black oxen tread the world,
> And God the herdsman goads them on behind,
> And I am broken by their passing feet."

It was about this time, too, that Mr. Yeats wrote that
most startling of all his lines, —

> "And God stands winding his lonely horn";

and "The Lake Isle of Innisfree," that so charmed Stevenson that he had to write its author, and say it cast
over him a spell like that of his first reading of the "Poems
and Ballads" of Swinburne and the "Love in the Valley"
of Meredith.

There is no greater lyric poetry anywhere in the writing
of Mr. Yeats than in "The Land of Heart's Desire"
(1894), that little folk-play whose constant boding and
final tragedy cannot overcome, either while it is playing
or as you remember it, the sing and lilt that are in the
lines. It tells of the luring away by a fairy child of the
soul of a newly married bride on May-Eve, and of her
death when her soul has passed to the "Land of Heart's
Desire" —

> "Where nobody gets old and crafty and wise,
> Where nobody gets old and godly and grave,
> Where nobody gets old and bitter of tongue,
> And where kind tongues bring no captivity."

It is a story out of folk-lore, and so far back in time, and
so far away from the life that we know is it, that all that
happens seems not only possible but inevitable.

"The Land of Heart's Desire" was the first play of

Mr. Yeats to be put on the stage, being presented at the Avenue Theatre in London in 1894; and it was also the first play of Mr. Yeats to be put on in America, being presented with Miss Mabel Taliaferro in the fairy's rôle as the curtain-raiser to Mrs. Le Moyne's production of "In a Balcony," in the spring of 1901. Fragile as is its charm, it crossed the footlights and made itself felt as a new beauty of the theatre. It was the lyrical interbreathings that appealed most to me, but the strife of priest and fairy for Maire Bruin's soul was very real drama. It was the fairy's song, however, that haunted me after I left the theatre, as it could not but be. It haunts me still, coming into my mind whenever I think of Mr. Yeats, as inevitably as the last lines of "The Countess Cathleen," or as "The Lake Isle of Innisfree," or "The Valley of the Black Pig," or "The Rose of the World," or the ecstasies of Forgael and Dectora, or the song in "Deirdre." "The lonely of heart is withered away" is its burden, a burden that will not out of mind.

"The Land of Heart's Desire" has probably been most often played, counting American performances as well as performances in Ireland and England, being played as frequently by amateurs as by professionals in this country, but the prose play "Cathleen ni Houlihan," because of its national theme, has had more playings in Ireland. Its effect upon the stage is very different from its effect in the study. Read, it seems allegory too obvious to impress. The old woman, Cathleen ni Houlihan, with "too many strangers in the house" and with her "four beautiful green fields" taken from her, is so patently Ireland

SCENE FROM "CATHLEEN NI HOULIHAN"

possessed by England, all four provinces, that one fails
to feel the deep humanity of the sacrifices of Michael
Gillane for her, his country, even though that sacrifice
be on his wedding eve. Seen and listened to, "Cathleen
ni Houlihan" brings tears to the eyes and chokes the
throat with sobs, so intimately physical is the appeal of
its pathos. He is, indeed, dull of understanding or hard
of heart who can ¦witness a performance of this play
and not feel that something noble has come his way. It
seizes hold of the Irishmen of the patriotic societies as
does "The Wearing of the Green," and even the out-
lander, little sympathetic to the cause of Ireland and holding patriotism a provincial thing, is moved in some strange
way he does not understand. Performance brings out its
homeliness, its touches of humor, its wistfulness, its nobility. It is with this thought of its nobility that every
thought of "Cathleen ni Houlihan" ends, that is every
thought of it on the stage. Off the stage it is, except to
him to whom the cause is all, something that falls short of
nobility, to many little more than eloquent allegory. In
the autumn of 1904 Miss Margaret Wycherly played
"The Land of Heart's Desire" and "Cathleen ni Houlihan" a few times in America, and "The Countess Cathleen"; and "The Hour-Glass" (1903) and "A Pot of
Broth" (1902), both plays in prose. "The Hour-Glass,"
a morality, was written after "Everyman" had won
Mr. Yeats, and "A Pot of Broth" was written, perhaps,
to prove that its author could do farce.

"The Hour-Glass" is based on a story that Mr. Yeats
found in Lady Wilde's "Ancient Legends of Ireland"

(1887), the story of a wise man who is saved from eternal damnation by the faith of a child. Mr. Yeats leaves the wise man the great scholar that he was in the old tale, a scholar whose teaching had taken away the faith of a countryside, but he changes the child who saved the scholar into Teig the Fool, and infuses into the record of the frantic hour, in which the wise man knows his life ebbing away as the sand falls, a spirit that is as reverent as the spirit of the old religious drama.

"A Pot of Broth" is a variant of a widely spread folk-tale in which a beggarman tricks a provident housewife out of a meal. He pretends a stone that he has, and which he gives her after his meal, makes good broth, but it is her chicken that has made the broth. It is a trifle, amusing enough, but remarkable chiefly for its difference from other work of Mr. Yeats. There is little doubt, I take it, in the mind of any one that it is not chiefly Lady Gregory's, as it surely is in its wording, and in its intimacy with the details of cottage life.

Prose also is "Diarmid and Grania," written in collaboration with Mr. George Moore and played at the last year's performance (1901) of "The Irish Literary Theatre." As this play as performed was in tone more like the writings of Mr. Moore than of Mr. Yeats, I have considered it among his plays rather than among the plays of Mr. Yeats.

His other prose play, "Where there is Nothing" (1903), is a statement of revolt against "the despotism of fact" that is perhaps as characteristic of the artist as of the Celt. The world would say that its hero, Paul Ruttledge, was mad, but no one that reads can deny him a large share of sympathy. This play was produced by the Stage Society in London in 1904. Lady Gregory having had a share in its creation, Mr. Yeats has since relinquished the theme to her; and now rewritten by her alone as "The Unicorn from the Stars," it would hardly be recognized as the same play.

His Paul Ruttledge, gentleman, becomes her Martin Hearne, coach-builder. Both are alike at the outset of their frenzy, in that they would be destroyers of Church and Law, both use tinkers as their agents of destruction, and both die despised of men. Both are "plunged in trance," but their trances differ. That of Lady Gregory's hero is cataleptic and directly productive of his revolt, from a revelation, as he thinks it is, that comes to him while he is "away." Paul Ruttledge, on the other hand, deliberately gives up his conventional life, and that as largely because of boredom as because of belief in its wrongness. One cannot, as one reads "Where there is Nothing," fail to see in its hero much of Mr. Yeats himself. He is not the professional agitator, literary or social, as was Oscar Wilde and as is Mr. Shaw, but he here delights in turning things topsy-turvy, just as they do, in a fashion that has been distinctive of the Irishman for many generations. Mr. Yeats is himself, often, like his hero, "plunged in trance," if one may call trance his "possessed dream," such as that in which "Cap and Bells" or "Cathleen ni Houlihan" came to him. The lyric came to him, he says, as a "vision," and so, too, the play. It is in the dedication to volumes I and II of "Plays for an Irish

Theatre," volumes containing "Where there is Nothing,"
"The Hour - Glass," "Cathleen ni Houlihan," and "A
Pot of Broth," that he tells us of the latter vision, and of
the beginnings of that collaboration with Lady Gregory
that taught her her art, and so profoundly influenced his.
So informing is it that I quote it in full.

My dear Lady Gregory: —
    I dedicate to you two volumes of plays that are in part your
own.
    When I was a boy I used to wander about at Rosses Point
and Ballisodare listening to old songs and stories. I wrote down
what I heard and made poems out of the stories or put them
into the little chapters of the first edition of the "Celtic Twilight," and that is how I began to write in the Irish way.
    Then I went to London to make my living, and though I spent
a part of every year in Ireland and tried to keep the old life in
my memory by reading every country tale I could find in books
or old newspapers, I began to forget the true countenance of
country life. The old tales were still alive for me, indeed, but
with a new, strange, half-unreal life, as if in a wizard's glass,
until at last, when I had finished "The Secret Rose," and was
halfway through "The Wind among the Reeds," a wise woman
in her trance told me that my inspiration was from the moon,
and that I should always live close to water, for my work was
getting too full of those little jewelled thoughts that come from
the sun and have no nation. I have no need to turn to my books
of astrology to know that the common people are under the
moon, or to Porphyry to remember the image-making power of
the waters. Nor did I doubt the entire truth of what she said
to me, for my head was full of fables that I had no longer the
knowledge and emotion to write. Then you brought me with
you to see your friends in the cottages, and to talk to old wise
men on Slieve Echtge, and we gathered together, or you gathered for me, a great number of stories and traditional beliefs.

You taught me to understand again, and much more perfectly than before, the true countenance of country life.

One night I had a dream, almost as distinct as a vision, of a cottage where there was well-being and firelight and talk of a marriage, and into the midst of that cottage there came an old woman in a long cloak. She was Ireland herself, that Cathleen ni Houlihan for whom so many songs have been sung and about whom so many stories have been told and for whose sake so many have gone to their death. I thought if I could write this out as a little play I could make others see my dream as I had seen it, but I could not get down out of that high window of dramatic verse, and in spite of all you had done for me I had not the country speech. One has to live among the people, like you, of whom an old man said in my hearing, "She has been a serving-maid among us," before one can think the thoughts of the people and speak with their tongue. We turned my dream into the little play, "Cathleen ni Houlihan," and when we gave it to the little theatre in Dublin and found that the working-people liked it, you helped me to put my other dramatic fables into speech. Some of these have already been acted, but some may not be acted for a long time; but all seem to me, though they were but part of a summer's work, to have more of that countenance of country life than anything I have done since I was a boy.

I should like also to quote in full Mr. Yeats's account of how "Where there is Nothing" passed into "The Unicorn from the Stars," as that account throws much light on the methods of collaboration that have added so greatly to the success of the dramatic movement, and that are especially valuable to beginners, whose plays, without reshaping in collaboration, might never win their way to the boards. But I have not the space for it all, and I must content myself with that portion of it in which Mr. Yeats confesses that belief of his in the *rapprochement* of scholar and tinker that one notes so often in Irish life. Speaking of Lady Gregory's rewriting of "Where there is Nothing" into "The Unicorn from the Stars," he says:—

Her greatest difficulty was that I had given her for chief character a man so plunged in trance that he could not be otherwise than all but still and silent, though perhaps with the stillness and the silence of a lamp; and the movement of the play as a whole, if we were to listen to hear him, had to be without hurry or violence. The strange characters, her handiwork, on whom he sheds his light, delight me. She has enabled me to carry out an old thought for which my own knowledge is insufficient and to commingle the ancient phantasies of poetry with the rough, vivid, ever-contemporaneous tumult of the roadside; to create for a moment a form that otherwise I could but dream of, though I do that always, an art that prophesies though with worn and failing voice of the day when Quixote and Sancho Panza long estranged may once again go out gaily into the bleak air. Ever since I began to write I have awaited with impatience a linking, all Europe over, of the hereditary knowledge of the countryside, now becoming known to us through the work of wanderers and men of learning, with our old lyricism so full of ancient frenzies and hereditary wisdom, a yoking of antiquities, a marriage of Heaven and Hell.

Interesting, however, as these plays in prose are, and significant of their author's desire to do work in a medium that was perhaps more immediately acceptable to the audience of the National Dramatic Society in its then culture, there is no doubt at all that the plays in verse are nearer his heart. They are himself, and in all of the prose plays there is a good deal of Lady Gregory. All this time that he was collaborating in these prose plays he was still dreaming over "The Shadowy Waters," retouching it, rearranging it, until it became in detail a very different play from the play that was published under that name in 1900. Its hero and heroine, Forgael and Dectora, are much as they were then, their fateful meeting in misty northern seas remains the central incident, and the climax is still their choice to be left alone in the Viking ship at the world's end; but more than half the lines are changed. "The Shadowy Waters" was staged in 1904, and with telling weirdness, but like many another author's best-loved and most elaborated work, it has not made the appeal of plays less favorite to him. Mr. Yeats has written that he has been brooding over "The Shadowy Waters" ever since he was a boy, and he told me, when I asked him once which writing of his he cared most for, "That I was last working at, and then 'The Shadowy Waters.'" It is too much to say that it expresses the dream of his life, but it is not too much to say that a dream that has haunted all his life is told here, or half told, for dream such as this eludes complete expression. "The Shadowy Waters" is a poem so long considered, so often returned to, so loved and elaborated and worked over, so often dreamed and redreamed, that one would expect to find in it its author's *credo*, if its author is one who could hold to one confession of faith. Few authors can, few authors should, and Mr. Yeats is not one of them that can or should. He wrote once that he would be accounted

> "True brother of that company
> That sang to lighten Ireland's wrong,
> Ballad and story, rann and song," —

and Nationalist though he still is he has grown more and
more preoccupied with art.  There was a time when a love
of the occult threatened his art, but from that the theatre
has saved him, if it has taken him from the writing of lyrics, in which his powers are at their highest.  To old Irish
legend, Mr. Yeats has, however, been true from the start,
and from the start, too, there has never been a time that
he has not been preoccupied with dream.  And if the two
loves to which he has been constant cannot be said with
exactitude to be in the story of Forgael and Dectora, because that story is not a reshaping of any one legend out
of old Irish legend, it is of the very spirit of the journeys
oversea in which that legend abounds, and it is steeped
in dream.  It would be here, then, that one would look
for an expression as like a *credo* as is possible to Mr.
Yeats, and here we do find it on the lips of Forgael, his
hero, who, can we doubt? speaks also for the poet himself: —

> "All would be well
> Could we but give us wholly to the dreams,
> And get into their world that to the sense
> Is shadow, and not linger wretchedly
> Among substantial things; for it is dreams
> That lift us to the flowing changing world
> That the heart longs for.  What is love itself,
> Even though it be the lightest of light love,
> But dreams that hurry from beyond the world,
> To make low laughter more than meat and drink,
> Though it but set us sighing?"

"On Baile's Strand" (1903) follows very closely the
story of Cuchulain's slaying of his own son as retold by
Lady Gregory in her "Cuchulain of Muirthemne" (1902).

Like Rustum he does not know who is the youth he is
fighting until he has given him his death wound. Its high
tragedy rends the more by the ironic setting of Blind Man
and Fool, two wastrels, one of whom might have prevented the tragedy, but would not because the fight
would give him and his fellow a chance to rob the larders
in houses whose owners were watching it. No one can
doubt the high intention of "On Baile's Strand," no one
can deny that its story is essentially dramatic, no one can
pass by certain passages without realization that here
is great verse, blank verse that is true dramatic speech.
Men remember Cuchulain's description of Aoife as men
remember Maud Gonne.

> "Ah! Conchubar, had you seen her
> With that high, laughing, turbulent head of hers
> Thrown backward, and the bowstring at her ear,
> Or sitting at the fire with those grave eyes
> Full of good counsel as it were with wine,
> Or when love ran through all the lineaments
> Of her wild body."

One remembers these things, but if one has not seen the
play on the stage, he does not bear with him memories
of beauty such as one bears always with him from even
the reading of "The Countess Cathleen" or of "The
Land of Heart's Desire." Nor is one moved by "On
Baile's Strand" as one is moved by other tellings of the
same world story, as one is moved by the epic telling of
it by Matthew Arnold in "Sohrab and Rustum," or even
by such a casual telling of it as is Mr. Neil Munro's
in "Black Murdo." If it were not for "Deirdre," in
fact, one would have to say that the verse plays of

Mr. Yeats after "The Shadowy Waters" grow, play by
play, less in poetic beauty, and that their gain in dramatic
effectiveness does not compensate for such a loss.

"The King's Threshold" (1904) is as near a play with
a purpose as Mr. Yeats has written. It vindicates the
right of the poet in Ireland's Heroic Age to sit at the highest table of the King, and as it was written and played in
1903, when its author was being accused of caring more
for his art than for his country, it looks very like a de-
fense. Seanchan, the poet, removed from his high seat
at the request of "Bishops, Soldiers, and Makers of the
Law," takes his stand on the King's threshold, with the
intention of starving himself to death there, as there is,
as the King says, —

> "a custom,
> An old and foolish custom, that if a man
> Be wronged, or think that he is wronged and starve
> Upon another's threshold till he die,
> The common people, for all time to come,
> Will raise a heavy cry against that threshold,
> Even though it be the King's."

It was at this time that the clamor against "In the
Shadow of the Glen" had stirred up a great deal of feeling against Mr. Yeats and the other managers of the Irish
National Theatre Society. And Mr. Yeats, it may be,
wrote the play not only to symbolize his contention that
the poet is as important to society as is the man of action,
but also to assert that poetry cultivated for its own sake,
the sake of art, is as necessary to a nation, to Ireland, as
what Ireland calls patriotism. By the way, he illustrated
the fact that that kind of patriotism that assumes the

King can do no wrong, — that is, that the Irish people can do no wrong, — and that whoever exposes their wrongdoing is no patriot, is a mistaken sort of patriotism.

Late in 1906 his "Deirdre" was successfully produced at the Abbey Theatre, Dublin. It presents only the last chapter of this, the saddest tale of the three heart-burdening tales that are known as "The Three Sorrows of Story-Telling," but it presents it so poignantly and with so keen an emphasis on the quick-passing of all things sweet, that it takes place, for all its slightness, with the world's greatest tragedies that are tragedies because of the overthrow therein of "queens . . . young and fair." There are few Irish writers whose concern is with things Irish who have not retold this, the greatest love story of Ireland, but none of them, from Sir Samuel Ferguson down to our own day, have retold it so nobly as Mr. Yeats, save only Synge, and his restatement of it, of the whole story from Deirdre's girlhood to her death, has about it a grandeur and triumphing beauty that make further retellings not to be tolerated.

It is not lines, "purple patches," one remembers from "Deirdre," but the whole play, its every situation, its setting. That setting so quintessentializes, in the words Mr. Yeats used to describe it, the romance of the old haunted woods where any adventure is possible, that I must quote it in full: —

A Guest-house in a wood. It is a rough house of timber; through the doors and some of the windows one can see the great spaces of the wood, the sky dimming, night closing in. But a window to the left shows the thick leaves of a coppice; the landscape suggests silence and loneliness. There is a door to right and left, and through the side windows one can see anybody who approaches either door, a moment before he enters. In the centre, a part of the house is curtained off; the curtains are drawn. There are unlighted torches in brackets on the walls. There is, at one side, a small table with a chessboard and chessmen upon it, and a wine flagon and loaf of bread. At the other side of the room there is a brazier with a fire; two women, with musical instruments beside them, crouch about the brazier: they are comely women of about forty. Another woman, who carries a stringed instrument, enters hurriedly; she speaks, at first standing in the doorway.

But if one does not carry in memory so many lines of "Deirdre" as one does of the earlier less dramatic plays, there are passages in plenty that arrest and exalt. One such is those lines of Fergus that so well describe one phase of the imagination of Mr. Yeats —

> "wild thought
> Fed on extravagant poetry, and lit
> By such a dazzle of old fabulous tales
> That common things are lost, and all that's strange
> Is true because 't were pity if it were not."

Another such is the song of the musicians, of Queen Edain's tower, "When the Winds are Calling There"; and another such, the crying of a woman's heart in Deirdre's offer to go with Conchubar that Naisi may be saved: —

> "It's better to go with him.
> Why should you die when one can bear it all?
> My life is over; it's better to obey.
> Why should you die? I will not live long, Naisi.
> I'd not have you believe I'd long stay living;
> Oh, no, no, no! You will go far away.

You will forget me. Speak, speak, Naisi, speak,
And say that it is better that I go.
I will not ask it. Do not speak a word,
For I will take it all upon myself.
Conchubar, I will go."

This is true dramatic speech, this has the accent of high tragedy, and weakly human as it is it does not take away at all from the queenliness of Deirdre. There are other passages that have such a tendency, however, true though they may be to the life they depict and to human nature of all time when in such a frenzy of fear and sorrow. Longer even than this heart's cry, however, I think I shall remember that line so near the opening of the play —

"She put on womanhood and he lost peace."

Lines greater than that are far to seek in English drama.

"The Green Helmet" (1910), a rewriting in a form of verse alien to the stage of the earlier prose "Golden Helmet" (1908), is hardly done out of any high intention, and although it is not wanting in a kind of strange and grotesque fascination, it is in result no higher than it was in intention. In fact the past five years, years much of whose time has been spent in forwarding the work of the Abbey Theatre, have not inspired Mr. Yeats to much work of importance. Mr. Yeats promises us more plays, but one cannot help wishing, if he must do verses other than lyric, he would put his hand now to a great epic. His "Wanderings of Oisin" is nearest this, near enough, for all the preponderance of lyric in it, to show that he could do it, were we without such lines of "large accent" as I have quoted from "The Countess Cathleen" to prove that beyond doubt. There is no better material for epic as yet unused than Irish legends, but there is none the old bards developed into epic proportions. There would be here the largest scope for the shaping power of the poet. Mr. Yeats must, of course, have thought of epic, but preferred drama as more in harmony with our time. Lionel Johnson said that Mr. Yeats took to drama because he liked to hear his lines finely spoken, but, surely, if that were his greatest delight, he could invent some way in which to bring story in verse to listeners. It were surely a lesser task than that of stimulating Mr. Dolmetsch to make a psaltery to which his lyrics may be musically spoken.

From the beginning, the verse of Mr. Yeats has had vocal quality, a quality that is unfortunately often rarer in good poetry than in verse that is good rhetoric. I cannot see that his interest in the psaltery, that developed after 1900, has brought about any change in the quality of his verse. There have been constant to it since "The Wanderings of Oisin" all the qualities that distinguish it to-day, — its eloquence, its symbols that open up unending vistas through mysteries, its eeriness as of the bewildering light of late sunset over gray-green Irish bog and lake and mountain, its lonely figures as great in their simplicity as those of Homer, its plain statement of high passion that breaks free of all that is occult and surprises with its clarity where so much is dim with dream. First one and then another of these qualities has most interested him. He has written in explanation of patriotic

verse, of folk-verse, of verse based on the old court romances, of symbolism, of Rosicrucianism, of essences, of
speaking to the psaltery, of dramatic art; and all the time
he has practiced poetry, the interest of the time resulting
in now the greater emphasis on one quality in the poetry,
and now on another quality. It would be superfluous to
do more than point out most of these qualities, but a
word on his use of symbols may help to a fuller understanding of his poetry. I am very sure that I read wrong
meanings from many of these symbols, as one who has
not the password must. They require definite knowledge
of magical tradition, and of the poet's interpretation of
Celtic tradition, for a full understanding. As the years
go by, I think their exact meaning will escape more
and more readers until they will have no more significance than Spenser's allegories have to us. Only to the
student deeply read in Elizabethan politics do these mean
to-day what must have been patent to the inner circle at
Elizabeth's court. Those symbols of Mr. Yeats that we
may understand intuitively, as we may "The white owl
in the belfry sits," other generations also may understand, but hardly those that have meanings known only
to a coterie. But we may read Spenser with enjoyment
even if all the inner allegories are missed, and so, too,
many read Mr. Yeats to-day, neglectful of the images
of a formal symbolism.

I do not know that I get more enjoyment from the
poetry of the verses entitled "The Valley of the Black
Pig" because Mr. Yeats's note tells us that it is the scene
of Ireland's *Götterdämmerung*, though it is an unques-

tionable gratification to the puzzle interest I have with my kind, and I would at times be more comfortable were I sure that the "Master of the Still Stars and of the Flaming Door" was he who keeps the gates of the Other World, the real world we shall enter when death sets us free of that dream men call life.  Mr. Yeats is not so kind to the men "in the highway" as the old Irish bards.  When they wrote enigmas they were apt to explain them fully, as does the poet of "The Wooing of Emer" when he tells what was meant by the cryptic questions and answers exchanged between that princess and Cuchulain.  When the symbolism is of the kind found in "Death's Summons" of Thomas Nash, which of all poems Mr. Yeats quotes oftenest, all cultivated men may understand —

> "Brightness falls from the air;
> Queens have died young and fair;
> Dust hath closed Helen's eye."

The difference between the symbol Helen and each one of the several symbols Mr. Yeats employs in "The Valley of the Black Pig" is the difference between a symbol universally recognized throughout the world and a symbol recognized by one people; but there is the further difference that one is intimately associated with the thing symbolized, is the name of a woman the context tells us is a queen and beautiful, and the other is only the scene of a battle that symbolizes the ending of the world.  It is more natural to use a beautiful woman as a symbol of all beauty than to use a black boar that shall root up all the light and life of the world as a symbol of the ending of the world.  But neither of these is a symbol that would be understood intuitively, as the rose used as a symbol of beauty or the wind as a symbol of instability. Sometimes Mr. Yeats's symbols are very remote, but perhaps they were remote in the old stories in which he found them. The details in

> "the phantom hound
> All pearly white, save one red ear,"

and "the hornless deer" which it chases, seem arbitrary. The hound, it is true, is known of all men as the pursuer, and the deer as the pursued; but does this knowledge suggest immediately "the desire of the man which is for the woman, and the desire of the woman which is for the desire of the man"? Mr. Yeats does not, as I take it, expect all his symbols to be understood so definitely as this hound and deer, which, of course, are not only symbols, but figures from the tapestry of fairyland. It is often enough, perhaps, that we understand emotionally, as in "Kubla Khan" or "The Owl." From some of his writing it would appear he believed many symbols to be of very definite meaning and to be understood by generation upon generation. In the note to "The Valley of the Black Pig" he writes, "Once a symbol has possessed the imagination of large numbers of men, it becomes, as I believe, an embodiment of disembodied powers, and repeats itself in dreams and visions, age after age."

This is but another phase of Mr. Yeats's belief that when a poem stirs us as by magic, it is a real magic has been at work. The words have loosened the seals that the flesh has fastened upon the universal memory which is subconscious in all of us, until that memory possesses us and we are one with all that has been since the beginning of time, and may in such moments live over all that has been lived. He thinks that in such moments the poet's magic brings before us the past and the unseen as the past and the unseen were brought before our pagan ancestors by the magical rites of their priests.

In his younger years Mr. Yeats held that poetry is "the words that have gathered up the heart's desire of the world." His heart's desire was simpler in those days than his heart's desire of after years. Then he had a child's wistfulness for little things and put lines in his poems of Blake-like innocence and freshness. "The brown mice" that

> "bob
> Round and round the oatmeal chest"

are out of memories of childhood, and many other of the similes of these early poems are out of the ways of wild little things that appeal so to children, perhaps because they are wild little things themselves. A later mood of Mr. Yeats is to hold of less account the things of out-of-doors, but still he uses as similes the ways of birds, as did the old Irish bards whose stories have so informed his. He never did describe nature for its own sake, but natural things gave him more figures than they do now, although always there have been in his lines many out of mythology. Summer days between Slieve Echtge and the western sea are, however, bringing the plovers and curlews and peewits back to his poetry. In the country of the Countess Cathleen, as everywhere in Ireland, you may hear "wind cry and water cry and curlew cry," and there, as all the world over, —

"Ill bodings are as native unto our hearts
As are their spots unto the woodpeckers."

It is from such knowledge of country things come the fine
lines about

"The dark folk, who live in souls
Of passionate men like bats in the dead trees"; —

and such lines are coming again into his verse, even into
the blank verse of his plays. The poems in which "the
strong human call" is heard are more than the many who
read Mr. Yeats hurriedly will think, and to those who
know his story they reveal again and again a great and
common sorrow. Whole poems and plays are often symbols of the poet's life. So may "The Countess Cathleen"
be taken as well as "The King's Threshold." "Ephem-
era," "The Dedication to a Book of Stories," "In the
Seven Woods," "The Old Age of Queen Maeve," "The
Folly of Being Comforted," "Old Memory," "Adam's
Curse," as well as the folk-poems of the first volumes, are
but little "dream-burdened," and passages elsewhere
have the human call. The feeling of Oisin nearing the
coast of Ireland is, for instance, the common joy on nearing the shore of the homeland at the end of exile: —

"Remembrance, lifting her leanness, keened in the gates of my heart.
Till, fattening the winds of the morning, an odour of new-mown hay
Came, and my forehead fell low, and my tears like berries fell down;
Later a sound came, half lost in the sound of a shore far away,
From the great grass-barnacle calling, and later the shore-weeds brown."

It is true, though, that the dream-drenched poems are
those most characteristic of the author, those that give a
note entirely new to English poetry. It is impossible to

pick out one as more representative than another where
so many are representative and where all are of the highest achievement. Nowhere is his own individual note
better sustained, however, than in the Michael Robartes
poems or in "The Rose of Battle" or "Into the Twilight"; and the hold that dream has of him and the
hold that human things have, chief among them love of
country, are told with utmost distinction and inevitability of phrase in "To Ireland in the Coming Times"
and in "To the Rose upon the Rood of Time."

I sometimes wonder, is the reason for the poet's holding
so devotedly to spiritual things of his kind not the very
same holding of his peasant countryman to the folk-tales
that take him to a world as rich and gorgeous-hued as the
Ireland about him is bare and gray, and to a church that
prepares him for a better world after death? A large part
of all poetry is the realization of the brevity of all beautiful things, — of bloom, of youth, of life; but no poet has
more often lamented "Fate and Time and Change" than
Mr. Yeats. It is, he says, "our narrow rooms, our short
lives, our soon ended passions and emotions put us out of
conceit with sooty and feeble reality." So the poet seeks
refuge in his own dream and in contemplation of the life
from which he came and to which he will return, and —
one almost dare say — in communication with which he
now knows such joy. The poet's life is little because he
has found out the littleness of earthly things; the peasant
holds life little because his share of it has been so poor. If
the peasant acquires riches by chance or by emigration,
he sees as the poet that all he can have is as nothing, so

short is the time he may hold it. Irish writers of the past have made this peasant only the jarvey wit; but if you read the old romances, or listen to the folk-tales still alive, you will learn that Mr. Yeats is at one with his countryman in this basic likeness.

There is a side of Irish life, the side the world knows best, that Mr. Yeats does not present, but that which he does present is true, though the poet's personality is so dominant that we get more of this than of Ireland in his poetry. So it should be, so it is with every artist. All the world can ask of him is his interpretation of what he knows. Yet so native is Mr. Yeats that the atmosphere of his poetry is the very atmosphere of Ireland. The artist and the setting of his art are in an unwonted harmony. No reader of Mr. Yeats who knows the brooding landscape of West Ireland can escape that realization, but only he who has met the poet amid the scenes that inspired his verse may know how complete is their accord. Such a meeting was mine one lowering August day, in whose late afternoon we walked in the Woods of Coole. Then I knew at last what Mr. Yeats meant by "druid charm" and "druid light." I felt the "druid charm" that was potent in gray skies over gray water and gray rock and gray-green woods; the bewildering "druid light" flashed out as the sun followed westward the trail to Hy Brasil, leaving in the Atlantic skies wild after-glow of winter yellow.

# CHAPTER IV

## MR. EDWARD MARTYN AND MR. GEORGE MOORE

THE announcement of Mr. Edward Martyn as playwright of "The Irish Literary Theatre" was, outside of
the narrow circle of his friends, a great surprise to all interested in letters in Ireland. But the almost simultaneous
announcement that Mr. George Moore was lending his
aid to the adventure was an even greater surprise. Mr.
Moore had, of course, written more than once of Ireland,
and there were many who had not forgotten the unpleas-
antnesses of "A Drama in Muslin" (1886), and Mr.
Martyn, though the author of "Morgante the Lesser"
(1890), was not known as its author, as he had published
it anonymously, and as it had not made enough of a stir
for its anonymity to be disclosed. Yet for the landlord-
author, who had turned his back on Ireland, to return to
his country with a greater interest in its life and its writers
than he had ever betrayed, was more remarkable than for
another landlord of the same family connection, comparatively a stay-at-home landlord, to turn from sport and
religion to the stage. Mr. Martyn had lived in London
and his love of music had taken him to the Continent, but
he had been something of a Nationalist, whereas Mr.
Moore had lost few opportunities to scoff at the country
his father had striven so unselfishly to aid. What of Mr.

GEORGE MOORE

Moore that was not French in 1899 was confessedly English.

Now that those interested have read "Ave," the first volume of the three of "Hail and Farewell," in which Mr. Moore is confessing the reasons of his return to Ireland and of his second departure from Ireland, they know that he had been mildly interested in Ireland as material for art as far back as 1894, and that it was Mr. Martyn who had interested him in the things of home. Mr. Moore tells us all about it more than explicitly in the "Overture" to his trilogy. In the first chapter he tells us that the interest faded away gradually, to be reawakened in 1899 by a visit paid him in London by Mr. Martyn and Mr. Yeats, who came to ask his help in founding a "Literary Theatre in Dublin." Then Mr. Moore learned the story of that theatre's inception, a story to him "disappointingly short and simple. When Yeats had said that he had spent the summer at Coole with Lady Gregory, I saw it all. Coole is but three miles from Tillyra [Mr. Martyn's estate in Galway]; Edward is often at Coole; Lady Gregory and Yeats are often at Tillyra; Yeats and Edward had written plays — the drama brings strange fowls to roost."

It takes Mr. Moore many pages to tell why it was he joined the three in their project, and many more pages to tell of their collaboration during the first two years of the three years that were the life of "The Irish Literary Theatre." The four are, indeed, the principal characters of Mr. Moore's "Ave" — I had almost said his novel "Ave" — himself, Mr. Martyn, Mr. Yeats, and Lady

Gregory, to mention them in the order of prominence that Mr. Moore gives them.

Lady Gregory and Mr. Yeats have learned their art, the highest and most difficult of all forms of literary art, so that each is sure in the shaping of fable and emotion to the stage, though neither is to drama native-born as was Synge. Mr. Martyn and Mr. Moore have neither of them, however, learned the art of the playwright. Mr. Martyn has the root of the matter in him, but he remains the amateur. Mr. Moore was once the amateur, even in the novel, in "A Modern Lover" (1883), for instance, true as that story is to the London art life and aristocratic life it is intended to reflect, but he has since then won his way, book by book, to the position, now that Mr. Hardy has given up the novel, of first novelist of the English-speaking peoples. Had he studied the play as painfully and as long as he has studied the novel, it may be that Mr. Moore had conquered it, too, though I doubt it, for the concentration necessary to drama is alien to his method as a novelist. As it is, his best plays are but the good journeyman work of one who is a skilled literary craftsman. Mr. Martyn has more originality of theme, more intimacy with Irish character, a surer instinct for effective situation, and more nobility of intention, though Mr. Moore's greater power over words gives his plays a dignity as art that the plays of Mr. Martyn do not attain.

Alone of the quartette that founded "The Irish Literary Theatre," Mr. Martyn is possessed of none of the instincts of the publicist. Lady Gregory has edited arti-

cles about ideals in Ireland at home, and on the lecture
platform she has stoutly fought the battles of "The Playboy of the Western World" in America; Mr. Yeats has
ever delighted in writing letters to the newspapers and he
has preached the evangel of the Renaissance from Edinburgh to San Francisco; and Mr. George Moore is a
controversialist pamphleteer even before he is a novelist.
In the few articles about the movement that Mr. Martyn
has written, brief articles all of them, there is, however,
clear indication of the spirit in which he wrote his plays,
if comparatively little discussion of his art. In the second
number of "Beltaine" (February, 1900), in an article
entitled "A Comparison between Irish and English Theatrical Audiences," Mr. Martyn declares that he sees in
Ireland, instead of the "vast cosmopolitanism and vulgar-
ity" of England, "an idealism founded upon the ancient
genius of the land." It is wholly in accord with the spirit
of this declaration that Mr. Martyn has written his more
important plays, all of them, in fact, but the satires on
weaklings and officials he calls "A Tale of a Town" (1902)
and "The Place Hunters" (1905). He writes little of the
peasants, being less interested in them than are Mr.
Yeats and Lady Gregory, and therefore less acquainted
with them. If one may judge from his writings the intimates of Mr. Martyn have been among his own landlord
class, the priests, and the politicians. It is the landlords
and middle-class people that occupy the foreground of
his plays, Peg Inerny in "Maeve" (1899) being the only
important character a peasant, unless Mrs. Font in "The
Enchanted Sea" (1902) can be called a member of a class

that she was born to, but from which her marriage removed her.

This question of the class the plays should present was one of those that led to the withdrawal of Mr. Martyn from the dramatic movement. A more definite cause, perhaps, was the unanimous determination of Lady Gregory, Mr. Yeats, and Mr. Moore that his "A Tale of a Town" could not be presented by "The Irish Literary Theatre" as he wrote it if the standards of that theatre were to be preserved. Its author's magnanimity in turning it over to Mr. Moore to be rewritten, — as it was, being presented as "The Bending of the Bough" (1900), — was revealed by Mr. Moore in "Samhain" (October, 1901), and very much more fully, if less kindly, in "Ave" (1911).

In its way their refusal to play Mr. Martyn's "A Tale of a Town" was as creditable to the other powers in the theatre as was his magnanimity in giving them the play to do with as they would. They knew their refusal to play it might lead him to withdraw his support of the theatre, and, in the end, it was a factor in bringing about that result. After their rejection of "A Tale of a Town," however, he still gave "The Irish Literary Theatre" his support, allowing it to put on his "Maeve," and in 1901 contributing to "Samhain" (October), "A Plea for a National Theatre in Ireland." Such a theatre Mr. Martyn had the power to give Ireland, but he did not give it, when it was thought he might, and in 1902 all hope of his giving his money for such a purpose was destroyed by his transference of a fund of fifty thousand dollars to the Catholic

Pro-Cathedral in Dublin "for the purpose of founding and supporting a Palestrina choir."

That Mr. Martyn was still a force to be reckoned with is revealed by the trouble Mr. Yeats went to, in "Samhain" of October, 1902, to explain why it was that the plays of the Irish National Dramatic Company were either folk-drama or drama whose life was the "life of poetry." Mr. Martyn had argued in "The United Irishmen," which up to the time of the presentation of "In the Shadow of the Glen" was a stanch supporter of the dramatic policies of Mr. Yeats, that the actors of the company should be trained to the drama of modern society. "The acting of plays like 'Deirdre,' and of 'Cathleen ni Houlihan,'" writes Mr. Yeats, "with its speech of the country people, did not seem to him a preparation. It is not, but that is as it should be. Our movement is a return to the people, like the Russian movement of the early seventies, and the drama of society could but magnify a condition of life which the countryman and the artisan could but copy to their hurt. The play that is to give them a quite natural pleasure should either tell them of their own life or of that life of poetry where every man can see his own image, because there alone does human nature escape from arbitrary conditions. Plays about drawing-rooms are written for the middle classes of great cities, for the classes who live in drawing-rooms, but if you would uplift the man of the roads you must write about the roads, or about the people of romance, or about great historical people."

Neither "Maeve" nor "The Enchanted Sea" can be

called a drawing-room play, though both introduce us to
"drawing-room people," but "The Heather Field" (1899),
Mr. Martyn's first play, and his greatest success, is a
drawing-room play, as in a minor way are "A Tale of a
Town" and "The Place Hunters." These last two plays
are failures; but they are not failures, I think, because
they are drawing-room plays, but because Mr. Martyn is
less effective with a full stage than with two couples or so,
and, principally, because he is less successful with social
and political questions than with those that concern the
individual.

Whatever value one puts upon "The Heather Field,"
it cannot be denied that it was a popular success and that
it was praised by critics whose judgment is discerning.
It is perhaps because it is a variant of the old theme of the
war between man the idealist and woman the materialist
that it so appealed to young men, troubled themselves as
to whether to follow their star or to accept the chains that
wife and children impose. It was enough for the audience
that witnessed its first performances in the Antient Concert Rooms, Dublin, May 9, 10, 13, 1899, that it showed
a man at war with the despotism of fact, as Ireland, pre-
eminently the Celtic Land, has so long been. It was not
remarkably acted, by an insufficiently rehearsed and not
very understanding scratch company, and yet it impressed its audiences more favorably than "The Countess
Cathleen" (1892), an unequivocally great poetic drama;
and these audiences were the most cultivated Dublin can
boast.

"The Heather Field" is the story of the going-mad of

Carden Tyrrell, a landlord of the west of Ireland. From
the first he is represented to us as a man to whom as to
so many of his countrymen dream is reality and reality
dream. His wife, to whom the realities are very instant,
urges him to do as others do, to entertain, to hunt, at
least to do something practical. For her he has abandoned
the ideal world he had built up for himself from his books
and his dreams and is trying farming. Yet his temperament is such that he must idealize even this. When the
curtain rises he is still busy with the project, long since
undertaken, of reclaiming a wind - swept heather field
fronting the Atlantic and of making it into the best
of pasture land. That reclamation and transformation
has become a passion with him, and soon we feel that it
is the symbol of that quality in him that is untamed, in-
curably "ideal." To free that field of rocks and to drain
its bogs he has mortgaged his estate, and, in the play, before the success or failure of his undertaking is proved, he
mortgages almost all that remains to him to improve the
land below, which the draining of the heather field has
turned into a swamp. His wife, to prevent this last folly,
strives to have control of his property taken away from
him, but his friend, Barry Ussher, believing that restraint
would make Tyrrell mad indeed, so intimidates a hesitat-
ing physician that Mrs. Tyrrell fails in her most natural
plan to save herself and her child from ruin by having
her husband declared incompetent, and, if necessary, restrained. With his friend's assistance Tyrrell has won
his fight against his wife. Obstinacy in the treatment of
some tenants that his debts have driven him to evict

rouses such hatred against Tyrrell, until then a loved landlord, that the police hold it necessary to follow him with
an escort that he may not be shot by his people. To avoid
being so followed, Tyrrell keeps within doors and so in-
tensifies his malady. The catastrophe comes when, on
his boy's first spring search for wild flowers, the child
brings him a handful of heather buds from the heather
field. Their message is that the mountain will revert to
waste again. Even in his "ideal domain" reality has as-
serted itself. His ideal world crumbles for the instant,
and his reason with it, and forever. But after a moment's
agony ideality triumphantly reasserts itself, and in mad
ecstasy Tyrrell, his years fallen from him, passes from
sight crying out at the beauty of a world that is to him
now forever a world of mornings in which, as he says,
"the rain across a saffron sun trembles like gold harp-
strings through the purple Irish spring . . . The voices
— I hear them now triumphant in a silver glory of song!"
Such is the play, "aching and lofty in its loveliness."

Is this ending, or is it not, sadder than the catastrophe
of "Ghosts"? Certainly to "Ghosts" it owes something,
and to "The Wild Duck" more than something. A quality as of Ibsen pervades the play, and it has, too, back of
it a background of nature and of thought that is beautiful in the way the background of nature and of thought
is beautiful and compensating in the plays of Ibsen.

In his introduction to "The Heather Field," which
was published before its presentation, Mr. Moore writes,
"Although all right and good sense are on the wife's side,
the sympathy is always with Carden." So it was on the

presentation of the play in Dublin, Mr. Yeats writing in
"The Dome," "Our Irish playgoers sympathized with
this man so perfectly that they hissed the doctors who
found that he was mad." Such an attitude is characteristically Irish; and equally characteristically English was
the reception of this play when Mr. Thomas Kingston
presented it at a matinée at the Strand Theatre in London.
Mr. Yeats is again the authority: "The London playgoers . . . sympathized with the doctors, and held the
divine vision a dream." Mr. Moore praises "The Heather
Field" more forthrightly in "Samhain" of October, 1901,
holding that "'The Heather Field' has been admitted
to be the most thoughtful of modern prose plays written
in English, the best constructed, the most endurable to
a thoughtful audience." Patriotism or kinship, love of
paradox or desire to assuage feelings hurt by the rough
treatment of "A Tale of a Town," may any or all of them
be called upon to explain so sweeping a statement. But
none of such motives could account for its praise by Mr.
Beerbohm in the London "Saturday Review." "Max"
is often paradoxical, but he is not paradoxical here: "Not
long ago this play was published as a book, with a preface
by Mr. George Moore, and it was more or less vehemently
disparaged by the critics. Knowing that it was to be
produced later in Dublin, and knowing how hard it is to
dogmatize about a play until one has seen it acted, I con-
fined myself to a very mild disparagement of it. Now that
I have seen it acted, I am sorry that I disparaged it at all.
It turns out to be a very powerful play indeed." I have
quoted Mr. Yeats and Mr. Moore and Mr. Beerbohm,

not only because I have not seen the play on the stage, but because, on reading it, its effect is one that puts my judgment at sea. Years ago as I read it it gripped me hard, but when I read it now and think it over now, I am at a loss to see why, done as it is done, I should have been so moved by it. Now I am moved greatly by but two situations. Both of these are in the last act. One of them is Tyrrell's revulsion against the bad news that his brother Miles brings from Dublin of the mortgagee's refusal to extend. His wife tells their friends that she is ruined, that "pretty nearly all" their property is mortgaged, but Tyrrell cries out, "All, do you say? No — not all. This vulture cannot touch the heather field! My hope, — it is my only hope, and it will save me in the end. Ha, ha! These wise ones! They did not think the barren mountain of those days worth naming in their deed. But now that mountain is a great green field worth more than all they can seize, (*with a strange intensity*) and it is mine — all mine!"

The other situation that moves me greatly is that at the very close of the play, that from which I quoted a while back, in which Tyrrell's madness becomes evident in his belief that he is a youth again, with all the world before him to do with as he will.

The characters in "The Heather Field" are less rigid than those in the later plays, but even in this play you feel about them, as you feel so often about the characters of Hawthorne, that they are characters chosen to interpret an idea rather than children of the imagination or portraits done from observation of life.

As one recalls the motive and situations and background
and symbolism of "The Heather Field," not having read
the play for some time, it seems far finer than when
one returns to it. Fine, too, it must seem to any one reading a scenario of it and not offended, as one reading it constantly is, by the inability of its dialogue to represent
more of the person speaking than his point of view. The
dialogue of Mr. Martyn is almost never true dramatic
speech, and not only not true dramatic speech, but despite the very clear differentiation of the characters, with
little of their personality or temperament in it.

"Maeve" has always seemed to me a lesser play than
"The Heather Field," and it now leaves me even colder
than of old. Nor, though I can see how fine in conception was the character of Mrs. Font in "The Enchanted
Sea," does that one character seem to me, now, to redeem
the undeveloped possibilities of the situations of the play,
the incomplete characters of Guy and Mask and the
failure of the dialogue assigned to the characters to
approach true dramatic speech. "Maeve" is the better
play of the two. With all its shortcomings it has about
it an unearthliness of atmosphere, a quiet coldness of
beauty that has come of the thought Mr. Martyn had, as
he wrote it, of the moonlight on the Burren Hills in his
home country. In this one respect Mr. Martyn has done
what he would, for he holds that "the greatest beauty
like the old Greek sculptures is always cold."

Mr. Martyn calls "Maeve" "a psychological drama in
two acts." It relates the story of the last day and night
in the life of a visionary girl, the hereditary princess of

Burren in Clare, in the west of Ireland. On the eve of her marriage to Hugh Fitz Walter, a rich young Englishman, whom she will wed only for her father's sake, to re-establish him in his position as "The O'Heynes" among the neighboring gentry, she wanders off into the Burren Hills with her old nurse Peg Inerny. Peg has fascinated Maeve O'Heynes with tales of "the other people," convincing Maeve, as she is convinced herself, that she changes from the old vagrant peasant whom the country-side half fears into Queen Maeve, the great Amazon of the Cuchulain legends. Maeve O'Heynes in her own dreams has seen great heroes and heroines of Ireland's legendary past, and she believes that they still live among the fairies as many a peasant to-day beside Peg Inerny believes. So Maeve follows Peg to the mountains, though it is her wedding-eve, to see these great people of old time and to meet a lover she has seen in vision, the ideal man of her dreams. She finds her way home several hours later through the white moonlight of the bitter March night. Then, in a sort of trance, looking out of her window in the half-ruined castle to the ruined abbey, the mysterious round tower, the stony mountains, she beholds the vision of Queen Maeve, with an attendant troupe of harpers and pages, rise from the cairn and approach the castle. As the troupe returns from castle to cairn Maeve's spirit passes with it under the Northern lights into the land of the ever-young of Tir-nan-Ogue. When her sister goes to call her to make ready for her wedding, she finds Maeve sitting still and cold at the open casement. Maeve has found the supernatural lover, once human, of "boyish face closehooded with short gold hair," and again only "a symbol of ideal beauty," to be truly a "Prince of the hoar dew," for he is death. Maeve has renounced life and sought "perfection in what unfolds as death."

Mr. Yeats explains the play ("Beltaine," February, 1900) to "symbolize Ireland's choice between English materialism and her own natural idealism, as well as the choice of every individual soul." Does it follow that the lesson of "Maeve" is that it were better for Ireland to be depopulated in her pursuit of national individuality, of ideal beauty, than to drift along to complete Anglicaniz-ation, even though that bring riches, peace, and content? An austere policy, surely, if I read rightly the meaning of Mr. Yeats.

"Maeve" was not so well played at its production dur-ing the second season's performances of "The Irish Liter-ary Theatre" in February, 1900, as "The Heather Field" had been performed in 1899, but it was almost as enthu-siastically received. It has not won for itself, however, reproduction outside of Dublin, as did Mr. Martyn's first play, which was played in New York, at the Carnegie Lyceum, in April, 1900, and which was revived in London in 1903.

If objection be made to "The Enchanted Sea" as a reflection of "The Lady from the Sea," it can be replied that the call of the sea that may not be resisted is as old as the heart of man. Sea fairies, mermaids and mermen, and the voice of the waters tugging as irresistibly on the tired spirit as the undertow on the body tired with long swim-ming, are in Gaelic literature from the beginning, and

before Mr. Martyn had written of the sea enchantment
it had lent its charm to many of the stories of "Fiona
Macleod." It was two years after its publication in 1902
that, on April 18 and 19, 1904, "The Enchanted Sea"
was put on at the Antient Concert Rooms, Dublin, by
"The Players' Club." It was not well played, but according to Mr. Standish James O'Grady it was much better,
seen and listened to, than read. Writing, in his "All
Ireland Review," of its production, he puts it on record,
"I never saw an audience so attentive and at the same
time so undemonstrative. It was like being in church."
The audience probably felt the dignity of conception back
of the insufficiency of execution in the play and its inef-
fectiveness of presentation. The story that Mr. Martyn
dreamed to carry over the footlights is of Mrs. Font, a
peasant woman who has sent her husband, a gentleman,
to his grave a broken-spirited man because of her sacrifice
of his honor to advance their material position. When the
curtain rises, Mrs. Font has been thwarted, by the death
of her son, in her lifelong dream of obtaining possession
of the Font estates. The estates have reverted to her
nephew, Guy Font, a strange boy, who has been brought
up by the peasantry of the west coast and so has come to
share many of their beliefs. He is fascinated by the sea by
which he lives, and his family's friend, Lord Mask, has been
drawn to him, although there is such disparity in their
years, by this love of the sea which he and the boy have in
common. Mrs. Font wishes her daughter to marry Mask,
but the young people are but half in love with each other.
Agnes Font cannot share his visionariness, as her other

lover, Commander Lyle, plainly sees. So the North of
Ireland man never gives up hope of winning her. Mrs.
Font vulgarly throws Mask and Agnes together, in her
determination that they shall make a match of it, and as
vulgarly tells Lyle the girl is not for him. Mask cannot
but marry Agnes, Mrs. Font thinks, if Agnes has a large
fortune. To secure the fortune and the lord for her
daughter, Mrs. Font determines to get Guy Font out of
the way. Her purpose coincides with her peasant belief
that he is a "changeling," and is really of the sea people.
So she goes with him to a sea cave he is fond of visiting,
and only she comes from the cave. She is suspected, but
before the officers come for her, she learns that her crime
has defeated its own end. Mask is driven mad by the loss
of his friend and, seeking to join him by the sea, is overwhelmed and drawn out by the undertow. As the officers
come to arrest her, Mrs. Font hangs herself from the
landing of the great staircase of Font Hill with the rope
Guy used there as a swing.

"The Enchanted Sea" is cruder, colder, more amateur-
ish than the two other plays of its class, full of the sort
of talk that falls from the lips of a boy of seventeen just
awakened to ideals. Its characters act as openly and as
petulantly as children. Mrs. Font, really fine in conception, is in realization only a typical villain of the cheap
melodrama; and Commander Lyle, of the Royal Navy, a
man of thirty, is as childish in love as a schoolboy whose
beloved takes an ice from his rival at a church festival.

What Mr. Martyn could have done with "A Tale of a
Town," had he been willing to learn when opportunity

was his with Mr. Yeats and Mr. Moore and Lady Gregory, is partially shown in the rewriting of the play by Mr.
Moore into "The Bending of the Bough." The motives
remain as they were, and, in essentials, the action is the
same, the first act being little different in the two plays.
The four other acts, however, Mr. Moore has almost
entirely rewritten, and though everywhere the fundamental brainwork is Mr. Martyn's, the last acts are finer
in the revised version. Mr. Moore makes far more plausible the girl, Millicent Fell, for love of whom, and a life of
ease, the political leader Jasper Dean gives up a leadership through which he could largely right his country's
wrongs. Not only does Mr. Moore make believable the
action of the play, but he puts words on it, which, if not
true dramatic speech, reveal, after the manner of the
novelist, just what are the thought and emotion of the
characters, and the words are in themselves beautiful.

In "A Tale of a Town" the political situation from
which evolves the action of the play is the unification by
Jasper Dean of the corporation of a town, unnamed, on
the west coast of Ireland, to prosecute a lawsuit against
an English town, Anglebury, which owes the Irish town a
large indemnity, promised the Irish town when it gave up
a line of steamers in the interest of the Anglebury line of
steamers. After uniting all the various elements save the
place hunter Alderman Lawrence against Anglebury,
Dean gives up the leadership because his fiancée, whose
uncle is the mayor of the English town, turns against him
because he is opposed to the interests of her set. To hold
her he betrays his town.

"A Tale of a Town" is so crude, so naked, so obvious, so uninspired, one wonders why it can be taken seriously at all. But the reason is not far to seek. The play is true, in the main, to the life it depicts, and there is vehement feeling back of its satire; and truth and intensity of feeling cannot be denied effect on the stage any more than on the rostrum. Where it falls short of reality is in the dialogue of the aldermen. No politicians, even when egged on by their envious womankind, would ever give themselves away as do these of "A Tale of a Town." They are as frankly self-revelatory as if they were characters in a morality play.

It would, perhaps, be inexact to call Mr. Martyn a misogynist, but he has that attitude toward women of some priests his countrymen, as of many priests of all creeds, that there is something belittling if not degrading in absorbing association with women. His feeling is not at all the commoner feeling of men that leads them all to cry, "The woman tempted me." Women tempt Mr. Martyn no more than they did Ruskin, but he seems to feel that the majority of them are nuisances if not baggages. So strong is this feeling in "A Tale of a Town" that it leads him to make Millicent behave in a way no Jasper Dean in real life would ever stand, for Jasper Dean is not a man pronouncedly uxorious until his abject surrender at the end of Act IV.

There are almost as many indictments of women as there are of England in the plays of Mr. Martyn: Mrs. Tyrrell in "The Heather Field" and Mrs. Font in "The Enchanted Sea," as well as all of the women in "A Tale

of a Town" save Miss Arabella Dean. In "Maeve," the
heroine and Finola are sympathetically presented, and
there is a kind of attraction as well as decided repul-
sion in Peg Inerny. But such sympathy as Mr. Martyn
does express here seems to be expressed not because the
women are fellow human beings, but because Maeve and
Peg Inerny symbolize Ireland's resistance to English
ways and because Finola is filled with loving-kindness for
Maeve. Agnes Font in "The Enchanted Sea" escapes the
pillory rather inexplicably, for she is poor, weak girlhood
unable to understand the other-worldly idealism of her
cousin and Lord Mask. But since Mrs. Font was altogether repulsive and the men either too dreamy for
"common nature's daily food" or too hard in the way
of the Black North, Mr. Martyn felt, I suppose, that his
hearers would be utterly alienated were there not some
one in the play sympathetic in the ordinary way of human
nature.

"A Tale of a Town" was put on for the first time at
Molesworth Hall, Dublin, late in October of 1905, by
Cumann nan Gaedheal, not very notably, but it was
hailed by the Irish Ireland newspapers as admirable
propagandist material, "The United Irishmen" declaring
that "an Irish play which brings home to us, as this does,
the secret of the endurance of foreign government in this
country, is a national asset."

Mr. Martyn has not cared enough for "The Place
Hunters" (1905) to publish it in book form, contenting
himself with its printing in a little periodical. It is, as its
title indicates, a fellow of "A Tale of a Town," but it has

not back of it intensity of feeling enough to lift itself out of farce.

Between "The Place Hunters" and "Grangecolman" is an interval of seven years, but it is the Mr. Martyn of the earlier plays, still faithful to Ibsen and still of a dialogue more formal than that of life, that we find in this play of his middle age. As you read "Grangecolman" you think of "Rosmersholm," as you thought of "The Wild Duck" when you read "The Heather Field." "Grangecolman" is the story of a daughter's frustration of her elderly father's intention to marry his young amanuensis, by playing the rôle of the family ghost, long fabled but never seen, and being shot by the girl she feels is driving her out of her home. Katherine Devlin is another creature of her maker's misogyny. She is a bitter, barren woman of suffragette type, whose marriage and career as a doctor have been alike failures, and who has alienated herself from all, even her mild father, by her selfishness and discontent. It is she who has brought Miss Clare Farquhar into her father's home to render him those services in his pursuit of heraldry and genealogy that were irksome to her, and so she herself is responsible for his dependence on his secretary, which, when once the daughter recognizes it, threatens annihilation of what little pleasure she has in her life. Her husband is a dreamy sort of man, slack-fibred and pottering, who goes about waving the banner of the ideal and refusing to work. The fifth character of the play is the butler, Horan. All are clearly characterized, but if the dialogue is less stiff than that of the earlier plays, it is little more distinctive of the people who speak it, and in the latter part of the play labored and stodgy. "Grangecolman" is a picture of life as we all know it, and there is in it a fidelity of purpose that gives it a kind of effectiveness. There is not in it, however, any keenness of vision, any deep reading of life, any great underlying emotion, to relieve its abject sordidness. There is no gusto, no beauty, no intensity of bitterness even, to make its sordidness interesting in any other than a pathological way.

As one reads "Hail and Farewell," one might readily come to believe that Mr. Martyn is only an eccentric character, "gotten up" by Mr. Moore for a novel. Mr. Martyn is, in reality, a very vital force working for the nationalization of Irish art, if not an artist himself. The pity is that he is not wholly an artist, for he might have been. He knows and is interested in classes of Irish society that the dramatists of the Abbey Theatre have not tried to depict, and had he realized twelve years ago what a chance was his to learn the art of the stage, with the help and collaboration of Mr. Moore, Mr. Yeats, and Lady Gregory, he might now be what he seemed to be after the triumphant production of "The Heather Field," the Irish playwright who had adapted the modes of Ibsen to the presentation of the life of Irish landlords and bourgeois politicians.

But Mr. Martyn would not realize that ideas — and he is rich in ideas — constitute the larger part of originality; he thought technique in drama must come from the man himself, too. Such technique, of course, comes most often from the study of other drama. Certainly it was an original possession of none of the dramatists of the Celtic Renaissance, and Mr. Martyn might have been content to be a fellow learner, along with the rest of them, from one another, and from all the great dramatists of the world. It may be that Mr. Martyn never would have attained style, but he could, I think, have learned to make his characters express themselves in a way nearer to true dramatic speech than the lifeless dialogue of his that only just manages to give you their thought, with none of their mood of the moment or of their personality.

In every one of Mr. Martyn's plays the plot is interesting, save in "The Place Hunters"; in every other play it is significant; and in all it is come largely of his individual experience of life. Back of all the plays but these two political satires there is brooding that is deep if not passionate. In all the characters are natural, though some of them are unusual in the way of the unusual characters of Ibsen. And all the plays are marred, "The Heather Field" less than any other, by the fumbling touch of the amateur. Ironically, Mr. Martyn is strong where most Irishmen are weak — in his plot construction: even Mr. Yeats, who never praises with his tongue in his cheek, owning to "the triumphant construction of the 'The Heather Field'"; and weak, where most Irishmen are strong, in the dialogue. It would not have aided Mr. Martyn, for the kind of play he prefers, to have listened to the speech of the peasant as Lady Gregory has listened to it, but he might have learned, with such compeers, how to select and to condense from actual upper-class speech a speech that would represent the thoughts and emotions and personalities of his characters. It is far more difficult, of course, to write dialogue for upper-class people, save humorous dialogue, since, as many from Wordsworth's day on have pointed out, upper-class people do not express their thoughts and emotions as frankly as do the folk. As Mr. Yeats puts it, they look into the fire instead.

Amateur as he is, however, Mr. Martyn has one play to his credit that he who has read will remember, "The Heather Field." It is often thus with the amateur. We need go no further than Mr. Martyn's countryman who gave us "The Burial of Sir John Moore" for witness. Mr. Martyn has, too, like other amateurs, given suggestions to others that they have realized as fine art. It is more than likely, for instance, that Mr. Yeats had in his mind some memory of Peg Inerny when he created Cathleen ni Houlihan. There is, too, about the best plays of Mr. Martyn, a quality of a certain kind. They have the distinctness of objects seen under the bright hard light of late winter, when the sun grows strong, but when the winds are still keen from the northwest and there are no leaves as yet on the trees.

There are many characterizations of Mr. Martyn in his kinsman's "Ave." He is now "a fellow . . . with an original streak of genius in him, and very little literary tact"; but he is more generally characterized in some such fashion as this, which Mr. Moore makes a deliverance of his own: "A good fellow — an excellent one, and a man who would have written well if his mother had n't put it into his head that he had a soul. The soul is a veritable pitfall." However that may be, it was the discovery, or at least suppositious discovery, that he had a soul, a soul in harmony with the melancholy soul of Ireland, that drove Mr. Moore back to Dublin, and, for moments, even farther west to the home country of his family about Lough Gara in Mayo. This discovery was foreshadowed in "Evelyn Innes" (1898), in which Mr. Moore grows curious about the belief in ancestral memory and other esoteric beliefs of Mr. Yeats; it is latent in the introductions to "The Heather Field" and "The Bending of the Bough"; and it is made manifest in the parts of the latter play that are Mr. Moore's. Who most helped him to the discovery it is not easy to say, but an interest in his country entered into and possessed him as Kirwan's ideas entered into and possessed Dean. No doubt Mr. Yeats helped him to find his soul, and Mr. Russell, but it must be it was Mr. Martyn through whose agency the first glimmerings of such a recognition began to break upon his mind. Is it only dramatically that Mr. Moore wrote when he put upon Kirwan's lips in 1900 the words, "Life is the enemy — we should fly from life "? But whether this is only a dramatic repetition of what he might have heard any time from "A. E." had he chosen to listen, there is no doubt that Mr. Moore did discover a new quality in himself in the late nineties after he became intimately associated with the new Irish movement. There is a wistfulness of feeling and a beauty of thought in his writing, from "Evelyn Innes" on, that there was not in it before "Evelyn Innes."

There are those who think the greatest excellence of Mr. Moore is as an art critic, and that "Modern Painting" (1893) is his great book. Mr. Moore himself says that "Esther Waters" (1894) is his only book that he can read with admiration and content; and those particularly interested in the Renaissance will hold out for "Evelyn Innes" or "The Lake" (1905). To me "A Drama in Muslin" (1886) is the best story of Mr. Moore in his earlier realistic manner and "The Lake" in his later manner, a manner that is now wistful and now mellow, as in "A Drama in Muslin" his manner is uniformly as hard as winter sunshine.

Mr. Moore is, as I said at the outset, a hard-working amateur in "A Modern Lover"; three years later, in "A Drama in Muslin," he writes with authority and insight; as he does, too, in "Parnell and his Island " (1887), though here with scant sympathy; but it is not until "Evelyn Innes" that he becomes deeply concerned with beauty of subject or beauty of background, or, except at haphazard, possessed of any mastery of style. "Evelyn Innes" is very well written, — in spots, — but "The Lake" is of a wholeness of good tissue that is attainable only through an art that has labored long and earnestly to achieve beauty. Had Mr. Moore never recaptured his ancestral tradition, had he remained the writer that Paris and London had made him, he had never written so finely as he writes in "The Lake." An infancy and boyhood in Ireland; a youth in London; the ten years from twenty-one to thirty-one in Paris; eleven years of hard writing in London, years comparatively lean after those of luxury that anteceded them, brought Mr. Moore at forty-two to a knowledge of what was beautiful and significant in his home country. He and Mr. Martyn were not many years apart when they began to write about Ireland, but Mr. Moore had back of him not only ten years of writing, but back of that ten years of living life as an art in Paris and his attempts in the art of painting and his years of discussion of art in the studios. Mr. Martyn, at home, had been more concerned with religion and nationality and politics, and a shift to art as the principal career of life after forty — "Morgante the Lesser" was no more than an incursion into art, about as much of his life as a trip to Bayreuth — is only in rare instances productive of results interesting to others than the "artist." The difference in the achievements of the two men is not so much the result of the difference of the powers with which both were gifted as the result of the difference of time at which the will began to work to realize those powers. Had Mr. Martyn begun soon enough and had he been enough interested in his writing he might have made drama as full of insight and beauty and as true to human nature as are the novels of his kinsman. It is another irony of Mr. Martyn's life that it was he who should have led Mr. Moore to the subject on which Mr. Moore was to do his most harmonious and beautiful work, though it is possible, judging from "Parnell and his Island," that Mr. Moore might in the end have found his own way back.

After his wont Mr. Moore puts his intimates into books made out of Irish life. In "Evelyn Innes" Ulick Dean, fashioned in the first version of the novel after Mr. Yeats, is the only wholly Irish character. Evelyn is not Irish at

all, and her Scotch father is given the musical interests
of Mr. Dolmetsch, a Bohemian, I believe. But Sir Owen
Asher has in him much of Mr. Moore himself, though most
of Mr. Moore that is there is the English Mr. Moore.
There is something of Mr. Martyn in Monsignor Mostyn,
though an actual and not a potential ecclesiastic is drawn
upon for the basic characteristics of the character. In the
second version of "Evelyn Innes" there is more of Mr.
Russell than of Mr. Yeats in Ulick Dean, at least in his
appearance and sayings, though Mr. Moore could not
divest his composer of the personality of Mr. Yeats.
There is less of Ireland in "Sister Theresa" (1901) than in
"Evelyn Innes," but "The Untilled Field," short stories
written after the removal of Mr. Moore to Dublin and
gathered together in 1903, are wholly concerned with
Ireland. As Mr. Moore makes Jasper say to Millicent in
"The Bending of the Bough": "It is the land underfoot
that makes the Celt. Soon you will feel the fascination of
this dim, remote land steal over you." It was when this
æsthetic homesickness overtook Mr. Moore that he grew
to feel lonely in England, at least momentarily, and to
believe that "we are lonely in a foreign land because we
are deprived of our past life; but the past is about us here
[he is speaking through the mouth of Dean and in Ire-
land]; we see it at evening glimmering among the hollows
of the hills."

In "Memoirs of my Dead Self" (1906) there are chapters which tell of the return of his thought to his boyhood
in the west and that record his wish to be buried with his
father by Lough Gara; and all three volumes of "Hail and

Farewell," the first of which was published in 1911 as
"Ave," and the second in 1912 as "Salve," are the fruit
of his ten years' partial residence in Ireland, 1901–11.

Our concern with Mr. Moore here, however, is with
Mr. Moore the dramatist, so I shall not dwell on the
short stories and the novels save to say that they, more
than any writing of his, reveal his inherent dramatic
power. By dramatic power I mean not his power of situation and evolution of dramatic technique, but his power
to change his point of view with the character he is creating. A sensual exquisite himself whose predominant
thought is of woman, and of woman from a standpoint
closely akin to an epicure's toward an ideal meal, Mr.
Moore can identify himself with people in whom there
is none of himself but the essential humanity common
to mankind. Most wonderful of many wonderful real-
izations of viewpoint so different from what is his personally is his realization of the attitude of Father Mac-
Turnan, an old priest, celibate by nature, who put aside
his books, as ministering to the pride of the intellect,
and sat, night after night, with them by his side in the
study, but always unopened, while he was knitting socks
for the poor of his parish. Better known, of course, than
this character of Father MacTurnan is that of Father
Gogarty in "The Lake," but for all his sympathetic
elaboration of this bemused and distraught cleric the
character is never wholly opposed to that of Mr. Moore
himself as is the character of Father MacTurnan.

It is this power of Mr. Moore that makes him the great
novelist that he is, this power of identifying himself with

the personality and this looking out on life from the view-point of Esther Waters or Lewis Seymour, or Edward Dempsey or Rose Leicester, of Kate Lennox or Mr. Innes. Such a power is akin to one of the greatest powers of the Gael, his quick sympathy with what appeals to him in others, his momentary absorption in their interests, and his passing possession by their purpose. It is this habit of his nature that makes the Gael tell people what they wish to hear, it is this that makes him so courteous, it is this that makes him so good an actor. And the power that makes one man a good actor, a real actor, — not one who happens to fit a part, but one who can change his per-sonality from part to part, — is but another manifesta-tion of the power that enables a man to identify himself wholly, now with this character, now with that, in a story which he is writing. If a man can express such identifica-tion in dialogue, he can, if he master dramatic construc-tion, make himself into a dramatist; if he express it in subtle analytic writing about the character, it gives him one of the great powers of the novelist, a power which, if it is united with the power of story-telling, makes him a great novelist, and, oftentimes, even if he be but a fair story-teller, a great novelist. The English novel has been famously deficient in story-telling ability since Scott's day, and Mr. Moore is no exception to the rule. As, however, the emphasis of all his stories is on character, his deficiency in narrative power matters hardly at all.

Mr. Moore is, then, Ireland's greatest novelist because he has in greatest measure — in full measure — this greatest gift of the Gael, the gift of dramatic impersonation of all manner of men in all their changing moods. A personality as intense as was that of Meredith, as is that of Mr. Hardy, Mr. Moore has not always one attitude, as have both Welshman and Saxon of the Saxons, however completely they write from the standpoint of each character they create. By the side of the characters of Meredith is always Meredith, high-hearted and confident, and by the side of the characters of Mr. Hardy is always Mr. Hardy, lamenting what woe fate has brought them, but by the side of Ned Carmady or Oliver Gogarty, the Mummer or Montgomery, Sir Owen Asher or Ulick, there is seldom Mr. Moore. He almost never plays chorus to his characters, either through a commenting character or by direct interposition in the manner of Thackeray, though, of course, the characters again and again express his views. So in "The Wild Goose," in which Ned Carmady represents one year's outlook of Mr. Moore, there is only one choric observation.

When one considers how alien to Ireland were all the interests of Mr. Moore for years, his rendering of the Irish characters of "The Untilled Field" and "The Lake" is realized to be all the more remarkable. It is not easy to pick up threads that one has dropped in a period of one's life that is dead and done, but Mr. Moore has picked them up more than once. From time to time he had, of course, made visits home, writing "A Mummer's Wife" in Galway in 1884 and finding there then, no doubt, the material for "A Drama in Muslin" and the sketches of "Parnell and his Island"; but these visits were none of them of long duration until his "return" in 1901.

It is far easier to paint in the background of landscape remembered from childhood than it is again to get into touch with people parted from in childhood. The landscape changes little in far-off, lonely places, but people nowhere are what they were when the past years are sufficient to bring up beside the old folks a new generation with ideals changed. Ireland, for all the agitation of the Land League, was landlord Ireland when Mr. Moore got "A Drama in Muslin" from Ireland; Ireland was passing to the peasant proprietor when Mr. Moore returned to it to write "The Untilled Field" and "The Lake." Social and economic questions, however, interest Mr. Moore only as they concern the individual, but the changing conditions in Ireland cannot be prevented from finding their way here and there into his writing through the changes they have brought about in the people of whom he writes, though many of those he writes of are survivals from an older generation.

There are glimpses in his writing of many phases of Irish life, his characters varying all the way from such old-timers as his Cousin Dan, who, as he himself intimates, might have come out of the pages of Lever or Lover, to the very modern Father Gogarty, whose outlook is on an Ireland that "perhaps, more than any other country, had understood the supremacy of spirit over matter, and had striven to escape through mortifications from the prison of the flesh." One wonders, at times, if Mr. Moore, who joined the cause of Mr. Martyn and Mr. Yeats, self-confessedly, to have his finger in a new literary pie, really felt the landscape as he says he does in his books, or whether he just momentarily caught the power of seeing it through their eyes. Can one who was once so resolute a realist really appreciate "faint Celtic haze; a vision of silver mist and distant mountain and moor"? Perhaps he can, as a good actor appreciates a part, alien to his sympathy, that he is playing. But whether or not Mr. Moore learned to love the lonely landscape for a while, he eventually tired of it, as his Father Gogarty tired of it. Surely Mr. Moore is speaking personally as well as dramatically when he writes, "This lake was beautiful, but he was tired of its low gray shores; he was tired of those mountains, melancholy as Irish melodies, and as beautiful."

Almost any novelist, sooner or later in his career, dabbles in drama, and Mr. Moore no doubt would have attempted drama in the natural course of things, even if he had not been interested in "The Independent Theatre" and thus led to a situation in which consistency demanded that he write a play. It was his articles on the drama, gathered into "Impressions and Opinions" (1891), that provoked Mr. G. R. Sims to taunt him into "The Strike at Arlingford" (1893). In "Our Dramatists and their Literature," one of these papers, Mr. Moore, in hitting all the heads of all the contemporaneous dramatists, so stung Mr. Sims that he said he would give a hundred pounds for a stall from which to witness a performance of "an unconventional play" written by Mr. Moore. Mr. Moore accepted the challenge, and "The Strike at Arlingford," as I have said, was the result, Mr. Sims having agreed to withdraw the word "unconventional" on Mr.

Moore's objection that he would be at the mercy of Mr. Sims' judgment if the word was retained. "The Independent Theatre" played the play and Mr. Sims paid the money. It was perhaps just as well for Mr. Moore that the adjective was withdrawn, for the play was little less conventional than "The Second Mrs. Tanqueray" or "Sowing the Wind," to mention two successes of that year by play-makers that took their art a little more seriously than Mr. Sims. In a way, too, "The Strike at Arlingford" is unoriginal. Lady Ann Travers is only a more fortunate Hedda Gabler who in the end accepts the protection of her Chancellor Brack, the capitalist Baron Steinbach, after her Lövberg turned labor agitator, John Reid, has, like his prototype, made a wreck of his life. "The Strike at Arlingford" has its excellences: its plot is logically unfolded; it is believable; it is true to human nature; it has moments of intensity. Had Mr. Moore power of dialogue it might have been a fine play, for the characterization is what one would expect from so conscientious a depicter of life as Mr. Moore, and the problem, a man's choice between his love and his duty, one that has never failed to appeal to men. Mr. Moore is careful to tell us that, in his own conception of the play, "the labor dispute is an externality to which I attach little importance."

Its performance and publication, though neither event was of very much more than journalistic importance, served to give Mr. Moore something of a position as an authority on the drama, coming as they did after his association, since 1891, with "The Independent Theatre." So it is that we find him collaborating with Mrs. Craigie in "Journeys End in Lovers Meeting" (1894), which served for a year or so as one of the little plays that characterized the repertoire of the Irving-Terry Company. Just what was Mr. Moore's share in this play I do not know, but that, slight as it is, it served as apprentice work in the art of collaboration there can be no doubt, or that it added to his familiarity with the stage.

It is certain that Mr. Martyn and Mr. Yeats were glad of the assistance of Mr. Moore in founding "The Irish Literary Theatre," not only for the prominence of his name as novelist and as Moore of Moore Hall, and for his known provocativeness in pamphleteering and his capacity for drawing the fire of opponents, but for what knowledge he had of playwriting and for what experience he had in getting together and training actors for special performances such as those of "The Independent Theatre."

I have already spoken of what Mr. Moore did to "A Tale of a Town" to make it "The Bending of the Bough." From the beginning of Act II on to the end, he rewrote almost all of it, retaining only now and then an eloquent or a biting line from Mr. Martyn's play. Mr. Moore changes the scene of the play from Ireland to Scotland, that its allegory may not be so obvious; he develops Kirwan's character until he becomes not only a sort of composite spiritual portrait of the leaders of the Renaissance but a believable leader of men; and he makes Millicent's moulding of Dean to her will human, as I have said, and — Dean being the weakling that he was — inevitable. Mr. Moore cuts the play down where it is stodgy, he expands it where expansion realizes for you more of the character and motives of his people, he infuses into it more of the spirit of the movement, and he makes its patriotism wider in its appeal, a bigger and a better thing, at once more concrete and more concerned with the things of the spirit.

"Diarmid and Grania" (1901), the prose play written in collaboration by Mr. Yeats and Mr. Moore, I write of here rather than in the chapter devoted to Mr. Yeats, because, as the legend is shaped in the play, it has more of Mr. Moore than of Mr. Yeats in it. As neither of the collaborators was satisfied with the play as produced, and as neither has been willing to give it up to the other to rewrite, "Diarmid and Grania" has never been published. The notices of its production, on October 21, 1901, at the Gaiety Theatre, Dublin, are so full, however, and the legend on which it is based so familiar, that it is possible to say as I have said, when one knows well the work of both authors, whose influence is dominant in it. It seems, from the notices, to have been finely played by the Benson Company, which was brought over from England especially to produce it. The results of "the scratch company" of the second year's performances, even though these were transferred from the Antient Concert Rooms to the better stage of the Gaiety Theatre, were not very satisfactory artistically, but the third year's experiment was in every way more successful. "The Daily Express" of Dublin, in those days very much interested in Irish Ireland, thus records, on October 22, 1901, the impressions of the first night. "The 'house' was not merely

crowded, but representative. We counted among the
audience the heads of all the great professions in
Dublin, a considerable number of literary critics, and
an extremely large representation of 'le monde où l'on
s'amuse.' The Gaelic League, which flooded the gallery,
was very friendly to Mr. Moore and Mr. Yeats, and became enthusiastic over Dr. Douglas Hyde ['The Twisting of the Rope,' by Dr. Hyde, was played by him and
a company of amateurs, in Irish]. Between the acts of
'Diarmid and Grania' several members of the 'gods' sang
a number of Gaelic songs with great gusto and a good
deal of musical ability."

There are several versions of the old legend, some of
them cynical, leaving Grania in the end lighter even than
Helen of Troy; others closing with Diarmid slain by the
boar as Adonis is slain, and Grania weeping his death.
In all it is Grania who tempts Diarmid to take her away
from Finn on the eve of her wedding to the old king. In
some he goes willingly, in love with her, in others unwill-
ingly, ashamed of his disloyalty to Finn, but under *giesa*
not to refuse a woman's request. In the play of Mr. Moore
and Mr. Yeats Diarmid and Grania "do not live," says the
"Daily Express," "the exciting life of flight from cromlech to cromlech. They settle down very comfortably in
the monotony of a prosperous farm. Diarmid busies
himself with his sheep. Grania . . . begins to pine for
the society from which she has wilfully cut herself off,
and to think more and more of the grim old warrior Finn.
Then Finn comes upon the scene, patches up a sort of
truce with Diarmid, and becomes more friendly with

Grania, his lost sweetheart, than Diarmid is able to tolerate. Mutual recriminations ensue between Diarmid and Grania, and finally Diarmid goes forth to his portended death, with the taunts of Grania and the rude jeers of the Fianna ringing in his ears. As the play closes, the Fianna bear away the body of Diarmid, Finn comforts the weeping Grania, and we remember the words of the legend that 'some say she was married to Finn.' The curtain falls — a happy touch of purely modern cynicism —upon the solitary figure of Conan, the Thersites of the play, the prophet of evil chances, the scorner of high things, the prompter of foul suggestions."

As the play was being written a good deal of discussion about it found its way into the newspapers. It was rumored that it would be translated into Irish, and then back again, by Lady Gregory, into English, but no such fantastic scheme as that Mr. Moore tells us of in "Ave" was suggested in any of the paragraphs that came my way. Because they could not agree on the kind of diction they were to use in the play, Mr. Yeats, who wanted a peasant Grania, agreed, writes Mr. Moore, to his suggestion that he write the play in French. Mr. Moore gives these as the words of Mr. Yeats: "Lady Gregory will translate your text into English. Taidgh O'Donoghue will translate the English text into Irish, and Lady Gregory will translate the Irish text back into English." "And then," Mr. Moore makes himself reply to Mr. Yeats, "you'll put style upon it."

More remarkable than the scheme was the actual attempt of Mr. Moore to realize it. On leaving Galway, where he and Mr. Yeats had been collaborating at Coole, Mr. Moore began the second act in French. He gives us enough of the dialogue (pages 370 to 376 of "Ave") to show us his high pride in his French, the tolerance of his humor, and his idea of the kind of style the play should have.

If Mr. Moore had given the subject to Mr. Yeats and to Lady Gregory, as he had some thought of doing, it would only have been a return of a subject already theirs by right of their long discussion of it together. Lady Gregory was not yet working upon it for "Gods and Fighting Men" (1904); but it was she who had reduced it to the proportions of a scenario for them to work upon. This scenario was published in "Samhain" of October, 1901, that all of the audiences of the play might be in possession of the story as a Grecian audience was in possession of the story of Elektra. And did not Mr. Moore say in his speech at the dinner given to the supporters of "The Irish Literary Theatre" in February, 1900, in speaking of his collaboration with Mr. Yeats in "Diarmid and Grania": "It would be difficult to name any poet that Ireland has yet produced more truly elected by his individual and racial genius to interpret the old legend than the distinguished poet whose contemporary and *collaborateur* I have the honor to be"?

The story, of course, had been retold only less often than the story of Deirdre by Irish writers, in one form or another, but there had been no memorable play made out of it. Mr. Yeats had met it in "The Death of Dermid," which Sir Samuel Ferguson included in "The Lays of the

Western Gael" (1864), as well as in the direct translations of such scholars as Mr. Standish Hayes O'Grady and in the versions of such popularizers as Dr. Joyce. One cannot, not having read the play, declare it is not what Mr. Moore would have it, "that dramatic telling of the great story which Ireland has been waiting for these many years," but it does not seem so to have impressed those who saw it and heard it at the performances in the Gaiety Theatre.

Now that Lady Gregory has done her "Grania" (1912), it is hardly likely that Mr. Yeats will return to the story, and with the waning of Mr. Moore's interest in old Irish legend it is very unlikely that he will wish to rewrite the play. It would seem we have lost it, whatever its value, until the "literary remains" of Mr. Moore are given to the public.

The quarrel with Mr. Yeats over "Diarmid and Grania," coming as it did at the end of the three years' venture of "The Irish Literary Theatre," explains why Mr. Moore wrote no plays for the Irish National Dramatic Company and its successors on through the Abbey Theatre Players. He was still interested, however, in the "cause" as far as it was possible for one of his temperament and taste, and he was conspicuous on first nights at the Abbey Theatre down to the time of his departure from Dublin in 1911.

Since "Diarmid and Grania" (1901) Mr. Moore has published the two books of his that since "A Drama in Muslin" (1886) reveal his deepest knowledge of Irish life, the volume of stories of varying length to which he gives that title, so symbolic, "The Untilled Field" (1903), and "The Lake" (1905), but there are few incidents in either that he is likely to develop into plays. "The Lake" could not be dramatized, but if it could be dramatized, it would be as little likely to be presented in Ireland as "The Tinker's Wedding." Mr. Moore, for all that he was born a Catholic, would not hesitate any more than did the son of the Protestant minister to put a priest into a realistic modern play, and that, of course, would be a mild audacity for Mr. Moore now that he has published the scenario of "The Apostle" (1911). His Paul, in "The Apostle," a "thick-set man, of rugged appearance, hairy in the face and with a belly," is wonderfully alive, and his Jesus is a distinct and realizable personality, if not the Jesus of Christian dream. It is a curious illustration of Mr. Moore's almost disciple-like attitude toward Mr. G. W. Russell that he should make his Christ talk like "A. E." It seemed to me, as I read the words that Mr. Moore puts first on the lips of Jesus, that they were phrases that I had heard on the lips of Mr. Russell. They are of the very quality of his speech and writing: "How beautiful is the evening light as it dies, revealing every crest; the outline of the hills is evident now, evident as the will of God." And now each time, as I reread them, they sound in my ears to the remembered rhythm of Mr. Russell's voice. Should Mr. Moore ever evolve a play from this scenario, and the play be played — and why should it not, now that the way is so plainly blazed by the score and more of miracle plays of the past decade? — it will have to be chanted as

"A. E." chants his verse, as one would wish mass to be chanted.

Only a year ago Mr. Moore made his last adventure of the theatre. With the help of Mr. Lennox Robinson he dramatized "Esther Waters," but later he threw out all the latter's work, feeling, no doubt, about it as Mr. Martyn felt about Mr. Moore's rewriting of his "A Tale of a Town"; and when it was put on, in the early winter of 1911–12 by the Stage Society, "Esther Waters" the play was like "Esther Waters" the novel, solely the work of Mr. Moore. The critics seem agreed that it was long drawn out and undramatic, but that it was well written and well acted. I suppose that the preoccupation with "Esther Waters" that this dramatization reveals is because "Esther Waters" was written in that period of his life when Mr. Moore was most himself. After ten years in London he had escaped considerably from the French influence of his young manhood, and his genius had not been warped out of its true plane, as he would doubtless now say, by Irish mists. Mr. Moore must have felt that there was something not wholly himself in much of "The Untilled Field" and in much of "The Lake," that the minds of Mr. Yeats and Mr. Russell had in a way dominated his mind, and that not even the hardly tolerated Mr. Martyn had been without influence upon him.

Such a realization is not the professed motive for the return of Mr. Moore to England, but I have no doubt at all that it is somewhere in the back of his mind, where he would like it to be hidden and forgot. At any rate, by the time of his return to England, Mr. Moore had come to see clearly that the Celtic episode of his maturity was closed.

It is not, I think, particularly difficult for one who understands the old-fashioned camp-meeting "getting of religion" to understand this "Celtic episode." Mr. Moore got Celtomania; a sort of "spiritual consumption," he calls his possession in one place, as a certain other type of sinner "got religion" in the old shouting days. That is, Mr. Moore wrought himself up partly in the spirit of the Playboy, and was wrought up to some degree willy-nilly until he could write his speech of February, 1900, on "Literature and the Irish Language," and, finally, a little later, could return happily to the country that until then he could endure only now and again.

But as a matter of fact the motive that led Mr. Moore back to Ireland matters not at all to literature. What beauty of writing that return led to matters a great deal. Had he not returned to Ireland, we should not have had a good deal that adds to the joy we win from satiric laughter, we should not have had "Hail and Farewell"; had he not returned we should not have had a book that adds to the treasure of beautiful feeling and beautiful writing there is in English literature, a treasure that there is no chance of ever having too large; we should not have had "The Lake," which is Ireland, West Ireland, Catholic Ireland, a land under gray skies that the priests its masters would, too many of them, make a land of gray lives.

# CHAPTER V

## MR. GEORGE W. RUSSELL ("A. E.")

SYNGE is the one instinctive dramatist of the earlier group
of writers of the Celtic Renaissance, the one to whom
drama was the inevitable medium for the expression of
the best that was in him. Yet even Synge came to write
plays only through an external stimulus, the urging of Mr.
Yeats on their meeting in Paris. It was fortunate for the
Irish drama, this meeting, and fortunate for Synge. If he
had not been brought to the theatre of his own country,
he would probably never have written anything of first
importance. Mr. Yeats himself, of course, had been interested in verse plays from boyhood, but he, for all the
energy he has expended in learning his own particular
art of the stage, speaks more beautifully through his lyrics
and the lyrical passages of his plays than through their
passages that are dramatic speech, and not only more
beautifully but with more of dignity and power. Nor
is Lady Gregory, any more than Mr. Yeats, essentially a
dramatist. Her great power is the power of dialogue, and
dialogue, of course, is as often employed in the service of
the story as in the service of the play. Yet it is not difficult to understand how in Lady Gregory the dialogue and
in Mr. Yeats the love of the spoken word led, when opportunity was made, to writing for the stage, and for success on the stage. But in the case of "A. E." it is as diffi-

GEORGE W. RUSSELL

cult to find a foreshadowing of the playwright in the mystical poet as it would be to see in all but all of the essays of "The Treasure of the Humble," any proof that their author was a playwright. To those who knew Mr. Russell only through his verses, and were unaware of the versatility of the man, his turning dramatist was as surprising as Emerson turned dramatist would have been to the America of anti-slavery days.

It was not, of course, because of an impulse from within that Mr. Russell attempted drama in "Deirdre" (1902), but because the young enthusiasts of Ireland's national literary movement wanted plays that should be at once native in quality and the work of writers of standing. It did not seem a strange request to Cumann nan Gaedheal to ask Mr. Russell for a play. What if he had never written a play? He was hardly in their estimation more of an amateur than Mr. Yeats or Mr. Moore or Mr. Martyn, who had written plays for "The Irish Literary Theatre" that had achieved success of a kind, and he was surely as ardent a Nationalist as any of these. So he was asked for a play to be played at the Spring Festival of 1902 by the Irish National Dramatic Company that was forming, and he did what he was asked to do, blocking it all out in six hours, and finishing it sufficiently in three days for it to be put in rehearsal. It was in the summer following its first presentation that I saw it again in rehearsal in a little hall back of a produce shop in Dublin, and got to know Mr. Russell as playwright before I read his play. One of the actors, himself maker of verses and plays, gave me his copy of "Deirdre," with cues marked. I had seen

notices of its first performance in the Irish papers, and I
had written Mr. Russell to see if I could get a copy, but
he had not yet published it. Then he wrote me of young
poets I met this night in Dublin, and the names on the
lips of the enthusiasts we talked to, and their names
were names Mr. Russell had written me of four months
before. Here were they introducing me to his work as
he had thus introduced me to theirs: "There are many
poets here who write beautiful lyrics who are quite unknown out of Ireland because they never collected them
from the pages of obscure magazines. . . . I have seen
many verses signed 'I. O,' 'Alice Milligan,' 'Ethna Carberry,' 'Oghma,' 'Paul Gregan,' which I enviously wish
I could claim as my own. . . . I think myself many of
these unknown poets and poetesses write verses which no
living English writer could surpass." The best of the
verses of some of these and of others among his following Mr. Russell collected in "New Songs" (1904), which
bore out much that he claimed for them.

It was to six of these young poets he dedicated his last
volume of verse, "The Divine Vision" (1904), as he
had dedicated his two earlier volumes to poet-mystics,
"Homeward" (1894) to Mr. Charles Weekes and "The
Earth Breath" (1898) to Mr. Yeats. The young writers
(for they were almost all writers as well as actors) we met
this Saturday night in Dublin, one and all, looked to
"A. E." as leader, and some of them looked to him as
high priest of their cult, as seer of that ancient type that
combined as its functions the deliverance of religious
dicta, prophecy, and song. My thoughts went back to

our Concord of half a century ago, yet I wondered was Emerson's fascination as compelling as this.

It was in a commonplace-looking editorial sanctum that I found "A. E." on the following morning, at 22, Lincoln Place, to which he had descended from his office in the Irish Agricultural Organization Society, to edit "The Homestead" in its editor's absence. I was to see him, in the hour I was to spend with him there, in many rôles. First was that of one of the beginners of the Irish Literary Revival. He has himself given the credit to Mr. Standish James O'Grady for furnishing the initial stimulus to the movement, in his "Heroic Period" and "Cuchulain and his Contemporaries" of 1878 and 1880; but to "A. E." and Mr. Yeats and Dr. Hyde also is due much of the credit. Mr. Russell said that when he came up to Dublin, a boy from Lurgan, there was no independent thought in Dublin, but now he thought there was a good deal, and he and his fellows of the Hermetic Society, he took mild pride in believing, had had something to do with the change. Even then, as a boy, he could not read most English literature, and so he took to reading the literature of the East, the Bhagavad-Gîta and the Sufis. From his reading of these, with other young men that somehow found each other out, came the Hermetic Society, at whose meetings everything mystic from the Upanishads to Thomas Taylor was discussed. From the study of the universal, he said, they came at last to the national, to the study of the ancient folk-lore and stories of their people, which, had it not been for the Danes and Normans, would have been shaped into literary form long before now, when, he said, they were only being so shaped.

His disciples had told me the night before that "A. E." had helped them much in the National Dramatic Company, painting scenery for them, designing costumes, and aiding in a hundred other ways. He was silent about these matters and not very proud of the play. "Of course," he said, "I was very familiar with the story of Deirdre, and I had thought of its dramatic effectiveness, but I knew nothing of the stage and I was very much surprised it went so well." That it went well, I, who had seen it but the night before, could testify, though that rehearsal could give but a suggestion of the beautiful stage pictures it presents when played in the costume of the Heroic Age. Despite its intensely dramatic situations, it is, however, essentially a decorative rather than a dramatic play, and its exalted prose is seldom true dramatic speech. But you carry from it the memory of beautiful pictures, and a feeling that something noble has passed your way, to enter into and become a part of you.

As we were talking of the "movement," in came a young Roscommon landlord, and with him another of its phases and my discovery of Mr. Russell, man of business, organizer of the Irish Agricultural Organization Society. The talk was now of the erection of a hall, and Mr. Russell seemed as familiar with stone and lime and sand as with mysticism and poetry, which we had discussed, and with painting, which we were considering in a few minutes, when Mr. J. B. Yeats, Jr., arrived, to talk over an exhibition of his pictures to be held in Dublin the following week. A few days later I was reading Mr. Russell's review of Mr. Yeats's pictures, but before I left 22, Lincoln Place, I had a mental picture of "art critic" added to the already long list of titles after "A. E.'s" name, and I had still another evidence of his impressiveness. Mr. J. B. Yeats, Sr., his son said, would be around to have Mr. Russell sit for him next morning, in order to get on with the two orders he had of portraits of the mystic, one of them from an admirer in America. It was pleasant on leaving him to go away with his laugh ringing in my ears as a surety that the high seriousness of his purpose, and the higher serious-ness with which some of his admirers take him, had not dulled his sense of humor.

Eight o'clock the next evening saw us in the eminently Philistine suburban street where was the little house of conventional exterior that sheltered the high dreams of "the Irish Emerson." Once entered, his embodied visions attract you from all four walls of the study. Piles of them in corners make you wonder is Mrs. Russell a saint. The pictures are of Irish landscape; of "the Other People"; of heroes and heroines of Ireland's prehistoric days; of souls that have yet to be born; of souls that have passed through incarnation after incarnation, never to rise above an animal existence; of souls whose every rebirth has taken them to higher spirituality, and that now wait to pass along the "path of liberation" into that immortality from which they shall never be born again. These visions have come to him, as the visions whose presence he records in his poetry, in all places — as he left the office and looked down the sun-gilded streets at close of day; as he wandered in the mountains under the stars with peasants who had "second sight"; as he talked with fellow Hermetists in meeting-rooms in back streets whose shabby interiors grew rosy gloom as the talk turned on mysteries.

To us Mr. Russell talked much, talked kindly of all men, talked well of many things, said startling things of society and art and poetry so gently that you did not think until afterwards that in another you would hold them gages of combat. I can hear him yet, as I sat and tried at the same time to listen to him and to look at his flaming-hearted spirits with luminous angel wings and flashing halos enveloped in an atmosphere in which "the peacock twilight rays aloft its plumes and blooms of shadowy fire" — I can hear him saying, "You can't read Shakespeare, can you?" As I thought over this question later, I understood. Then I was too far rapt by the pictures to wonder at it greatly. Later came to mind Emerson's declaration that Homer, Milton, and Shakespeare "do not fully content us," that the "heavenly bread" is to be found in Zoroaster, Plato, St. John, and Menu. Both Emerson and Mr. Russell fail to use art as the standard. To the mystic, to whom this world is not reality, what appeal may have its seeming truths and shows as compared to the certain truth of the idealists and the beauties of the eternal life? The deep human knowledge, the great pageants of Shakespeare's kings and queens, are but "glories of our blood and state . . . shadows, not substantial things."

Mr. Russell talked very simply of his pictures, of how their subjects came to him, and of his enjoyment in thus recording them. He does not consider himself a painter, but he thinks there was the making of a painter in him had he had instruction in his earlier years. This attitude towards his various powers, as well as the attitude towards him of ardent young countrymen of his, came out in a story he told us of a boy that he found waiting for him one night at a street corner near his home. The boy timidly asked him was he not Mr. Russell, and then walked silently by his side until the house was reached. They entered and the boy mustered up courage to say he had waited for him two hours at the head of the street. "A. E." had been waiting for the boy to say what brought him, but he was obliged to encourage the boy before he would out with it. Said "A. E.," "You came here to talk with me. You must be interested in one of the three interests I have given much time to. Is it economics?" "No," replied the boy, indignantly. "Is it mysticism?" continued "A. E." "No," cried the boy, almost angry at such an interest being attributed to him. "It must be literary art, then?" "Yes," said the boy, with a sigh, his haven reached at last. "A. E." soon found the boy an exquisite who thought the literary movement was becoming vulgarized through so many people becoming interested in it. Finally the boy turned questioner and found that "A. E." was seeking the Absolute. Having found this out, he again sighed, this time regretfully, and said decidedly that "A. E." could not be his Messiah, as he abhorred the Absolute above everything else. He was infected with Pater's Relative, said Mr. Russell, "which has fallen like a blight on all English literature." So the boy — he was not yet twenty-one — went out into the night with, I suppose, another of his idols fallen.

As this boy came to "A. E.," so come scores of others, and most of those that have real troubles go away comforted, to return for advice and counsel and friendship, as their need is. This I knew before I met "A. E.," and his kindness I felt and certain magnetism, but the qualities that make him the leader of men, and hierophant to his personal following, do not lie on the surface to be quickly distinguished by every comer. Neither, we are told, did Emerson's, who was leader of men and hierophant. I thought often of "A. E.'s" pictures as I looked at the pictures of Watts in the Tate Gallery in London, and I have thought more often of them since I have come to know haloed Rosicrucian drawings and strange symbols in such books as our own Wissahickon mystics, Kelpius and his brethren, brought with them to "The Woman in the Wilderness" from Germany late in the seventeenth century. How notable the impression of Mr. Russell's paintings and visions upon two Irish writers the English-speaking world reads to-day may be learned from their exploitation in Mr. Stephen Gwynn's "The Old Knowledge" (1901), whose Owen Conroy owes being to "A. E." and his pictures, and from Mr. George Moore's "Evelyn Innes" (revised edition, 1901), whose Ulick Dean has his appearance and his power of seeing visions.

As the evening wore on, Mr. Russell picked up a manuscript collection of poems — that we were to have two years later as "The Divine Vision" — and read us several. Most distinctly of these I remember "Reconciliation," which he chanted most lovingly of all he read. It is a poem I do not pretend to understand in detail, but I do feel its drift, and I can never read out its stately music, or even read it silently, without hearing his sonorous chanting. Many of his poems are like this poem in that you must content yourself with their general drift and not insist on understanding their every phrase. I suppose to the initiate mystic they are more definite, but I doubt whether some of them are more than presentations of emotions that need not be translated into terms of thought for their desired effect.

To Mr. Russell poetry is a high and holy thing; like his friend Mr. Yeats he is at one with Spenser in believing it the fruit of a "certain enthousiasmos and celestial inspiration"; it is his religion that Mr. Russell is celebrating in his verses, many of which are in a sense hymns to the Universal Spirit, and all of which are informed by such sincerity that you do not wonder that his followers make them their gospel. In his own words: —

The spirit in man is not a product of nature, but antecedes nature, and is above it as sovereign, being of the very essence of that spirit which breathed on the face of the waters, and whose song, flowing from the silence as an incantation, summoned the stars into being out of chaos. To regain that spiritual consciousness, with its untrammelled ecstasy, is the hope of every mystic. That ecstasy is the poetic passion. . . . The act which is inspired by the Holy Breath must needs speak of things which have no sensuous existence, of hopes all unearthly, and fires of which the colors of day are only shadows.

About a score of the less than tenscore poems of "A. E." are definitely declarations of belief, but declarations so personal, so undogmatic, that you would hardly write him down a didactic poet at first reading. "A New Theme" tells of his desertion of subjects "that win the easy praise," of his venturing

> "in the untrodden woods
> To carve the future ways."

Here he acknowledges that the things he has to tell are "shadowy," that his breath in "the magic horn" can make but feeble murmurs. In the prologue to "The Divine Vision" he states the conditions of his inspiration: —

> "When twilight over the mountains fluttered
> And night with its starry millions came,
> I too had dreams: the songs I have uttered
> Came from this heart that was touched by the flame"; —

that is, the flame of his being that, "mad for the night and the deep unknown," leaps back to the "unphenomenal" world whence his spirit came and blends his spirit into one with the Universal Spirit. This same union through the soul's flame "A. E." presents in his pictures, and in his prologue to "The Divine Vision" he writes that he wishes to give his reader

> "To see one elemental pain,
> One light of everlasting joy."

This elemental pain, as I take it, is the pain of the soul shut up in its robe of clay in this physical, phenomenal world, and so shut off from the spiritual world, the world of the unphenomenal or unknowable. The "everlasting joy" I take to be the certainty of eventual union with the Universal Spirit in the unphenomenal world, a union and a joy anticipated in the occasional temporary absorptions of the soul into the Universal Spirit in moments that Emerson experienced as "revelation" and Plotinus as ecstasy.

"A. E.'s" friend, Mr. Charles Johnston, records the two young Irishmen's joint attempts to attain ecstasy, when he writes of those days when "we lay on our backs in the grass, and, looking up into the blue, tried to think ourselves into that new world which we had suddenly discovered ourselves to inhabit." Do not think this ecstasy too rare and wonderful a thing. To Plotinus it meant an utter blotting-out of self, a rapture of peace, and to Mr. Russell it frequently means that he is entirely "heart-hidden from the outer things," but I suspect it means sometimes mere lift of the heart through lungs full of fresh air, or through green fields for tired eyes, or through mountain air for worn nerves, or through skies thick-sown with stars for the vexed spirit.

The typical poem of "A. E." is that in which the sight of beautiful things of this phenomenal world in which we live lifts his soul to participation in the Universal Spirit. It is most often through some beauty of the sky at sunset, when

"Withers once more the old blue flower of day,"

as in "The Great Breath"; or at twilight, when

"Dusk wraps the village in its dim caress,"

as in "Dusk"; or at night, when

"The yellow constellations shine with pale and tender glory
In the lilac-scented stillness,"

as in "The Singing Silences"; or at sunrise, when there is

"Fire on the altar of the hills,"

as in "Dawn"; — it is most often through some beauty of the sky at such times that he becomes one with the Universal Spirit in "the rapture of the fire," that he is "lost within the 'Mother's Being,'" he would say; that the soul returns to the Oversoul, Emerson would say. There are ways by which the soul homes other than these — sometimes it is

"By the hand of a child I am led to the throne of the King,"

but it is most often by way of beauties of the sky. Some reasons are not far to seek. From sunset to sunrise the poet is free as he may be from the treadmill of the "common daily ways," and the high moods he tries to express are most easily symbolized by skyey images — massed clouds and sweeping lights of diamond, sapphire, amethyst; the still blue black of heaven thrilling with far stars; the purples of twilight horizons. In his use of these splendid symbols he is but following Proclus, whom he found quoted by Emerson as saying that "the mighty heaven exhibits, in its transfiguration, clear images of the splendor of intellectual perceptions, being moved in conjunction with the unapparent period of intellectual natures."

How important the symbol is to "A. E." — as important as it is to Emerson — may be gathered from "Symbolism," which, read in the light of what I have quoted, needs, I hope, no further interpretation.

"Now when the giant in us wakes and broods,
Filled with home-yearnings, drowsily he flings
From his deep heart high dreams and mystic moods,
Mixed with the memory of the loved earth things:
Clothing the vast with a familiar face;
Reaching his right hand forth to greet the starry race.

"Wondrously near and clear the great warm fires
  Stare from the blue; so shows the cottage light
  To the field laborer whose heart desires
  The old folk by the nook, the welcome bright
  From the housewife long parted from at dawn —
  So the star villages in God's great depths withdrawn.

"Nearer to Thee, not by delusion led,
  Though there no house-fires burn nor bright eyes gaze:
  We rise, but by the symbol charioted,
  Through loved things rising up to Love's own ways:
  By these the soul unto the vast has wings
  And sets the seal celestial on all mortal things."

In this poem is the proof of how intimately "A. E."
could write of the sweet things of earth did he so choose.
But he does not so choose, except rarely, and sometimes
he leaves out the statement of beautiful material things
by which he customarily bids farewell to earth in his as-
piration to spiritual things, and writes only of unearthly
things — as of some girl that he, an Irishman living in the
Dublin of to-day, loves in the Babylon of three thousand
years ago, to the annihilation of space and time. This is
written in the very spirit of Emerson's declaration that
"before the revelations of the soul, Time, Space, and Nature shrink away." Need I quote further to show that
"A. E.," like Emerson, holds that the true poet is he who
"gives men glimpses of the law of the Universe; shows
them the circumstance as illusion; shows that Nature is
only a language to express the laws, which are grand and
beautiful; and lets them, by his songs, into some of the
realities"? Emerson yearns that "the old forgotten
splendors of the Universe should glow again for us," and
"A. E." believes that we at times attain "the high

ancestral Self"; his restless ploughman, "walking through the woodland's purple" under "the diamond night,"

> "Deep beneath his rustic habit finds himself a King."

"A. E.'s" poems on death are little different from those in which he celebrates the soul's absorption into the Universal Spirit, since death means to him only a longer absorption into the Universal Spirit or sometimes such absorption forever. In the event of this last, he in some moods sees

> "Life and joy forever vanish as a tale is told,
> Lost within the 'Mother's Being,'"

or no sense of individuality in souls in heaven; in other moods he sees individuality preserved after death among those "High souls," that, —

> "Absolved from grief and sin,
> Leaning from out ancestral spheres,
> Beckon the wounded spirit in."

So sustained is the habitual altitude of Mr. Russell's thought, so preoccupied his mood with spiritual things, that the human reader must feel lonely at times, must feel the regions of the poet's thought alien to him. At such times it is a positive relief to find the poet yearning for the concrete sweet things of earth. It is perhaps only in "Weariness" that Mr. Russell's high mood does fail, but I rejoice when that failure makes him acknowledge —

> "Fade the heaven-assailing moods:
> Slave to petty tasks I pine
> For the quiet of the woods,
> And the sunlight seems divine.

> "And I yearn to lay my head
> Where the grass is green and sweet;
> Mother, all the dreams are fled
> From the tired child at thy feet."

It is love, love of country, love of countryside, and love of woman that he writes of when he does write of "loved earth things." "A Woman's Voice" and "Forgiveness" are poems so simple that none may misunderstand; they have the human call so rare in "A. E.," but it is not a strong human call.  Of such love songs he has written but few — poems out of the peace and not out of the passion of love; of passion other than spiritual ecstasy and rapt delight in nature there is none in his verse.  Although he has been given "a ruby-flaming heart," he has been given also "a pure cold spirit."  Only about a fourth of his poems have the human note dominant, and even when it is so dominant, as when he writes of his country, he is very seldom content to rest with a description of the beauty of place or legend; the beautiful place must be threshold to the Other World, as "The Gates of Dreamland," which he finds at the end of "the lonely road through bogland to the lake at Carrowmore," Carrowmore, the great cemetery of the great dead of prehistoric Ireland under Knocknarea near Sligo; or the legend must be symbol of some mystic belief — "Connla's well is a Celtic equivalent of the First Fountain of mysticism."

He can draw starkly, when he will, a picture of bare Irish landscape: —

> "Still rests the heavy share on the dark soil:
> Upon the black mould thick the dew-damp lies:
> The horse waits patient: from his lowly toil
> The ploughboy to the morning lifts his eyes.

> The unbudding hedgerows dark against day's fires
> Glitter with gold-lit crystals: on the rim
> Over the unregarding city's spires
> The lonely beauty shines alone for him."

In "In Connemara" and "An Irish Face," poems with earthly titles, you expect only things earthly, but in these, too, he uses the picture of the concrete only as the symbol of the universal.   The reason Mr. Russell must take you to the supernatural in these poems is because he sees spirits everywhere he goes in Ireland.  "Never a poet," he writes, "has lain on our hillsides, but gentle, stately figures, with hearts shining like the sun, move through his dreams, over radiant grasses, in an enchanted world of their own."  Start "The Memory of Earth" and you think you are to read one of the many fine poems of twilight in our literature, but the fourth line undeceives you: —

> "In the wet dusk silver sweet,
>   Down the violet-scented ways,
>   As I moved with quiet feet
>   I was met by mighty days.
>
> "On the hedge the hanging dew
>   Glassed the eve and stars and skies;
>   While I gazed a madness grew
>   Into thundered battle-cries.
>
> "Where the hawthorn glimmered white,
>   Flashed the spear and fell the stroke —
>   Ah, what faces pale and bright
>   Where the dazzling battle broke!
>
> "There a hero-hearted queen
>   With young beauty lit the van.
>   Gone! the darkness flowed between
>   All the ancient wars of man.

"While I paced the valley's gloom
Where the rabbits pattered near,
Shone a temple and a tomb
With the legend carven clear.

"Time put by a myriad fates
That her day might dawn in glory;
Death made wide a million gates
. So to close her tragic story."

And so it is in "A. E.'s" score and more poems that are suggested by Irish places and Irish legends and Irish loves. Never an Irish exile but will have a dear home place brought before him by such lines as

"The Greyhound River windeth through a loneliness so deep
Scarce a wild fowl shakes the quiet that the purple boglands keep";

and a story of the home place brought before him by such lines as

"Tarry thou yet, late lingerer in the twilight's glory;
Gay are the hills with song: earth's fairy children leave
More dim abodes to roam the primrose-hearted eve,
Opening their glimmering lips to breathe some wondrous story";

and a girl of the home place brought before him by such lines as

"Dusk, a pearl-grey river, o'er
Hill and vale puts out the day —
What do you wonder at, asthore,
What's away in yonder grey?"

but all these poems, of which these lines are the fine onsets, lead past "the dim stars" and "unto the Light of Lights."

A man that believes that his spirit is one with the Universal Spirit cannot but be an optimist if he believe that Spirit is the Spirit of Good, and that a Platonist must believe. Yet "A. E." so longs to be rapt into everlasting union with the Universal Spirit that he tires of the earth, where that union is interrupted by the necessities of daily life. The fairies call to him and he would away —

> "'Come away,' the red lips whisper, 'all the world is weary now;
> 'T is the twilight of the ages and it's time to quit the plough.
> Oh, the very sunlight's weary ere it lightens up the dew,
> And its gold is changed and faded before it falls to you.'"

But it is not always twilight to him, and there are many blither moods. Over against these lines you may put,

> "I always dwell with morning in my heart,"

and

> "Oh, but life is sweet, is sweet."

Earth is not an unhappy place, but he sighs sometimes for the happiness unalloyed of heaven.

When we come to consider the technique of Mr. Russell's art, we find him anything but Emersonian. Mr. Russell has, in general, command of form, melody, harmony, distinction. Who reads carefully will remember many fine lines; who reads only once will be as one lost in sun-filled fog like that of "A. E.'s" own Irish mountains, but he should be patient, he should wait and look again and again, and finally he will see, even if earth be still dimmed with fogbanks, much of the heavens, free of fog, and radiant with cold white light.

> "Forest glooms
> Rumorous of old romance"

and

> "But joy as an Arctic sun went down"

are the kind of lines rarest in his verse; more characteristic are,

> "Hearts like cloisters dim and grey,"

>> "the great star swings
> Along the sapphire zone,"

> "The Angel childhood of the earth,"

> "Glint the bubble planets tossing in the dead black sea of night,"

> "The old enchantment lingers in the honey heart of earth."

There are comparatively few "purple patches" in Mr. Russell's poetry, for the reasons that each poem depends for its chief appeal on one mood or thought or dream immanent in it, rather than on any fine phrasing. The effort to catch the meaning of the verse — seldom apparent at first glance — prevents the noting of as many purple lines as there are. Nor when noted are such lines readily memorable, since they are apt to lack association with known and loved things to bring them home to the reader. And again the poems are very short, — intimations, suggestions rather than expressions, — and their intangible themes are often much alike, and poem becomes confused with poem in the memory.

It may be that to those to whom the Other World is very instant, as it is to many Irishmen, or to those that go about daily preparing for the world beyond the grave, as did our Puritan ancestors of the seventeenth century, these poems of Mr. Russell's speak familiar language, as they of a certainty do to the mystic, but to the many modern art lovers who hold to Pater's "New Cyrenaicism,"

— as Mr. Russell would say, "those under the blight of the Relative," — as well as to the man in the street, their language is new and difficult to understand. But the poems have found their audience — there is no doubt about that — and they are regarded as oracular by hundreds. This is the more curious in that there is so little personality in them, surprisingly little when one knows how strong is the personality of the man that made them. But this lack of personality follows naturally on the mystic's creed — he must put into his writings chiefly his relation with God, — for all other relations are as nothing to that, — and if he attain his desire he is rapt away from himself and his fellows into oneness with God.

Quality, a very definite quality, these verses of Mr. Russell's have, but it is an almost unchanging sameness of quality; almost all his verses, as I have said, have the same theme. So there is a monotony about them, and their reader is apt to cry out that mysticism is inimical to art. It may well be that this unswerving following of one theme is of definite purpose; that Mr. Russell feels that he as Irishman and mystic has a mission, as indeed Mr. Charles Johnston owns. Speaking of Irishmen, in "Ireland" (1902), he says, —

We live in the invisible world. If I rightly understand our mission and our destiny, it is this: To restore to other men the sense of that invisible; that world of our immortality; as of old our race went forth carrying the Galilean Evangel. We shall first learn and then teach, that not with wealth can the soul of man be satisfied; that our enduring interest is not here but there, in the unseen, the hidden, the immortal, for whose purposes exist all the visible beauties of the world. If this be our mission and our purpose, well may our fair mysterious land deserve her name: Inis Fail, the Isle of Destiny.

Very like Emerson this, too, but very Irish. Let us not forget that Berkeley and Scotus Erigena were Irishmen.

I do not wish to overemphasize the influence of Emerson on "A. E.," and indeed it is no greater than Emerson's influence over M. Maeterlinck. I believe Emerson was as much guide as master, that he pointed "A. E." the way to the mystics. I might dwell on the resemblance between thoughts common to the two much more than I have — there are even lines of the younger man's that show the influence of lines of the elder. But that is not my object. I wish to point out that Puritanism in Ireland has flowered up into the mystic poetry of "A. E.," into poetry of that strange quality, cold ecstasy, as Puritanism in America has flowered up into the mystic poetry of Emerson, poetry of cold ecstasy. In England, so far as I know, Puritanism, that has given us so great a poet as Milton, has never so flowered. Crashaw was born of a Puritan father, but it was through the Old Faith his greatest inspiration came, and his ecstasy, as that of his latter-day disciple, Francis Thompson, is warm ecstasy, not cold like that of the two Puritan poets. Henry More, Platonist and seer of visions, never attained ecstasy in his poetry. It may be that it required transplantation of Englishmen into Ireland and into America to bring about this phenomenon. Nor is it the only quality these two earliest bodies of English colonists alike developed. But it is more than dangerous to dogmatize where so many races went to the making of a people as went to the making of Anglo-Irishmen and Americans.

How different are the types of Anglo-Irish I could not but ponder as we left "A. E.'s" home and went out into the chill rain of that August night. To the right hand, as we walked with "A. E.'s" disciples, they pointed to Maud Gonne's house. "Irish Joan of Arc" they call her, leader of men whom men worship at first sight; most exciting of Ireland's mob orators, all proclaim her, a very Pytho whose prophecies stir unrest and tumult! And here next door the Quietist, the man of dreams and visions, to whom all the war of the world is of as little moment as all other unrealities, since here in this world he has begun already the real, the spiritual life. Both are types that have been as long as Ireland has been; both Pytho and priest were among the high order of druid and druidess of old time; agitator and reconciler, by Mr. Russell's belief, might well be reincarnations of the wise women and wise men of prehistoric days. To the world Maud Gonne is more representative of Ireland than Mr. Russell, but he is just as truly a symbol of Ireland as she: to those who know Irish history the thought of her quiet monasteries of the seventh century, whence she sent out teachers to all of Europe, is as recurrent as her political agitation of the nineteenth, and to those who know her countryside the memories of soft sunny rains and moonlit evenings are as lingering as those of black angry days and wild blind nights. Her very colors, her grays and greens and purples, proclaim her peace. It is of this peace and of the greater peace of that unphenomenal or spiritual world,

that lies nearer to Ireland than to any Western land, that
Mr. Russell is interpreter.

You may think of Mr. Russell as you will, as organizer
of the Irish Agricultural Organization Society, as stim-
ulator of the Irish Literary Revival, as economist, playwright, poet, painter, preacher, but always as you put by
his books you will think of him as mystic, as stargazer,
wandering, as he so often tells us in his poems, on the
mountains by night, with his eyes keener with wonder at
the skies than ever shepherd's under the Star of Bethle-
hem; you will see him, the human atom, on the bare
Dublin mountains, thrilling as he watches the sweep of
world beyond world; and yet, atom that he is, the possessor of it all; — you will think of him as stargazer whose
"spirit rolls into the vast of God."

# CHAPTER VI

## LADY GREGORY

WHEN one stops to think how much of the blood of the Gael, Irish and Scotch, there is in us in America, one realizes that we owe a debt of gratitude to Lady Gregory second only to that owed her by "The Men of Ireland and Alban" themselves. For it is Lady Gregory, in her "Cuchulain of Muirthemne" (1902) and in her "Gods and Fighting Men" (1904) and in her "Book of Saints and Wonders" (1908), who has done more than any other writer of the Gaelic countries to bring home to us the wonders of Gaelic romance. That they should have to be brought home to us is a shame to us. With so much of Irish and Scotch blood in us the names of the heroes of the Red Branch and Fenian Cycles should not be so foreign in aspect and sound as they undoubtedly are, and their deeds should be as familiar as those of Robin Hood. A hundred years ago our grandfathers had, indeed, "Ossian" on their shelves, as we had in boyhood Dean Church's stories of Greece and Rome, or, in some cases, the stories of his doings in their memories, learned from their parents were they old-country born, or of their nurses were it their privilege, as it was that of many more Americans of the second half of the nineteenth century, to have as foster mothers "kindly Irish of the Irish."

LADY GREGORY

To her own countrymen the work of Lady Gregory, valuable as it is, is not the revelation it is to us. Those of them that have not been brought up on the stories that she translates could read at least many of them in the "Old Celtic Romances" (1879) of Dr. P. W. Joyce, or in the versions of the Cuchulain and the Finn legends by Mr. Standish James O'Grady (1878 and 1880), books that somehow or other never came to be widely read in America. Mr. Yeats admits it was Mr. O'Grady that "started us all," that is, the writers who began the Renaissance in the late eighties. It may be, of course, that the added beauty and dignity the stories take on in the versions of Lady Gregory will inspire to nobler writing poets and dramatists and novelists that already owe much to Mr. O'Grady or Dr. Joyce or to the scholars they were sent back to by these popularizers. It is certain that the writers of the younger group, the group of those that are only now nearing distinction, owe much to Lady Gregory. After all is said, however, her work is to be judged not for its value to others, but as in itself an art product, of a class kindred to "The Wanderings of Oisin" of Mr. Yeats, although differing in form. I am not forgetting, of course, that she is following faithfully, or rather as faithfully as an artist may follow, the old legends. She has, she owns, clarified them, condensed them, left out contradictory episodes, woven now and then a Scotch version of an incident into a cycle arranged in one complete whole from many Irish versions. When Lady Gregory has owned this she has owned that she has added something more of her own than a "connecting sen-

tence." Although she has labored carefully to keep herself out of the stories, and although, if you have read only
her versions of them, you may feel that she has succeeded
in keeping herself out of them, you will recognize, if you
turn to her originals in O'Curry or in Whitley Stokes or in
Standish Hayes O'Grady, that she has added that all-
important thing, a personality. Some scholars object to
this as "too literary." And some literary men would
rather have the old stories, they say, "just as they are."
There is the crux. How can we get them, even in an exact
translation, "just as they are"? We cannot. This is not
the place to discuss this most vexed question of translation, but I must go into it so far as to point again to the
fact that we are more likely to have made upon us, by an
interpretative translation, an effect more nearly like that
made upon the listener contemporary to the time of the
making of the story than if the translation were literal.
We are always forgetting the so obvious fact that the
kind of metaphor or descriptive epithet of this sort or
that, which would make a certain effect on the listener of
the tenth century, will make a very different effect on
the reader of to-day. As Lady Gregory points out, the
description of the contortion of Cuchulain in his fight
with Ferdiad seems very unheroic to us, and is therefore best left out of the translation, or, if retained, con-
veyed in terms that will make an effect on us similar to
the effect the detailed description had on the audience of
the old bards. Here again, however, is trouble. How can
we get that effect? We cannot surely, but an imaginative
translation by one who is scholar and *littérateur* both will

take us nearest to it. We want, as a matter of fact, both kinds of translations, the interpretative and artistic translation of Lady Gregory and the literal translation of Mr. Standish Hayes O'Grady. The one is needed to check the other. We would have a gauge by which to measure how much such a translator as Lady Gregory has taken from and added to the old story. We would know how great is the freedom in which we willingly acquiesce, remembering that the translations which we treasure as great in literature are in greater or less measure "free." So checking Lady Gregory's translations we find that they represent a fair measure of freedom, as so checking the verses of FitzGerald's "Omar Khayyám" we find in them the utmost measure of freedom, a freedom indeed that, in certain verses, is virtually a re-creation.

Many, both scholars and literary men, object to the kind of English into which Lady Gregory translates the stories of Ireland's heroic age, her "Kiltartan English," the English of the people of her home country on the borders of Clare and Galway, the English made by a people who think in Irish. This familiar language, they say, has lessened the dignity of the old tales, bringing them all to one level by a diction and style that is one, whether they are romance or folk-tale. This objection can be taken, however, only to the Cuchulain stories, which were court romance, and not to the Finn stories, which come out of the thatched houses. This "Kiltartan English" seems to me, in its more familiar moments, less imposing than that in which I first heard stories of Finn McCool told by our old gardener, Lawrence Kelly of County Wexford, but it may be I remember less clearly the homeliness of his "discourse" than its "grand speaking." It is, however, as peasant English, a fitting medium for the telling of the stories of Brigit and St. Patrick in her "Book of Saints and Wonders," for Brigit and Patrick are still household words among all the children of the Gael. But by its very difference from the English of all other artists in words, save of a few of her own country and generation, and from such conversational English as I know well, this "Kiltartan English" brings me a foreign quality. I feel that the art of these tale-tellers is an art of another race than the English, just as I feel that the art of the teller of Beowulf is an art of another race than the English. The literature in our ancestral tongue is not to me English until it sloughs off the Germanic sentence-structure of Anglo-Saxon. Here lies, I think, the greatest difficulty in translating Old English literature. And it will not be successfully translated, I think, without the use of the syntax of some dialect that preserves an archaic sentence-structure.

To me, then, it seems singularly fortunate for Lady Gregory to have her "Kiltartan English" to fall back upon to give that foreign flavor that we intuitively feel the need of in a translation. There may be a slight loss of dignity through its use, but there is a great gain in folk atmosphere.

In quoting to show the style of Lady Gregory I should quote description rather than narrative, as the description seems to me better as well as briefer. The three famous tales of Old Irish literature, "The Three Sorrows of Story-Telling," are "The Fate of the Children of Usnach," comparable, in the great wars it led to, to the rape of Helen; "The Fate of the Children of Lir," a story that has as its base the folk-tale that underlies "Lohengrin," but which takes us back farther into the past in its kinship to "Medea"; and "The Sons of Tuireann," which has been called the Irish Odyssey. Of these the first is incomparably the finest story, and Lady Gregory has told it nobly in "Cuchulain of Muirthemne," but it alone of all the stories in her three books of translations has enough of humanity in it to put it side by side with the story of Sigurd and Brunhilde or the story of Paris and Helen. When one remembers that Greek and Scandinavian literature may boast five stories each, at least, but little short of these their greatest stories, and that Irish literature has but "Diarmuid and Grania" to boast as in any way comparable to the story of Deirdre, it must be admitted that early Irish literature representing Ireland's heroic age is not so beautiful as the literature that represents the heroic ages of Scandinavia and Greece. "The Fate of the Children of Usnach" is rich in beautiful detail of incident and of description of nature; it preserves for us much of the inner life of old time; and it has dignity of proportion. It has not the fundamental weakness, as great art, of most of these old Irish stories, their characters' lack of interest because of their lack of body, their lack of personality, their running to type rather than moulding into individuals; yet the feats performed by Cuchulain are so wholly superhuman, most of them, that they often put their doer beyond our sympathy, and at their worst make him absurd.

Goshen College Students' Library Association

If these stories were simply extravagant folk-fancy, such as the Jack the Giant Killer story, to delight children, we should not quarrel with this quality in them, but there is so much in them of dignity that we must take them seriously, as we take Homer. When their heroes are definitely gods we can accept almost any of their deeds, so we can delight in the earlier stories of "Gods and Fighting Men," the stories of the Tuatha de Danaan, Lugh and Angus, Midhir and Etain, Bran and Connla, as we cannot in those of Finn and Goll and Cuchulain and Conchubar, who, because of their historical setting and more definite characterization, have more of the appeal of humanity. We know Cuchulain, in Lady Gregory's pages, as a small dark man, constant in love in comparison with his fellows, faithful to his friends, loyal to his king; and we know Finn as a fair old man of ruddy countenance, a lover of women, somewhat pompous and somewhat quarrelsome; but neither hero is a clear-cut personality like Sigurd or Ajax. If either Cuchulain or Finn were surely a god we should accept his deeds as now we cannot accept them, and were either brought home to us as wholly human and divested of his supernatural powers, and given a personality, we should be far more moved by his fortunes.

It is in enchantments, visits to worlds oversea and under wave, and in praises of the beauties of this world, its woods, its waters, its real wonders, and in the celebration of sorrow and delight that "Gods and Fighting Men" is at its best, not in the celebration of happy loves, or of wild loves, or of great victories. So it is that

Gabhra, where the Fianna were broken, is finer than "The Battle of the White Strand," where they won against great odds.

Finer, however, than any narrative power possessed by the old Irish bards is their power in the lyrical passages so freely interspersed throughout the stories, and in the lyrics that come into them on the lips of the poets and warriors and on the lips of the women who have lost their lovers in fight. The farewell of Deirdre to Alban and her lament over Naoise, the song of the woman from oversea to Bran, the poem Finn made to prove his power of poetry, the sleepy song of Grania over Diarmuid, the lament of Neargach's wife, the song of Tir-nan-Og that Niave made to Oisin, and Oisin's own praise of the good times of the Fianna—these are the passages in which the old tales reach their highest poetry. Once read, these remain in memory, but certain episodes and certain sayings remain also. Mr. Yeats has picked out one of the sayings in his introduction to "Gods and Fighting Men" that will do for sample. It is the answer of Osgar dying, to the man who asks him how he is: "I am as you would have me be." Starker even, perhaps, is the absolute simplicity of the description of that last fight in "The Battle of the White Strand," in which Cael and Finnachta go, locked in each other's arms, to their death under the waves without a word.

Wild nature is always about these warriors. The storm in the trees, the sorrow of the sea, the clatter of wild geese and the singing of swans find echo in the poems that praise them. We see, too, at times, fields heavy with harvest,

and often the apple trees in bloom and the cuckoo calling among them, — indeed, the sweet scent of apple gardens, like the keenness of the winds of spring, beautiful as
are the phrases that present them, become almost stock
phrases. Always, too, there are wonders of the other
world about the heroes; women from undersea and under-
ground come into their halls as naturally as the members of their own clans, and the twilight mists unfolding
from familiar hills will reveal their marvelous duns, white-
walled with silver or marble, and thatched with the wings
of white birds.

There has been frequent quarreling in certain quarters
with Mr. Russell and Mr. Johnston and Mr. Yeats for
introducing mysticism and a definite symbolism and
the ways of Eastern thought into their versions of Irish
mythic tales and their records of Irish mood. There will
be found some justification for such practices in Lady
Gregory's translations. Manannan, the sea-god, is here
presented doing tricks like those of the East Indian fakirs;
Finn is reincarnated in later great leaders of the Gael; and
in "The Hospitality of Cuanna's House" there is out-and-
out allegory, to say nothing of a possible symbolistic interpretation of episodes in almost every other story. Even
the willful obscurity of the modern poetry can be paralleled by the riddling of Cuchulain and Emer.

It is, perhaps, because Lady Gregory has found the old
stories not only in the dignity of their bardic presentation, but also in the happy familiarity of their telling by
the people of the thatched houses in her own district, that
she has been able to bring them so near to us. From these

same people, too, she has got some of her stories of St. Bride and Columba and poems and stories of recent and contemporary inspiration, poems and stories that have to do with humble life as well as with the highly colored heroic life that those who live bare lives themselves are so fond of imagining. In her "Poets and Dreamers" (1903) are records of this collecting and of her study of local ways about Coole and on the Connemara coast and in the Aran Isles. One of the most interesting of her chapters is that on the poet Raftery, whose poems Dr. Hyde has published. Blind and bitter, Raftery wandered about Connacht until about 1840, when death took him, an old man, but still vigorous in mind and spirit. Another chapter of "Poets and Dreamers" is "On the Edge of the World." Each reading of this is to me like a return to West Ireland, the very quality of whose life it gives. It should be the first chapter of the book turned to by the reader, for it gives one the note on which to read all. As Lady Gregory drives by the sea, people about her on the roadside and in the cabins are singing in Irish. The little experiences of the day are, for them, experiences to brood over; and for her, too. And this thought is the last of her brooding: "The rising again of Ireland, of her old speech, of her last leader [Parnell], dreams all, as we are told. But here on the edge of the world, dreams are real things, and every heart is watching for the opening of one or another grave."

There is creative writing in these essays of Lady Gregory's, for all that she is playing middleman between her people and the reading public of the English - speaking world in many of them; and, as I would emphasize again, in her three books of translations. But, after all, translation will not content, and the essay that is not self-revelation will not content, the writer who would have his writing a "reading of life." So it is not surprising that Lady Gregory turned toward drama. And yet I do not ever feel, after many readings of her plays, that Lady Gregory took to drama because of any overmastering impulse toward this most difficult of all literary forms. She has learned to handle some orders of drama pleasantly, the farce more than pleasantly, and, very recently, the folk-tragedy nobly; but had it not been that plays of other than romantic tone were needed for the Abbey Theatre as a foil to those of Mr. Yeats and of Synge, I doubt whether it is drama that Lady Gregory would have chosen as the medium through which to express her reading of life. I can just as well imagine her shrewd kindliness of judgment upon the foibles and virtues of her countrymen in stories whose form is very like that employed by Miss Barlow in her "Irish Idylls" (1892) as in these so original little plays that she has wrought out without precedent, under the tutelage of Mr. Yeats.

It is more than likely, as I say, that had it not been that drama was needed for the Abbey Theatre she would not have attempted drama. But more than likely it is, too, that had she written plays not made to order they had reached wider through Irish society and plumbed deeper into Irish life. Lady Gregory knows Irish life, from bottom to top, as few Irishwomen and few Irishmen of her day know it; she has large heart, wide tolerance, and abounding charity; and yet she was long con-

tent to limit her plays of modern Ireland to farce, at
times of a serious enough purpose, but because it is farce,
not of the first seriousness. It may be, of course, that
Lady Gregory knows best of any one her own powers, and
it is true that in the plays she has written she is at her best
when they are at their merriest. I cannot, however, but
feel that this is a success of intention rather than a success
of instinct. She would have them the most successful in
a quality as far removed as might be from that quality of
troubled dreaminess which is the best of the dramas of Mr.
Yeats. Synge, it must be remembered, did not begin as
a writer of comedy, and there is little of that ripe irony
that has no precedent in English literature in that first
play that he wrote for the Abbey Theatre, "Riders to the
Sea" (1903). Is it a coincidence that later, as he found
his bent for that sort of writing that culminated in "The
Playboy," Lady Gregory turned at times to historical
drama and a farce that grew as serious as comedy? There
is, of course, in all her plays serious indictment of national weaknesses, sometimes obvious indictment, as in
"The Deliverer" (1911), which records, in terms of folk-
biblical allegory, his countrymen's desertion of Parnell;
sometimes indictment not so obvious, as in "The Canavans" (1906), which rebukes that shoneenism in high
places which has for generations been one of the curses
of Ireland. To him who knows only a little of Irish life
it is easy to see the meaning but superficially concealed by
the farcical bustle, the laughter, and the lamentations.
But to him who looks but on the surface there is merriness enough and wittiness enough and wisdom enough

to make his loss of the deeper meaning, for him, but a little loss.

There are enough characters presented, too, peasants generally and townsfolk of the lower class, to make the farces a "reading of life." What is wanting to him who looks for more than what farce may do is the largeness of utterance that will make a "reading of life" memorable. Take "The Image" (1910), for instance, in which Lady Gregory is attempting more than in "Spreading the News" (1904) or "Hyacinth Halvey" (1906). This play, the longest that Lady Gregory has written, is what the stage would call the character farce. She owns it a presentation of dreams of old men and old women which crumble at the touch of reality, but it is not only this, but a symbolizing of the proneness of all Ireland to accept as certainties on the eve of realization what are really only signs that point to possibilities in a far to-morrow. In the play four old men of a little village on the west coast are debating what they will do with their share of a windfall that has come to the village in the shape of two whales that have drifted up on the beach. When the priest determines that all the proceeds from the sale of the oil from the whales be spent on something that will benefit the whole community they plan a statue (one of them is a stone-cutter) to some great celebrity. The motives that lead them to choose Hugh O'Lorrha are telling satire not only of Irishmen, but of all men. It would hardly be, however, in any other country than Ireland that the name of the one come at by way of accident would, unidentified for some time by any, be finally revealed as that of the hero of a folk-tale. Four days after the whales had come ashore, days wasted in planning what the village will do with the prize money, and unutilized in securing the blubber and rendering out the oil, the quartette learned that "the Connemara lads have the oil drawn from the one of them, and the other one was swept away with the spring tide."

Though "The Image" be farce, its characters are the characters of comedy, and its purpose whole-heartedly serious. And even "Spreading the News" has its lesson, of rumor's wild riot in Irish crowds. On the slightest grounds the reciting of an errand of helpfulness is turned by quick imagination into a story of a murder. Lightly sketched as are the people here, from a caricature of a magistrate to the more serious presentment of Mrs. Fallon's "nice quiet little man," they are very true to Ireland. Slighter even are the butcher and the postmistress and the model sub-sanitary inspector in "Hyacinth Halvey," though all are fully understood and fully blocked out in their author's mind, if impossible of complete realization within limits so narrow; but the farce itself is not lifted into dignity by any noble underlying attitude. "The Jack Daw" (1907) has rumor again as its motive, as had "Spreading the News," but it is not the motive of the play or any of its incidents that is the best thing about it, but the character of Michael Cooney, of the "seventh generation of Cooneys who trusted nobody living or dead." He is, of course, caricatured, but he has possibilities of personality, and he could have been worked into the fullness of a universal character had "The Jack Daw " been comedy, we will say, instead of farce. Of all her characters, that of

Hyacinth Halvey is most nearly rounded out, but then Lady Gregory has taken two little plays in which to present his portrait, "The Full Moon" (1911) recording some of his later experiences in Cloon and his final departure from the town, his introduction to which was recorded in the play bearing his name.

"The Workhouse Ward" (1908), reaching from wild farce to sentimental comedy, is hardly more than a dialogue, but it is given body by the truth to Irish life out of which it is written, that quarreling is better than loneliness. Lady Gregory has disowned "Twenty-five" (1902), which is frankly melodrama, her only other experiment in which, in her plays of modern Ireland, is "The Rising of the Moon" (1903). This play relates the allowed escape from a police officer of a political prisoner through that prisoner's persuading the officer that "patriotism" is above his sworn duty to England.

Of the plays that may be called historical, "The Canavans" (1906) is the best, because it is of the peasantry, I suppose, who change so little with the years, and whom Lady Gregory presents so amusingly and so truly in her modern farce comedy. "Kincora" (1903) takes us all the way back to the eleventh century, deriving its name from Brian's Seat on the Shannon and ending with his death at Clontarf. It is undistinguished melodrama. "The White Cockade" (1905) is better only in so far as it involves farce, farce in the kitchen of an inn on the Wexford coast just after the Battle of the Boyne. "Devorgilla" (1908) is of a time between the times of the two other historical plays, of the time a generation later than the coming of the Normans to Ireland. It is pitched to a higher key than any other of her historic plays, and it is held better to its key, but its tragedy is far less impressive than the tragedy of "The Gaol Gate" (1906) which pictures the effects upon his wife and his mother of the imprisonment of an Irish lad of to-day, and their learning that "Denis Cahel died for his neighbor." This little play is out of the life that Lady Gregory knows and can deal with; it is finely conceived and finely executed, lingering in the mind as does the keen heard rising from some bare graveyard fronting the Atlantic.

Just why Lady Gregory, who has rendered in prose so well old legends, should render old Irish historic life so much less well I cannot explain. Sometimes I think it is because she has found less of that history than of that legend among the people. Yet in "A Travelling Man" (1907), her little miracle, somewhat in the manner of Dr. Hyde's, that brings Christ into a modern peasant home, she has made a play of a tender and reconciling beauty. With the success of "A Travelling Man" and "The Gaol Gate" before me I cannot say it is because her genius is for farce; and to say that it is because her genius is for the plays of modern peasant life does not help to account for the fact.

The idiom of all these plays is racy of the soil, and when it need be, eloquent with the eloquence that is almost always in the English of the Irish. It is full of wise saws and proverbs, quips and quirks of expression, the picturesquenesses and homelinesses of speech that are characteristic of a peasant to whom talk is the half of life. These range from sayings like those of the clowns of

Elizabethan drama, such as "He had great wisdom, I tell you, being silly-like, and blind," and such country wisdom as "What would the cat's son do but kill mice," up through the elaborate maledictions of the two old paupers in "The Workhouse Ward" and such delightful asperities as that of Maelmora anent his bitter sister Gormleith, "You were surely born on a Friday, and the briars breaking through the green sod," to aphorisms that have an accent of eternity, as, "It is the poor know all the troubles of the world," and "The swift, unflinching, terrible judgment of the young."

The characters, even when they are purposely almost caricatures, have in them the possibility of complete portrayals. There is no flagging of the invention in any of them, no slipshod or careless composition. Her technique, too, at least in farce, is masterful, and in her plays of modern life of other form adequate. That she could master historical drama, as I have said, I must doubt, but that she need restrict herself so largely to farce and farce comedy in her plays of modern life, I do not for a moment believe. "The Gaol Gate," in fact, proved that she need not so restrict herself, and "MacDaragh's Wife" (1911), written by Lady Gregory at sea on her way to America, but perhaps for that all the fuller of the wild old life of her native Connacht. It would almost seem that with "Grania" (1912), a tragedy too, following "MacDaragh's Wife," Lady Gregory is widening the scope of her work, as she well can, now that there are other dramatists to provide comedies and farces for the Abbey Theatre. It is a haunting story that "MacDar-

agh's Wife" tells, and largely a true story, the story of a
piper who, though a pauper, draws all the countryside to
the funeral of his wife, draws them, through the wild lamenting of his pipes, from the fair where they are sporting to follow, with a full fellowship, to the grave, her who
died all but alone. Lady Gregory tells us in a note just
what of it she gathered from old people about her girlhood's home at Roxborough, and what about her home
of to-day at Coole, how she has shaped it, and what emotion is back of it, the "lasting pride of the artist of all
ages."

As Lady Gregory had restricted herself, until recently,
in the forms of modern life which she wrote of and in the
kinds of people she selected to write of, so, too, she had
restricted herself, until recently, in the motives she considered. It is true that the motive most recurrent in her
plays, that of fear of the opinion of the neighbor, an attitude probably sprung of the clan system, is dominant in
Irish life; and it is equally true that the motive most
notably absent, love, was until yesterday far from a dominant motive in the Irish life that Lady Gregory presents: yet there are many other motives that, in true
comedy, and even in farcical comedy, might well have
place. That these motives are not there is, I think, not
only that Lady Gregory, self-effacingly, put into her
plays what was wanted to make them foils to the plays of
Mr. Yeats and Synge, but also because of the practice
of one type of gentlewoman in literature, of which Jane
Austen is characteristic. And yet the mere mention of
Jane Austen increases the wonderment that Lady Greg-

ory has not written of people of every condition in her
neighborhood, whether that be London or Dublin or Gort,
as Miss Austen did of people of every condition in her
neighborhood, whether that be Steventon or Bath or
Chawton. It can hardly be said, even, that "Grania,"
her last play, is a play about love. In her note to the
play, Lady Gregory declares, "Love itself, with its shadow
Jealousy, is the true protagonist!" And yet, I think, it
is Jealousy only that is the true protagonist. There is
much talk about love, but it is not from love, but from
jealousy that the action of the play arises. Among
all this talk about love, among many eloquent sayings
about love, true readings of love, there stands out most
clearly in my memory this part of a speech of Finn, a
speech uttered before Grania had turned from him to
Diarmuid —

And as for youngsters, they do not know how to love because there is always some to-morrow's love possible in the
shadow of the love of to-day. It is only the old it goes through
and through entirely because they know all the last honey of
the summer-time has come to its ferment in their cup, and there
is no new summer coming to meet them forever.

This I remember not only for its thought but for its
style, the rhythm of its prose. It is Lady Gregory at her
best, as "Grania" as a whole is Lady Gregory at her best
in tragedy. If "Grania" in every detail were as inspired
as its explanation of the queen's quick turn from Diarmuid to Finn, it would be a great play, indeed. Grania
is no light woman, and yet she turns, in the old legend,
from the man who sacrificed all but all for her, on his death,

to the High King who brought about his death, with a
suddenness inexplicable. Lady Gregory makes that sudden turn plausible, for two reasons. One is that for seven
years of wandering all over Ireland, Diarmuid by his own
will, and because of loyalty to Finn, had kept Grania a
maid, making her his wife only after he found her being
carried off by the King of Foreign. The other reason is
that as Diarmuid lies dying, wounded to death by that
King of Foreign whom he has killed, his thoughts are all
of his long-delayed disloyalty to Finn, and not at all of
Grania. Thus, she justifies herself, speaking to Finn: —

*Grania.* He had no love for me at any time. It is easy to know
it now. I knew it all the while, but I would not give in to believe it. His desire was all the time with you yourself and Alm-
huin. He let on to be taken up with me, and it was but letting
on. Why would I fret after him that so soon forgot his wife, and
left her in a wretched way?

*Finn.* You are not judging him right. You are distracted
with the weight of your loss.

*Grania.* Does any man at all speak lies at the very brink of
death, or hold any secret in his heart? It was at that time he
had done with deceit, and he showed where his thought was,
and had no word at all for me that had left the whole world for
his sake, and that went wearing out my youth, pushing here and
there as far as the course of the stars of Heaven. And my thousand curses upon death not to have taken him at daybreak, and
I believing his words! It is then I would have waked him well
and would have cried my seven generations after him! And I
have lost all on this side of the world, losing that trust and faith
I had, and finding him to think of me no more than of a flock of
stars would cast their shadow on his path. And I to die with
this scald upon my heart; it is hard thistles would spring up out
of my grave.

I have spoken of Lady Gregory as translator, as collector of folk-lore, as essayist, and as dramatist; but there is another rôle in which she has brought no less advantage to the Celtic Renaissance, though it is a rôle that has not brought her, as have these other, the joys of recapturing or of creating beautiful things. Always objective, though never wholly able to subordinate personality, however near she may have come to effacing it in her plays, Lady Gregory has in this rôle considered herself solely as an agent in the service of Irish letters. The Irishman is naturally a pamphleteer, and Mr. Yeats, poet of the Other World though he be, can give as good blows in controversy as Mr. George Moore. Almost all who have part in the Renaissance have skill in the art of publicity. They have needed no publicists to fight their battles as the Pre-Raphaelites needed Ruskin. Still, in some measure in the way of publicity, and in large measure in other ways, Lady Gregory has been to the Celtic Renaissance what Ruskin was to that last renaissance of wonder. She has edited pamphlets on things national and artistic in Ireland, she has helped Dr. Hyde and Mr. Yeats in their collecting of folk-lore and to a deeper knowledge of the people; she has been one of the forces that have made possible the Abbey Theatre, giving to it her power of organization as well as plays and patronage. More than this, she has welcomed to Coole Park many a worker in the movement, who in the comfort of a holiday there has been refreshed by the gray and green land so near the sea and reinspired by the contact with that Irish Ireland so close to her doors. Like Ruskin, Lady Gregory is a great patron of letters, but like Ruskin she is much more. Lady Gregory is an artist in words who is to be valued as a presenter of Irish life, past and present, with a beauty that was not in English literature before she made it.

# CHAPTER VII

## JOHN MILLINGTON SYNGE

It is Synge himself who puts the just phrase on what his life was to him, and it is, as it could not else be, from the lips of his Deirdre that it falls. "It should be a sweet thing to have what is best and richest, if it's for a short space only." It is Deirdre alone of his men and women that is introspective at all, Deirdre — and Naisi when he is mastered by thoughts of home that will not down. Synge wrote the play of her triumph over death as he himself was dying, and he wrote it with high heart, and, what is higher, gladness, despite his foreknowledge of his doom. It was to fulfill his dream of the most queenly girl of old Irish legend that he wrote "Deirdre of the Sorrows," but he could not keep out of his writing, had he wished to keep it out, his own love that death was so soon to end, and the thoughts of what was the worth of life. "It should be a sweet thing to have what is best and richest, if it's for a short space only." It is not a new saying, but it is not to be identified with the proverbial "a short life and a merry," with which some confuse it, and of Synge it was a true saying. There are those who, because of the irony of his writing, an irony that is new to literature, and, maybe, to some cruel, or at least disillusionizing, may think there was little joy for him; but the truth is there was never a writer in whom there was more joy. This "strange still

JOHN MILLINGTON SYNGE

man" as he was even to those who knew him best, gentle or simple, found all life that was natural life, even of the barest and rudest, as thrilling as first love. It is this man, to his enemies at home the sated Parisian, who knew a gusto in living greater than that of any English writer since Borrow. Let no one forget those lines with which Christy Mahon cries defiance to the Mayo folk who have known his greatness and his fall: "Ten thousand blessings upon all that's here, for you've turned me a likely gaffer in the end of all, the way I'll go romancing through a romping lifetime from this hour to the dawning of the judgment day." I do not deny that these words are in a sense wrung from the Playboy, but what I do hold is that they prove how vital was the genius of the man who wrote them, who saw the joy there was yet in life for this braggart wastrel just as he saw that even such a miserable boyhood as Christy's knew a kind of poacher's joy in running wild on the bogs. Even for poor Nora, turned out on the roads with a tramp for companion, there is the joy of the road once she learns to know it. The tramp knows it surely: —

You'll be hearing the herons crying out over the black lakes, and you'll be hearing the grouse and the owls with them, and the larks and the big thrushes when the days are warm: and it's not from the like of them you'll be hearing a tale of getting old like Peggy Cavanagh, and losing the hair off you and the light of your eyes, but it's fine songs you'll be hearing when the sun goes up, and there'll be no old fellow wheezing the like of a sick sheep, close to your ear.

Of like gusto, too, is the joy of Martin Doul and Mary Doul in their blindness; and the joy of the three tinkers in the escape of themselves and their half-sovereign from the priest and in the prospect of "A great time drinking that bit with the trampers in the green of Clash." And from such joys as these, wild and earthy and rallying, his exultations range to the exalted serenity and sadness of Naisi and Deirdre as they look back on their seven years of love in Glen Masain, of love almost too perfect and too happy to be human.

Yes, joy is as distinctive as irony and extravagance of the writing of Synge, joy in mere living, in life even at the worst, and joy, too, in life at the best. "It should be a sweet thing to have what is best and richest, if it's for a short space only." It was for a short space of years that Synge had "what is best and richest," hardly for the seven years of his great lovers. He did not have it when his thought homed to Ireland in 1899, as a result of a meeting with Mr. Yeats in Paris. His writing, then, was of little moment, but it grew better when, at home again, he realized what Irish life was to him, when once renewed contact with the Irish peasant brought back the familiarity that had been his in the nursery. It was the Wicklow glens, to which memories of his people drew him, and the Aran Islands, where he went to study Irish — until then little more than a book language to him — and to live a life perhaps "more primitive than any in Europe," that enabled him to find himself. Further 'prentice work, though of a new sort, followed his sojourns in Wicklow and Aran, but by 1903 his art had matured to the ripe power of "In the Shadow of the Glen" and "Riders to the Sea," which, after adjustment to the stage, were put on respectively October 8, 1903, and February 25, 1904, at Molesworth Hall, Dublin. "The Tinker's Wedding" which has been played only once, and then in London, dates from about the same time. "The Well of the Saints" was produced on February 4, 1905, at the Abbey Theatre, Dublin, and "The Playboy of the Western World" on January 26, 1907, at the same place, to the accompaniment of an uproar that a certain element of Irishmen have considered it proper to create ever since on its first appearance in all cities whatsoever, whether in Great Britain or America. One wonders what they would have done had he made it as biting as Ibsen made "Peer Gynt." "Deirdre of the Sorrows," which Synge left unrevised, was first produced at the Abbey Theatre on January 13, 1910, the last of the six plays of his maturity. It was in the years from 1902 to 1909 that he had "what is best and richest"—a full life, lived largely in the Ireland that he loved; the artist's joy in making that life into a new beauty, a beauty that was all compact of exaltation and extravagance and irony; and love for a woman in whom his man's life and his artist's life were united, for her who embodied his dream of Pegeen Mike and added her life and her art of the stage to his dream of Deirdre, as day by day it emerged from his mind. And so great was his joy in these good things that his precarious health, and even his year-long last illness, could not, while he had any strength, lessen the high spirit of his writing. There is none of his plays more vital than "Deirdre of the Sorrows."

And yet this joy that is basic in Synge, this exaltation,

is no more basic than emotions and attitudes of mind
that are often, in other men, at war with joy and exaltation — irony and grotesquerie, keen insight into "the
black thoughts of men," and insistent awareness of the
quick passing of all good things, *diablerie* and mordancy.
Strange, then, should be his love passages and strange,
too, they are at times, ranging from the bizarre delight of
"In Kerry" to the triumphing nobility of Deirdre's farewell to Alban. One thinks of Mr. Hardy and one thinks
of Donne as one reads "In Kerry": —

> "We heard the thrushes by the shore and sea,
>     And saw the golden stars' nativity,
>     Then round we went the lane by Thomas Flynn,
>     Across the church where bones lie out and in;
>     And there I asked beneath a lonely cloud
>     Of strange delight, with one bird singing loud,
>     What change you'd wrought in graveyard, rock and sea,
>     This new wild paradise to wake for me . . .
>     Yet knew no more than knew those merry sins
>     Had built this stack of thigh-bones, jaws and shins."

One thinks of no other writer at all, however, when one
reads Christy's wooing of Pegeen, even when one puts
down the book in the quiet that always comes on one in
the presence of something great; one thinks of no other
writer, of course, when one sees the lovers and listens to
their words, on the stage, for one is rapt out of one's self
by the perfect accord of drama and actors at one in the
service of beauty: —

*Christy* (*indignantly*). Starting from you, is it? (*He follows
her.*) I will not, then, and when the airs is warming, in four
months or five, it's then yourself and me should be pacing

Neifin in the dews of night, the times sweet smells do be rising, and you'll see a little, shiny new moon, maybe, sinking on the hills.

*Pegeen (looking at him playfully).* And it's that kind of a poacher's love you'd make, Christy Mahon, on the sides of Neifin, when the night is down?

*Christy.* It's little you'll think if my love's a poacher's, or an earl's itself, when you'll feel my two hands stretched around you, and I squeezing kisses on your puckered lips, till I'd feel a kind of pity for the Lord God is all ages sitting lonesome in His golden chair.

*Pegeen.* That'll be right fun, Christy Mahon, and any girl would walk her heart out before she'd meet a young man was your like for eloquence, or talk at all.

*Christy (encouraged).* Let you wait, to hear me talking, till we're astray in Erris, when Good Friday's by, drinking a sup from a well, and making mighty kisses with our wetted mouths, or gaming in a gap of sunshine, with yourself stretched back unto your necklace, in the flowers of the earth.

*Pegeen (in a low voice, moved by his tone).* I'd be nice, so, is it?

*Christy (with rapture).* If the mitred bishops seen you that time, they'd be the like of the holy prophets, I'm thinking, do be straining the bars of Paradise to lay eyes on the Lady Helen of Troy, and she abroad, pacing back and forward, with a nosegay in her golden shawl.

Borrow, who comes to mind more often than any other writer as one reads Synge, chose to avoid love scenes, and Borrow's follower, Mr. Hewlett, for all his gusto, has no such exaltation as this. Had Harry Richmond taken to the road with Kiomi we might have known something like it. A chapter out of the early life of Juggling Jerry and his "Old Girl," done in the manner of "Love in the Valley," would be still nearer to it. As it is, this passage of the third act of "The Playboy of the Western World" stands alone. I doubt if Synge had read Meredith, and even had he, the life of the roads and their cottages that Synge knew so well was his master, and no writer at all. In a way, of course, the Irish-English of Dr. Hyde's translations of "The Love Songs of Connacht" was an influence, and you will find many expressions common to them and Synge. It is not important, however, whether these expressions have a common source, or whether Synge took them from "The Love Songs" rather than from his own note-book. Whatever their source it was Synge who made out of them a great style, his peasant style. It is another and a severer style that he uses in his "Deirdre of the Sorrows," the courtly subject demanding dignity and restraint. This latter style has borrowed some of the bare simplicity of the personal style of Synge, that style, I mean, in which he records his own experience in the Aran Islands or in Wicklow and Kerry.

Romancing, which is the very atmosphere of "The Playboy of the Western World," would be out of place in any telling of the greatest of old Irish legends; so it is that Synge has found for "Deirdre of the Sorrows," or rather for its great moments, an austere epic speech that seems native to the story. The passionate words are nobly adequate to the passionate resignation they have to tell, a resignation that has come of the unwilling belief of the lovers that so great a love as theirs cannot last longer "without fleck or flaw" than the seven years it has lasted. Says Deirdre, when she has come to know it is fate that they will return to Ireland, and death: —

The dawn and evening are a little while, the winter and the summer pass quickly, and what way would you and I, Naisi, have joy forever . . . It's this hour we're between the daytime and a night where there is sleep forever, and is n't it a better thing to be following on to a near death than to be bending the head down, and dragging with the feet, and seeing one day a blight showing upon love where it is sweet and tender?

*Naisi (his voice broken with distraction)*. If a near death is coming what will be my trouble losing the earth and the stars over it, and you, Deirdre, are their flame and bright crown? Come away into the safety of the woods.

*Deirdre (shaking her head slowly)*. There are as many ways to wither love as there are stars in a night of Samhain; but there is no way to keep life, or love with it, a short space only. . . . It's for that there's nothing lonesome like a love is watching out the time most lovers do be sleeping. . . . It's for that we're setting out for Emain Macha when the tide turns on the sand.

*Naisi (giving in)*. You're right, maybe. It should be a poor thing to see great lovers and they sleepy and old.

*Deirdre (with a more tender intensity)*. We're seven years without roughness or growing weary; seven years so sweet and shining, the gods would be hard set to give us seven days the like of them. It's for that we're going to Emain, where there'll be a rest forever, or a place for forgetting, in great crowds and they making a stir.

*Naisi (very softly)*. We'll go, surely, in place of keeping a watch on a love had no match and it wasting away. (*They cling to each other, then Naisi looks up.*)

And this is from the unfinished second act, that Synge thought would scarcely be worth preserving. I have quoted it rather than the great keen over the body of Naisi that brings the play to a close, because that must of necessity follow the old poem, and this is as Synge

imagined it.  Each is "a thing will be a joy and triumph
to the ends of life and time."

I have thrown what I have to say about the exaltation
of Synge to the forefront of what I have to say of him,
that all may be read in the memory of this emphasis
and of the exaltation of what I quote, no matter how
fantastic or grotesque or disillusionizing or even ghoulish
it may be.  Whatever other quality may be dominant at
any moment in Synge there is always, along with it,
exaltation.

It is the extravagance and grotesquerie, of both language and situation, that is the most immediately arresting of the qualities of Synge.  And this extravagance and
grotesquerie have marked his writing from the start.  The
old husband playing dead, that he may catch his young
wife with her lover, of his first play, "In the Shadow
of the Glen," is a very old motive, and familiar in the
meliorized form that made it known to the theatre in
"Conn the Shaughraun" (1875).  Before that, Crofton
Croker had given it currency, in "The Corpse Watchers,"
among those outside of the circles in which it was a familiar folk-story.  It might, indeed, be said of "In the Shadow
of the Glen" that it begins in the manner of Boucicault
and ends in the manner of Ibsen, for Nora Burke is in a
way a peasant Hedda Gabler.  Such a criticism would,
of course, be very superficial.  The story is a folk-story of
many countries and Synge was told the version he worked
from by the old shanachie of Inishmaan whom he calls
Pat Dirane in "The Aran Islands."  At moments the
play approaches farce, as when the supposed corpse rises

from the bed where he is stretched and drinks whiskey with a tramp who has happened in while Nora is gone to meet her young man. From such a situation it turns to keen pathos, as Nora sits with tramp and lover and the old husband she thinks dead, and listens to the wind and rain sweeping through the high glens about the hut and thinks of "the young growing behind her," and the old passing. Where else will you find cheek by jowl such sardonic humor as this and such poignancy of lament for the passing of youth? Nora speaks as she pours out whiskey for her young man: —

Why would I marry you, Mike Dara? You'll be getting old and I'll be getting old, and in a little while, I'm telling you, you'll be sitting up in your bed — the way himself was sitting — with a shake in your face, and your teeth falling, and the white hair sticking out round you like an old bush where sheep do be leaping a gap.

(*Dan Burke sits up noiselessly from under the sheet, with his hand to his face. His white hair is sticking out round his head. Nora goes on slowly without hearing him.*)

It's a pitiful thing to be getting old, but it's a queer thing surely. It's a queer thing to see an old man sitting up there in his bed with no teeth in him, and a rough word in his mouth, and his chin the way it would take the bark from the edge of an oak board you'd have building a door. . . . God forgive me, Michael Dara, we'll all be getting old, but it's a queer thing surely.

*Michael.* It's too lonesome you are from living a long time with an old man, Nora, and you're talking again like a herd that would be coming down from the thick mist (*he puts his arm round her*), but it's a fine life you'll have now with a young man — a fine life, surely.

(*Dan sneezes violently. Michael tries to get to the door, but before*

*he can do so Dan jumps out of the bed in queer white clothes,
with the stick in his hand, and goes over and puts his back
against it.)*
*Michael.* Son of God deliver us!

Equal extravagance and equal grotesquerie, and an
irony biting beyond any in any other of his plays, you
will find in "The Well of the Saints." This, too, is built
up out of Synge's experience of life in Aran and Wicklow.
Old Mourteen, a "dark man," who taught him Gaelic on
Aranmor, suggested Martin Doul, the chief character of
the play, and it was Mourteen told him, too, the story
of the well whose water would give sight to blind eyes. A
story told Synge on Inishere supplied the saint, and a
tramp in Wicklow the thoughts of Martin Doul and Mary
Doul as to the glory their hair would be to them in age.
As you read his travel sketches, in fact, you are always
coming on passages that very evidently are the suggestions for situations in this play or that, and sometimes
more than suggestions — stories and situations and very
phrases that you remember as on the lips of the peasants in his plays. In these travel sketches, too, you
find the background of the plays. There is but the germ
of "The Playboy of the Western World" in the story
told Synge in Inishmaan of the hiding there from the
police of the man that killed his father, but there is old
Mourteen's comparison of an unmarried man to "an old
jackass straying in the rocks," which later we find transferred to Michael James Flaherty almost as Synge
heard it — "an old braying jackass straying upon the
rocks."

It may be, too, that the famous Lynchehaun case confirmed Synge in taking the Aran story of the man who killed his father as the basis of "The Playboy," but it is little he got for his plays from his reading of "the fearful crimes of Ireland," and little that he got for them from any of his reading. There are situations in "The Tinker's Wedding" — the tying-up of the priest in the bag, for instance — that suggest as source "The Lout and his Mother," included by Dr. Hyde in his "Religious Songs of Connacht," but Synge records, in "At a Wicklow Fair," that a herd told him the story of the tinker couple that would be wed, as he and the herd met the man in the case in Aughrim.

No one who knows Ireland at all would hold that Synge's plays are typical of the Irish peasant generally, but any one who knows Irish literature at all, and the life of the roads in Ireland, will admit that wildness and extravagance are to be found in that literature from the beginning and in that life even at this day of supposed civilization. You will find one kind of extravagance in the distortions of Cuchulain in bardic literature, another kind of extravagance in "Little Red Mary and the Goat with the Chime of Bells" that your gardener tells you in a prosaic American suburban town; you will find the primitiveness of prehistoric life in the burning of poor old Mrs. Cleary by her neighbors in Tipperary (1895), to drive a demon out of her, and the savage that is but under the skin of all men in the description of the Spinsters' Ball at Ballinasloe in "A Drama in Muslin." Said an old shanachie to Synge on Inishere, when Synge had told him of a

stock exchange trick, "Is n't it a great wonder to think
that those men are as big rogues as ourselves?" It is idle
to pretend that it is not true that, in some moods, all men
the world over have sympathy for the rogue. Why do we
read of Reynard the Fox with delight, and Robin Hood,
and Uncle Remus, and not only in the days of our own
infantile roguery, but as grown men and women? This
man or that may say it is because of the cleverness of
Reynard, the daring of Robin Hood or his wild-woods
setting, and the resourcefulness of Bre'r Rabbit; but the
honest man will admit it is because of an innate and
deeply rooted human sympathy with roguery as well as
our natural human sympathy with the under dog and the
man hunted by a merciless or an alien law. Very often, if
the roguery is very great, or we are brought face to face
with its effects and realize it is a real thing in real life,
we will be shocked out of our sympathy with it, and
realize, as did Pegeen Mike, the difference between a
"gallous story and a dirty deed." But sometimes, if we
are a people living a primitive life, we will no more awaken
to the reality of the wrong of roguery than we would as
children have been able to sympathize with the farmer
whose pumpkin patch we raided on the eve of Hallowe'en.
A sneaking sympathy with roguery, however, is a very
different thing from a delight in extravagance. That, too,
is a universal passion, but not so native to the Teuton as
to Celt or Finn or Oriental. Its absence is what most
differentiates Old Norse literature from Old Irish, with
which it so early came into contact. It is in travelers'
tales and in the tales of seamen and in the writing that

was based on these, in rare moments of religious or romantic ecstasy, or in borrowings from Celt or Oriental
that you will find the most of what extravagance there
is in English literature. In America you find extravagance in our humor, and this humor, perhaps, owes as
much of its extravagance to an Irish ancestry as to an
environment of new wonders that could not be well
expressed save in hyperbole.

It is not only the extravagance of the change wrought
in Christy by unexpected hero-worship and an awakening
of self-confidence through love for the first time known
and returned that we wonder at, and the extravagance of
that hero-worship, but the extravagance of the imagination of his creator, and the beautiful extravagance of his
speech. The freshness and audacity of that imagination,
and the beautiful extravagance of that speech, a speech
modulated to a rhythm that Synge was the first to catch,
are in themselves enough to give distinction to almost any
subject. There was granted Synge more than this, however, — a keenness of vision into the pathetic humanity
of ugly things and a power to realize this with a beauty that
was granted to no one before, though to Swift it was
granted to see the ugliness as a bitter thing. Borrow had,
indeed, a glimpse now and then of the pathetic beauty
there is in ugliness, as in the story of Isopel Berners and
the Flaming Tinman, and Whitman, too; but no man
before Synge had the power at once to see the ugly subject as beautiful from a new angle of vision, humanize
it, irradiate it with a new glow of imagination, reveal it
through a style that for the first time ennobles English

prose drama as blank verse has long ennobled English verse drama.

Take "The Tinker's Wedding," for instance. The theme is the desire of a tinker woman, youngish if not young, to wed the man who has long been her mate; his mother's unstudied frustration of that scheme by stealing, to swap for drink, the can they were to give to the priest along with a half-sovereign for marrying them; and their joy, in the end, that they have escaped matrimony and the wasting of good money. And yet this theme is underlaid with an emotion so vital, the emotion of a wild free life, and invested with a pathos so poignant of the quick passing of all good things, that no understanding heart can but be profoundly moved by that pathos and racily rejoiced at that wildness.

It is thus, for instance, soliloquizes Mary Byrne, the rapscalliony old tinker woman of outrageous behavior of "The Tinker's Wedding." She is stealing the aforesaid can, in the absence of her son and his Sarah "to get two of Tim Flaherty's hens": "Maybe the two of them have a good right to be walking out the little short while they'd be young; but if they have itself, they'll not keep Mary Byrne from her full pint when the night's fine, and there's a dry moon in the sky." One thinks, as one reads, of Villon's old woman and her lament for yesteryear, but there are not many writers anywhere in the world, of old time or of to-day, who have such power of blending pathos and ugliness into beauty, and no other one that I know who can infuse humor into the blend, and make one at the one time laugh ironically and be thrilled as with great poetry.

There are those, of course, to whom this earthiness and wildness are repulsive, to whom old Martin Doul's love pleading to Molly Byrne is unendurable. A dirty "shabby stump of a man," a beggar, blind and middle-aged, is asking a fine white girl, young, and as teasing as an ox-eyed and ox-minded colleen may be, to go away with him. Not an exalting situation, exactly, as you read of it or see it on the stage, but once you see it on the stage, where its animality you would expect would be heightened, you realize — and it is strange to you that you do so realize — first of all its pathos, and again its pathos, and always, the scene through, its pathos. Had Molly gone with old Martin it would have revolted you, for it would have been unnatural, but since she did not, and since she was not the sort to be easily insulted, you only wonder at the power of passion and realize its pathos, and the irony of it.

There is, however, a situation ironical of love in "In the Shadow of the Glen" that is more appalling to some than any irony of "The Well of the Saints." I mean the scene at the end, where Nora, turned out by her husband and forsaken by her lover, goes out into the rain with the tramp, leaving husband and lover drinking together in utmost amity. The pathos of this and the irony of it are of a part with the pathos of the close of "Hedda Gabler." Hedda and Nora, selfish and willful both, if you like, are yet fine women both, and human, as Zenobia and Eustacia are human, and pathetic in their fates, with a pathos that even Hawthorne and Mr. Hardy have seldom the power to make us feel. But the fate of Nora was ironic as the fate of none of the others, for all three of them escaped the ennui and misery of life, while Nora but begins a new life, freer for the moment than her old life, but promising, in the end, only the old dull round.

The irony of it! "The irony of it" is always in Synge's writing even in its most exalted moments. A seven years' love "without fleck or flaw" is "surely a wonder," but it is just as surely ironical that it, like all good things, shall so soon come to an end. That, of course, is but the way of nature, and so we much question if, after all, the irony of Synge is more insistent than the irony of nature. If it is it is because he takes more care to uncover it, but basically his irony is but the irony of nature. He is in reality less ironical than Mr. Hardy, the great ironist of English literature of our day, and he is never bitter, for bitterness comes seldom except to the writer who is interested in morals, and morals interest Synge only in so far as they are natural. It is life — not any conventional way of life, or any ideal of life — that interests Synge, so he escapes ensnarement in any of the questions of the day. So frankly does he accept life that there is in him no note of protest whatsoever, which is again fortunate, for protest, too, will lead a man to morals and leave on his work the taint of a passing system of morality as it did even on Ibsen.

If there is symbolism to be found in Synge, it is there only by accident, never as the result of definite intent. He may have had, in the back of his mind, as he wrote "The Playboy of the Western World," the thought of chance making a man, of a man finding himself through

others believing in him who has no belief in himself; but
that there is in the play any parable of young Ireland losing its allegiance to a previous ideal of Ireland, I do not
for a moment believe. There is, of course, in "The Well of
the Saints" the old and oft-uttered truth that men prefer
blindness in many things to correct vision of them, that
truth that drives Mr. Shaw to blind anger. Synge has no
resentment against that truth, only interest in it as a fact
that is true of people as he sees them. The play is an
unforgettable symbol of that truth, but to make it such
was not why Synge wrote it. He wrote it with a purpose akin to that which inspired Burns to write his
"Jolly Beggars." He wrote it to make something beautiful out of the life of the beggars of the Wicklow mountains,
and I have no doubt he had a wild joy in the idea of it, in
the irony of its truth, in the grotesquerie of the situations
he garnered from his memory to illustrate its beauty and
truth.

Many wonders are possible even to-day in the wild life
of the roads and of the sea-haunted islands that Synge
knew, but he was wise to put "The Well of the Saints"
back a hundred years or more. Aran islanders told him
of rye that turned to oats in their fields and of phantom
ships that passed them at sea, but a miracle of healing
such as that of "The Well of the Saints" they were familiar with only in folk-song such as "Mary's Well," and
such a miracle, too, would hardly be attempted by a priest
of to-day.

Synge had the great advantage of writing all his plays,
after the earliest, for the stage. He knew as he wrote that

he could test that writing's stage effect in rehearsal and change it if need be. So he did change "The Playboy of the Western World," revealing the incident of the supposed patricide as a bit of narrative addressed by Christy to the admiring girls of the Mayo village, instead of, as he had intended, a scene on the stage in "a windy corner of rich Munster land." Had he written "Riders to the Sea" later, Synge would surely never have crowded into it incidents that took far longer in the happening than in the portrayal of that happening on the stage. It is this technical shortcoming that for me takes away somewhat from the exceeding beauty of this tragedy of Aran. The story of the finding of the clothes that tell of the death at sea of the last but one of the five sons of Maurya, and of the death on the very shore itself of the last son, is in its very nature a dirge, and demands a slower movement than is possible with its incidents arranged as he was content to leave them in the play as we have it. "Riders to the Sea" is less representative of Synge, moreover, than any other of his plays, for it is written on one note, the note of the dirge, of the dirge of the tides that sound their menace of the sea through Inishmaan. It is less representative of Synge because it has in it no humor, no quick changes of mood, no revelation of tumult of soul. It is less representative of Synge in that it is less original than any other of his plays, reminiscent in fact in all but its style, now of Ibsen, now of M. Maeterlinck, now even of Mr. Edward Martyn. And his style itself is not what his style was in "In the Shadow of the Glen," nor what it became again in "The Well of the Saints."

One wonders where that speech came from, that speech that is, as he would have it, "fully flavored as a nut or apple." Mr. Yeats and Lady Gregory tell us that he did not have it until he had been made free, through residence there, of the life of the Aran Islands. If one has read, however, the English of the prose translations of Dr. Hyde's "Love Songs of Connacht," one may see in their style the genesis of the style of "Riders to the Sea," and if one has read the "Dialogue between Two Old Women" of "The Religious Songs of Connacht," and "The Lout and his Mother," one may come to believe that these turned Synge toward the even more fully flavored and more rhythmic speech of the other plays. Perhaps, too, there were memories of the rhythm and of the flavor of the speech of him who made these words for Jasper Petulengro: "Life is sweet, brother, . . . there's night and day, brother, both sweet things; sun, moon, and stars, brother, all sweet things; there's likewise a wind on the heath. Life is very sweet, brother; who would wish to die!"

The speech of Connacht folk-song rendered into the English of Connacht by Dr. Hyde, however, and the speech of Borrow were no more than the start, if they were as much as the start, that put him on the right road. If ever a man made his style himself, it was Synge. He made it out of his memory and out of his imagination, using "one or two words only that I have not heard," he said, "among the country people of Ireland, or spoken in my own nursery before I could read the newspaper," but evolving from that memory by his imagination a speech that is in harmony with the imagination of the people, an imagination that is, he tells us, "fiery and magnificent and tender," though no such actual speech would be possible of reproduction from any one of them.

Synge is very definite in his statement of what he believes drama should be, and what he would make his own drama of Irish life, expressing his belief in the preface to "The Tinker's Wedding": —

The drama is made serious . . . not by the degree in which it is taken up with problems that are serious in themselves, but by the degree in which it gives the nourishment, not very easy to define, on which our imaginations live. . . .

We should not go to the theatre as we go to a chemist's or a dramshop, but as we go to a dinner where the food we need is taken with pleasure and excitement. . . .

The drama, like the symphony, does not teach or prove anything. . . .

Of the things which nourish the imagination, humor is one of the most needful and it is dangerous to limit or destroy it. Baudelaire calls laughter the greatest sign of the Satanic element in man; and where a country loses its humor, as some towns in Ireland are doing, there will be a morbidity of mind, as Baudelaire's mind was morbid. In the greater part of Ireland, however, the whole people, from the tinkers to the clergy, have still a life, and view of life, that are rich and genial and humorous. I do not think that these country people, who have so much humor themselves, will mind being laughed at without malice, as the people in every country have been laughed at in their own comedies.

In the preface to "The Playboy of the Western World" is this paragraph, completing his *credo* as to drama: —

On the stage one must have reality, and one must have joy; and that is why the intellectual modern drama has failed, and people have grown sick of the false joy of the musical comedy, that has been given them in place of the rich joy found only in what is superb and wild in reality.

Although there are only about forty characters, all told, in the six plays of Synge, and ten of these are in "Deirdre of the Sorrows," which for all its humanity is a play out of a life that is gone, there are men and women a-plenty to give us this "rich joy found only in what is superb and wild in reality." Nora is "superb and wild" in her longings, and Maurya in her sorrow; and old Martin Doul "superb and wild" in his dream of life in the South; Sarah Casey and Pegeen Mike "superb and wild" in the most direct sense of the phrase; and these are all real, if not representative of the poorer peasantry. And in the high way of romance who has dreamed what is more superb and wilder than the lament of Deirdre over Naisi! In the creation of character, as in style, and in technique of drama, Synge has done what he would. In only one of his plays, in "Riders to the Sea," are his leading characters representative Irish peasants; and even Maurya and her children, not only because of the isolation of their home in Aran, but because of the fate which has marked her mankind for death at sea, are somewhat apart from the fisher-people of the west coast. In all his four other plays of modern life, Synge has chosen characters who are, in his own words, "variations from the ordinary types of manhood," — chosen them because of his deep-seated love of the unconventional. In "In the Shadow of the Glen," Michael Dara, the herd, is a common type, and Dan Burke, the old sheep farmer, not an uncommon type, but the tramp and Nora, the one by his wandering and the other by her brooding, are "variations," though very human both. Of the cottager class, too, are Timmy the Smith, Molly Byrne, and the "villagers" of "The Well of the Saints," as are, too, the girls and men of "The Playboy of the Western World" other than the Mahons and Michael James. Shawn Keogh, indeed, is a cut above cottagers, being almost a strong farmer, and Michael James himself was, no doubt, of a similar cottager respectability before he took to shebeen-keeping. Almost all the other characters of these modern plays are, with the exception of the priest of "The Tinker's Wedding" and the saint of "The Well of the Saints," squatters, beggars, and tinkers. Among them, few as they are all told, are very differing personalities — Christy the Playboy and his father, "a dirty man, God forgive him, and he getting old and crusty"; Martin Doul, a "shabby stump of a man," "of queer talk," middle-aged and blind and a beggar; Michael Byrne, the hardy, thieving, unimaginative tinker; and the romancing young tramp who gallants Nora when her own husband turns her out on the road; — "variations" all, perhaps, but human, and compelling, all of them, our interest, and greater or less sympathy. And the women! Nora, whom we leave as road-woman, I have likened to Hedda Gabler, and Sarah Casey in externals to Isopel Berners, but I do not know to whom to compare the others save Mary Byrne, as slightly suggestive of Villon's old woman. Mary Doul, blind Martin's blind wife, has a general likeness to some old witch out of a fairy tale, but she is far from being a witch; and

Widow Quinn the incomparable might be compared, were she not too high-hearted, to the hag of "The Lout and Mother" in being

> "indecent-spoken, carneying, lying,
> Plausible, full of poems and prophecies and sharp edged."

Of the women of the cottager class, Nora, for all her wildness and bitterness, is the most lovable, and Molly Byrne the least lovable; the girls of "Riders to the Sea" are not fully enough individualized to make us feel we know them; but Pegeen Mike, Synge has put before us in appearance and temperament, character and personality. "A wild-looking but fine girl," he describes her, "with a divil's own temper," "the fright of seven town-lands" — as she says — "for my biting tongue," but susceptible of softening toward a boy of good looks and coaxing ways such as Christy. He gets around her with "his poet's talking" and his popularity, his "mighty spirit" and "gamey heart" until she gives him "words would put you thinking on the holy Brigid speaking to the infant saints."

There might be incongruity, if one were writing of any other than Synge, in speaking of Deirdre in such a company. Incongruity, however, is of the very texture of Synge's art, which has reconciled qualities, as I have said, never before reconciled in English literature. It is on Deirdre that Synge has lavished all the ideality that was in him, not because he had a dream of woman he wished to fulfill, but because to him Deirdre was all that was queenly. And yet even Deirdre is a "variation," as nobility and beauty must ever be. So lofty is she that words even in praise of her are almost impertinent. Just how lofty her words that I quoted at the outset show, as does also, by way of contrast, the mention of her here among these half-tragic, half-grotesque women of the cottages and of the roads. There is scarcely a poet, of all that have written of Ireland from the time of Ferguson to our time, that has not written his dream of Deirdre as he finds her in the old legends of Ireland, but to my mind no one of them has dreamed her so triumphantly as has Synge.

It is not, however, of such "variations" as Deirdre that the critics fall foul, but of the "variations" he puts on Irish roads and in Irish cottages when he presents the life of to-day. Why he replied to this criticism when to most criticism he was, if not indifferent, at least impervious, it is not easy to say. It is more than likely, however, that it was rather to explain his ideas than to justify his characters that he did answer. This criticism of the reality of his peasants began with his "Shadow of the Glen" and is still to be heard in many places to-day. It rose to its highest pitch of denunciation at the time of the production of "The Playboy of the Western World" in Dublin, but it was before that that he answered it fully, in the last paragraph of "The Vagrants of Wicklow," a travel sketch he made out of his wanderings in his native country. Here it is, as effective in its answer to subsequent criticism as to that which it was definitely intended to answer: —

In all the circumstances of this tramp life there is a certain wildness that gives it romance and a peculiar value for those who look at life in Ireland with an eye that is aware of the arts also. In all the healthy movements of art, variations from the ordinary types of manhood are made interesting for the ordinary man, and in this way only the higher arts are universal. Beside this art, however, founded on the variations which are a condition and effect of all vigorous life, there is another art — sometimes confounded with it — founded on the freak of nature, in itself a mere sign of atavism or disease. This latter art, which is occupied with the antics of the freak, is of interest only to the variation from ordinary minds, and, for this reason, is never universal. To be quite plain, the tramp in real life, Hamlet and Faust, in the arts, are variations; but the maniac in real life, and Des Esseintes and all his ugly crew in the arts, are freaks only.

It is well to consider all his characters in the light of this statement, I think, and to re-read, keeping in mind a possible further application of it, those phrases in the plays that so outrage many at their hearing in the theatre. I would not for a moment seem to want to soften the hardness of the life he pictures or to explain away his delightfully sardonic humor as in reality a reconciling sort of humor, but I do wish to say that the more I read him the less cruel and sardonic that humor seems. The impersonality of the man as dramatist grows on you as you read, you realize more and more his abstention from playing chorus to his characters, and you come to know that the seeming cruelty and sardonic joy are largely only the direct outcome of his courage in allowing Nature to speak for herself. If you turn again to the plays after learning of their background from his travel sketches, you see many things in a new light. The irony, the grotesquerie, the tonic earthiness never grow less, but one learns to discount somewhat the effect of the hardness of speech on the recipients of that speech, as through experience one learns — after one's second attendance at a wake — to discount something of the too voluble sorrow of keening.

That the candor of Synge, in allowing his people of hard nature or of careless nature to say the ruthless things native to their minds and temper, hurts many, there is proof every time one sees a play of his on the stage. You will hear women about you gasp with mingled surprise and disgust, their sensibilities wholly outraged, but unwilling laughter in their minds when the Widow Quinn says to Christy, after his praise of Pegeen, "There's poetry talk for a girl you'd see itching and scratching, and she with a stale stink of poteen on her from selling in the shop." Such gasps are nothing, however, to those they utter when they hear Mary Doul tell Molly Byrne "when the skin shrinks on your chin, Molly Byrne, there won't be the like of you for a shrunk hag in the four quarters of Ireland."

Very different is the kind of laughter aroused by the sly malice, native to the rogue story from the days in which its characters masqueraded as animals, that is revealed in the remark of Mary Byrne to the priest, "It's destroyed you must be hearing the sins of the rural people in a fine spring"; and different again the childish delight in the extravagance at Christy's threat to send Shawn Keogh "coaching out through Limbo with my father's ghost"; and still different the breathless, delighted wonderment in the sense of moral values exhibited by Michael James, when, fearing that Christy's threatened murder of Shawn, if carried out, would give his secret trade away, he jumps up with a shriek, exclaiming, "Murder is it? Is it mad you's are? Would you go making murder in this place, and it piled with poteen for our drink to-night?" Different, too, is the laughter at the Rabelaisian touches and at the farcical situations in which the plays abound.

If ever there were characters that lived a life apart from their author's, those characters are Synge's. It is in the verses and in the travel sketches that we get the man himself, the man back of the dramatist that gives to his characters a life independent of his own, a life that he knows partly in reality and partly in imagination, but that he himself has lived chiefly as an observer and imaginer. There is no humor in these verses and travel sketches, not even when he is describing a humorous scene such as that of the upsetting by pigs running wild of the constabulary busy about evictions on Inishmaan. We get the man himself, I say, in these verses and travel sketches, a man exulting in primitiveness, in wildness, in beauty of woman and child, in beauty of landscape; but exulting, more than in all else, in his own moods aroused by these things that he loved. Even here, however, he is at times almost impossibly impersonal, so that you feel in a certain description that there is no man between you and the thing described, but that, to adapt a phrase of Thoreau, it is the hills and the sea and the atmosphere writing. This impersonality persists even in "The Aran Islands," so large a part of which is very personal in that it is a statement of his daily life on Inishmaan. It is not, however, from the impersonal writing that I would quote, — though I would emphasize this impersonality because it is part of the very nature of the man, — but from the personal parts, because they reveal more of the positive part of him. After a day of storm on Inishmaan, the middle island of the three that make up the Aran group, Synge writes: "About the sunset the clouds broke and the storm turned to a hurricane. Bars of purple cloud stretched across the sound where immense waves were rolling from the west, wreathed with snowy fantasies of spray. Then there was the bay full of green delirium and the Twelve Pins touched with mauve and scarlet in the east." That is the Connacht coast, and this the next paragraph is Synge: "The suggestion from this world of inarticulate power was immense, and now at midnight, when the wind is abating, I am still trembling and flushed with exultation." And here is Synge again, in another temper, which came to him on the seas about Inishmaan: "The black curagh working slowly through this world of gray, and the soft hissing of the rain, gave me one of the moods in which we realize with immense distress the short moment we have left us to experience all the wonder and beauty of the world."

"The Aran Islands" is most memorable of his travel writings, because he spent more time on these rocks at the world's end and came closest here to the soul of Irish life. There are passages, however, in his description of the Kerry coast, and even in his newspaper sketches of the coast of Connemara, that tell not only of the places but of their visitor. "I got on a long road running through a bog," he writes in "In West Kerry," "with a smooth mountain on one side and the sea on the other, and Brandon in front of me, partly covered with clouds. As far as I could see there were little groups of people on their way to the chapel at Ballyferriter, the men in homespun and the women wearing blue cloaks, or, more often, black shawls twisted over their heads. This procession along the olive bogs, between the mountains and the sea, on this gray day of autumn, seemed to wring me with the pang of emotion one meets everywhere in Ireland, an emotion that is partly local and patriotic, and partly a share of the desolation that is mixed everywhere with the supreme beauty of the world."

The comment on Ireland, her ways and her place among the peoples, that many a dramatist would have permitted himself to express through some character chosen to play chorus to the action, Synge now and then permits himself in the travel sketches. In "From Galway to Gorumna," which he wrote for the "Manchester Guardian's" investigation of the congested districts, is one of such rare avowals, an avowal to treasure along with those of his all too short prefaces: "It is part of the misfortune of Ireland that nearly all the characteristics which give color and attractiveness to Irish life [he has been speaking of 'men dressed in homespuns of the gray natural wool, and the women in deep madder-dyed petticoats and bodices, with brown shawls over their heads'] are bound up with a social condition that is near to penury, while in countries like Brittany the best external features of the local life — the rich embroidered dresses, for instance, or the carved furniture — are connected with a decent and comfortable social condition."

It is this penury, perhaps, and its gray background, that by way of contrast emphasize so strongly the moments of splendor that Irish landscape knows. One such moment Synge saw as he looked southward across the bay from the Dingle peninsula toward Killarney: "The blueness of the sea and the hills from Carrantuohill to the Skelligs, the singular loneliness of the hillside I was on, with a few choughs and gulls in sight only, had a splendor that was almost a grief in the mind."

This splendor Synge found also in his own Wicklow, a lonelier country than Aran, if loneliness comes from absence of human life. And if there is not the loneliness of the sea in the inland glens that Synge knew so well, there is in them the equal loneliness of the mountains. It is this county of Wicklow that is the background of "In the Shadow of the Glen" and of "The Well of the Saints" and of "The Tinker's Wedding." And perhaps had not the Abbey Theatre grown to be a theatre for folk-drama and for poetic drama of court romance alone, Synge would have made Wicklow the background of dramas of a high life of yesterday. Certain it is that in these passages he is thinking of it: —

Every one is used in Ireland to the tragedy that is bound up with the lives of farmers and fishing-people; but in this garden one seemed to feel the tragedy of the landlord class also, and of the innumerable old families that are quickly dwindling away. These owners of the land are not much pitied at the present day, or much deserving of pity; and yet one cannot quite forget that they are the descendants of what was at one time, in the eighteenth century, a high-spirited and highly cultivated aristocracy. The broken greenhouses and mouse-eaten libraries, that were designed and collected by men who voted with Grattan, are perhaps as mournful in the end as the four mud walls that are so often left in Wicklow as the only remnants of a farmhouse. The desolation of this life is often of a peculiarly local kind, and if a playwright chose to go through the Irish country houses he would find material, it is likely, for many gloomy plays that would turn on the dying away of these old families, and on the lives of the one or two delicate girls that are left so often to represent a dozen hearty men who were alive a generation or two ago.

I have dwelt on these travel sketches of Synge not alone for their own sake, but because they are, as I have said, the background of the plays, and because they contain what are in a sense the diary notes out of which the plays grew. In a sense, too, they are a commentary on the plays, and as I have also said a revelation of the playwright. All must be read for a thorough understanding of the plays, though these alone should be a delight to all, even if they know no more of Ireland than that share of human nature which is axiomatically the same in all men of all races. If you do not read the travel sketches, you may fail to see how deeply sympathetic Synge is with the Irish peasant, and in no patronizing way. In "The Aran Islands" he takes the greatest care to disguise the identity of those he knew intimately lest they be pained by anything he wrote of them. No one could write with higher courtesy of those whose guest he had been than Synge. You, reading, are made one of their home circle, but no family secrets are betrayed. You are made aware of their weaknesses, but there is never any disloyalty; and always in his records of them their virtues of courage and endur-

ance, of adaptiveness and simplicity, of family stanch-
ness and communal helpfulness, outweigh the drunken-
ness and roguery that one expects from the primitive.
Synge is, indeed, not only loyal, but full of respect and
liking for the Aran Islanders, and of admiration for their
rich humanity.

It was out of his island life and out of his life of the
roads, and out of his mood, once he knew his doom, that
he made the twenty-two poems of his that are retained
of a great deal that he had written, most of it in his
younger years. That Synge faced his fate with bravery
the triumphant tone of "Deirdre of the Sorrows" that I
have instanced is proof, but there could not but be moments when the thought of death was too instant to be
denied. It was in such mood he wrote, either toward the
end, or in earlier moments of anticipation of it, "Queens,"
"On an Anniversary," "To the Oaks of Glencree," "A
Question," and "I've Thirty Months." There is in these
verses a certain morbidity, an almost ghoulishness, that
is very seldom present elsewhere in his writing. And yet
I may be wrong in attributing it to his certainty of ap-
proaching death, for there is a more intense preoccupation
with death in the plays of M. Maeterlinck's youth and a
greater ghoulishness in the verse of Mr. Hardy's youth.
It is of Mr. Hardy's verses that one thinks oftenest as one
reads these verses of Synge, and not only because of certain likenesses in subject-matter, but because of the im-
perfect mastery of both over the verse forms and a certain epigrammatic gnomic quality common to both. The
verses of Synge are not relatively so important in com-

parison with the rest of his writing as Mr. Hardy's verses
are in comparison with the rest of his writing, for they are
not needed to explain a philosophy of life as are Mr.
Hardy's verses. Fortunately, Synge attempted no philosophy, had the rare wisdom to rest content with observation.

In regard to poetry, as to all his art, Synge had,
however, definite views, though his verse is almost too
little in bulk to exemplify them. It was the poetry of exaltation, as it was the drama of exaltation, as it was the
exaltation in living, of change and speed and danger and
love, that meant most to him. He held further that "in
these days poetry is usually a flower of evil or good; but
it is the timber of poetry that wears most surely, and
there is no timber that has not strong roots among the
clay and worms." The verse of Synge, as all his art, was
so rooted, surely. "Even if we grant," he continues,
"that exalted poetry can be kept successful by itself, the
strong things of life are needed in poetry also, to show
that what is exalted or tender is not made by feeble
blood. It may almost be said that before verse can be
human again it must learn to be brutal."

It is sayings of this sort that bring to mind his kinship with Whitman, to whom he is also bound by the
freemasonry of the roads. Both men felt the call of the
road; both loved the changing landscape and the little
adventures of the caravansaries; both loved most of all
the men and women they met. Once only Synge seems
to have forgotten humanity when he took to the road,
that time which he has recorded in "Prelude": —

"Still south I went and west and south again,
  Through Wicklow from the morning till the night,
  And far from cities, and the sights of men,
  Lived with the sunshine, and the moon's delight.

"I knew the stars, the flowers, and the birds,
  The gray and wintry sides of many glens,
  And did but half remember human words,
  In converse with the mountains, moors, and fens."

It is to this, to the wandering wayside life of Synge, that one's thought of him always returns, and rightly, for it was the road that most inspired him. It is the memory of the road that most kindles him; and so it is always to the man of the road that he gives his most lyric passages; or, perhaps, I should say it is the speech that the thought of the man of the roads or of the woman of wild heart raises in his mind that is his most beautiful speech, with the very wildness of the wandering heart in it, and with the long swing that comes, with second wind, when you have been a day abroad on the road.

What if the words have now the clauber of the roads upon them, and even the muck, and now the reek of the shebeen or of the tinker's fire in a roadside ditch; they have, too, the bog smell, and the smell of the whin, the smell of ploughed land and of the sea, and they fall into cadences that are cadences of the wind and of the tides, of full rivers and clucking streams that sudden rains have filled, as well as the cadences of the voices of boy and girl and they love-making, and of the voices of the wild folk of the roads coaxing or loudly quarreling, and the voices of women and men, young and old, lamenting the hard way of life and of the sorrow that waits for all in the end.

Why quarrel with Synge, in short, because his style is of the very essence of life, and of nature, which is the background of life?

To attain a style that is his very self, that is of the very color of his life, and of the very color of the extravagant phases of the life of his country, to attain a style that embodies all this, and that for the first time sets English dramatic prose to a rhythm as noble as the rhythm of blank verse, is surely in itself title to greatness. But Synge has other titles, too. In the few characters that he has created, forty in all, characters all natively Irish, he has attained universality, because these Irish men and women, Nora and Martin Doul, Sarah Casey and Christy Mahon, Maurya and Deirdre, are so human that they are prototypes of men and women the world over. And of dialogue, where style and characterization blend, he has sure control. Each character of the six great characters that I have just mentioned speaks and acts just as such a character would, and not only these, but every other character that occupies the stage for more than a moment. Michael Dara and Timmy the Smith, the Priest or Philly Cullen, Bartley and Owen, each one has an individuality clearly defined.

There is less that is great in the structure of his plays than in any other component of them, but that structure always clearly reveals the action which arises from the emotion and theme underlying each, — the menacing sea in "Riders to the Sea"; the loneliness of the mountain glens that drives men fey in "The Shadow of the Glen"; the blindness, the blessed self-delusion of mankind, in

"The Well of the Saints"; the wildness of the life of the roads that law may not tame, in "The Tinker's Wedding"; the boy's finding of himself through his having to live up to a community's mistaken ideal of him, in "The Playboy of the Western World"; and the benison of death that prevents a great love from dying, in "Deirdre of the Sorrows."

Always the joy of making something beautiful out of his experience and dream of life is what inspires Synge to write, and though the intention to read life truly is a passion with him, there is never a suggestion of didacticism, or even of moralizing, though "The Well of the Saints" is unquestionably, whether he wills it so or not, a symbol of man's discontent with things as they are, his preference in some things of the lie to the truth. I think that Synge did not will to make "The Well of the Saints" a symbol, and that the play was to him but a reading of life, as life is, in his characteristic, exalted, ironic, extravagant way of writing, and that if he was aware of the symbolism, he was not keenly aware of it or much interested in it. He gives us life untroubled by the passing agitation of the day, and for that we should be thankful, and thankful, too, that he has given in his plays "the nourishment, not very easy to define, on which our imaginations live." His irony, as desolating to some as the irony of Swift, gives pause to all, as insight always will, but to me his extravagance is a joy unalloyed, and his exaltation, so rare a thing in modern literature, should bring to all men delight and refreshment of spirit. No reading, or seeing and hearing, of his plays leaves me with-

out a feeling of richness or without wonder and large content.  He gives back my youth to me, both in the theatre
and in my library, and, in the glow that is mine in such
recapture, I call him the greatest dramatist in English
that our stage has known in a century.  That I know him
to be on sober second thought, second thought that has
been concerned with his art, as I followed it developing
during the slow years from "Riders to the Sea" to "Deirdre of the Sorrows."

# CHAPTER VIII

THE YOUNGER DRAMATISTS — MR. PADRAIC
COLUM — MR. WILLIAM BOYLE — MR. T. C.
MURRAY — MR. S. LENNOX ROBINSON — MR.
RUTHERFORD MAYNE — "NORREYS CONNELL"
— MR. ST. JOHN G. ERVINE — MR. JOSEPH
CAMPBELL

ONE wonders whether it is not of himself Mr. Padraic
Colum is writing as "The dawn-man . . . in the sunset."
That phrase arrests one on the first page of his little book
of verse "Wild Earth" (1909), in the first poem, "The
Plougher." It refers, of course, to an elemental man of to-
day, to the peasant of the great central plain of Ireland,
who is "brute-tamer, plough-maker, earth-breaker," just
as truly as it does to the breaker of horses who drove
furrows with a tree-knee through primordial mould; and
it carries us in imagination back to the man of the Stone
Age by way of many other ploughmen, by way of the
last man we saw between plough-handles who appealed to
our imagination, a man limned against an April sky from
which the sun had passed to leave all the west that gold-
green that the greatest of Westmoreland dalesmen loved;
by way of that Dumfries peasant whose

> "conquering share
> Upturned the fallow fields of truth anew";

by way of Wayland Smith, whose anvils dot the shores

PADRAIC COLUM

of Britain; by way of Tubal Cain, "an artificer in brass and iron," of the seed of Cain, "a tiller of the ground."

One wonders is it not of himself that the poet writes, though what he writes takes us far from him, carrying us in thought halfway round the world and back through civilizations that have passed. But whether it is of himself that Mr. Colum writes or not, he is certainly, in a sense, "The dawn-man . . . in the sunset." The "Glory of the Gael" that is to-day, if it is "glory," is glory of sunset, of "purples and splendors" that pass; there are those who hold that the race that "went forth to battle," but "always fell," is already passed beyond the sunset, into the twilight, that twilight that is the time of day so surely symbolical of the writing of the many Irish poets that have followed after Mr. Yeats. Mr. Colum, however, whether his race be in twilight or sunset, is of the dawn. He is of the dawn not only because he is the youth, at oldest the young man, in his writing, who sees the world freshly and fresh, none the less fresh because he knows it old; but he is of the dawn because it is chiefly those things that are fundamentals, that come out of the beginnings of things, that interest him profoundly, that stir him deeply. Subtleties and complexities, decadent things, are not for him, but simplicities, primordial things, the love of wandering, and what is only less old, the love of land; and love of woman. These three things, and youth, and little else, concern him. Mr. Colum writes, indeed, in the dedication to "Thomas Muskerry" (1910) that he has set down "three characters that stood as first types in my human comedy, the peasant, the artist, the official, Murtagh

Cosgar, Conn Hourican, Thomas Muskerry." It is not, however, the official that Mr. Colum emphasizes in "Thomas Muskerry," but the man who longs for a quiet little place where he may be free from the nagging of his daughter and her children; and in Myles Gorman, in this same play, is sounded that other call that is recurrent in his work, the call of the road. We see more of wanderer than of artist, too, in Conn Hourican, though Mr. Colum calls the play he made for him "The Fiddler's House"; and here, too, the love of land is a motive — love of land and the wander-love battle in "The Land" (1905), with love of woman the deciding factor in the latter's victory.

Mr. Colum would not be an Irishman if nationality and religion were not also motives in his plays and poems, but it is only in his 'prentice work that either appears as a leading motive. From a good deal of writing, most of which appeared originally in "The United Irishmen," he has republished only the three plays before mentioned, "The Land" (1905), "The Fiddler's House" (1907), "Thomas Muskerry" (1910), his miracle play, "The Miracle of the Corn," and two stories in "Studies" (1907), and what he wishes to preserve of his verse in "Wild Earth" (1909).

It was through "The Daughters of Erin" that Mr. Colum came in touch with the dramatic movement. Their plays and tableaux in the Antient Concert Rooms in 1900 attracted his attention, and he wrote to the secretary, inclosing with the note copies of two plays that he had written — the dramatic achievement of his late 'teens. These plays were about the "Children of Lir," that one of "The Three Sorrows of Story-Telling" that is less poignant than the story of Deirdre only because it is less human, and about Brian Boru, the high king that beat back the Danes at Clontarf. Faery and mediæval history were not destined, however, to be Mr. Colum's field, and Mr. Fay, then stage manager of the Association productions, probably helped him on the way to his true field, the life of the peasant of the Midlands, by declaring them rubbish. Two years later Mr. Colum had learned enough about life and about the stage to write a play against enlistment in the English army that held the attention of audiences and was regarded as good propagandist "stuff." "The Saxon Shillin'," produced May 15, 1903, Mr. Colum has not republished, nor "The Kingdom of the Young" (1902), which like its predecessor was published in "The United Irishmen." With this last play, as its title indicates, Mr. Colum found his way to that subject of youth, which, whatever other one of his dominant motives his plays may involve, is always present. The hardness of youth is the theme of "The Kingdom of the Young," the hardness that came into the heart of a daughter, when driven into revolt by the older generation. She turns on her father in the end, determined that she will not be cheated of the joy of life as was he.

In "The Foleys," another little play of the same year, 1902, a play that for all its crudity and incompleteness is full of insight into Catholic Ireland, youth is again the theme, or the intolerance and self-righteousness of youth. "Eoghan's Wife" (1902) is only a monologue, only the old story of the woman who finds her home lonely and depressing because the wrong man is the man of the house. She looks out over "brown bogs with black water," wondering what is the way of escape from it all.

"Broken Soil," put on at the Abbey Theatre on December 4, 1903, is the first play of Mr. Colum with which, in after years, he was in any way content, but he was not too content with it, rewriting it in 1907 as "The Fiddler's House," and, I think, in the main improving it.

Mr. Colum, a youth with an appetite for reading as insatiable as his impulse to write, read not only his Ibsen but his M. Maeterlinck. Back of "Broken Soil" is Ibsen, back of "The Miracle of the Corn" is M. Maeterlinck. "The Miracle of the Corn" was put in rehearsal by the Irish National Theatre Society in 1904, but so far as I know it was never played by that organization, its first staging I have record of being by "The Theatre of Ireland" at the Abbey Theatre on May 22, 1908. Here again is youth a leading theme, the power youth has, if it be wistful and tender and pleading, to soften the heart of age. It may seem to some that the girl Aislinn is only a symbol, only the dream of his youth returned to the farmer Fardorrougha, who has hardened his heart even in famine time, but whether apparition, or child of the flesh and symbol, too, Aislinn is the bringer-back to Fardorrougha of the soft heart of youth.

As the Irishman in America is preferably a city dweller, it may be a little difficult for his fellow Americans of other ancestry to understand why the Irishmen at home were so concerned with Mr. Colum's next play, whose theme, as whose title, is "The Land." The cry for a home and a bit

of land, a cottage around a hearth and around the cottage
a few acres of your own, is a cry that has been heard in all
ages and among all people.  It is a cry that we all have
cried at times, gypsy-hearted though we be; it is a cry
that even the city-loving eighteenth century raised in all
the "Mine be a cot" poems, whether of Pomfret or Pope
or any other of the many who followed the same fashion,
and it is a cry that is especially loud in present-day
America.  But none of us can feel the call of the land, none
of us can desire it with more intensity than the Irishman
of to-day, city-dweller though we find his kin in America;
there is no one class of people anywhere in the world who
want the land as the Irish peasants of to-day want it.
Their fathers and grandfathers saw the fields that they
had farmed turned into pastures for cattle, as the Scotch
crofters saw their holdings turned into deer-parks; the
two generations of Irishmen now respectively in old age
and middle age have known what it is to be taxed out
of the places their improvements as tenants made more
valuable; and to-day those of the old folk that are still
alive and those of the middle years that are still in Ireland
are getting back to the land, along with the younger generation that desires it almost as ardently, but were not
born upon it, profiting by legislation that compels landlords to sell to the Government, which in turn sells to the
small proprietors.

The Irish peasant loves his bit of land far more than his
language, and even more, I think, in the bottom of his
heart, than he loves his church, although allegiance to
his church is a duty that he puts before any love.  A boreen

in bogland is not a lonely place to the Irish peasant if he have neighbors of long standing. It is the big city that to him at home seems the lonely place, despite the glamour of its lights, and its shops, and its ceaseless excitements.

The story of "The Land" is, as I have said, the story of the struggle between love of land and the *Wanderlust*, with the love of woman as the decisive factor in the latter's victory. Matt Cosgar is the son of a peasant farmer, the last of many that the hardness of Murtagh has driven to America, and he, too, goes in the end, after his father's will is broken, because the girl of his choice is restless and will not be content as a farmer's wife. Matt and Ellen, the fit and the strong, go to America, Cornelius and Sally, the hair-brained and the drudge, remain. Symbolic this is, of course, of the situation in Ireland to-day, or at least yesterday, but the characters are strongly individualized and show no tendency to harden into types. In "The Land" the restlessness of youth, its call to wander, is the motive that clashes with love of the home and of the home place. In "The Fiddler's House" there is youth desiring peace, and youth afraid of love, in Annie and Maire Hourican; and the call of the road to old Conn, the fiddler. Sacrifice is rare in youth, and if it were not that Maire is afraid of her love for Brian McConnell, and gives up her home and takes to the road with her father partly because she fears her love for her lover, fears her powerlessness with him, it would hardly be in the course of nature that she would sacrifice so much for her sister. It was a sure instinct that guided Mr. Colum so to make believable a sacrifice at first view seemingly so great. Even in this play, which Mr. Colum intends as a study of the artistic temperament, the land is a motive second only to the call of the road. Maire cared somewhat for the land, less than her sister cared, more than her father cared, though he too loved it in so far as the artist's gypsy nature will permit. It is the road and his music, however, that Conn cares for most, and in his expression of such love he attains to an eloquence that is Mr. Colum at his best: "I'm leaving the land behind me, too; but what's the land, after all, against the music that comes from the far strange places, when the night is on the ground, and the bird in the grass is quiet?" As one reads, aloud, as one must, one thinks now of the Old Testament and now of Synge.

Although Mr. Colum determined to put aside thoughts of dramas of old Ireland in 1900, he evidently could not keep the old legends out of his mind. They intrude now and then into his verses for all his modernity, and one of them, "The Destruction of the House of Da Derga," forced him to turn it into a play. "The Destruction of the Hostel" has not been published, but it seems to have pleased those who saw and heard it as played by the boys of St. Enda's School on February 5, 1910.

In the last play, too, of Mr. Colum, the ending is a parting, here the parting that death brings. Telling the fortunes of poor old Thomas Muskerry, who in the end dies a pauper in the workhouse where once he was master, the play opens our eyes to that life of the small town, deadliest of lives the world over, a life knowing neither the freedom of the farm nor the freedom of the city, as such life is lived in Ireland. In "Thomas Muskerry," as in "The Land" and "The Fiddler's House," the characterization is sure and true. One may take it that this is Ireland, Ireland on the average, as one cannot take it that what we have in the plays of Synge or Lady Gregory is Ireland on the average. Crofton Crilly, the son-in-law of the master, soft and big and blond, is an unsympathetic but memorable portrait. Unsympathetic and memorable, too, are the portraits of his son Albert and his daughter Anna, the one tricky and the other grasping, and the workhouse porter and the old piper haunt my memory as strange men I have met haunt my memory, year in and year out.

All three of these plays are, as I have said, sprung of domestic problems, sure proof that Mr. Colum is the peasant's son. The family, as he has pointed out in an article in "The United Irishmen," is not only what the family is, ordinarily, in northwestern Europe, but that plus that which the Irish family has inherited of the clan spirit. It was only yesterday in Ireland that the girl and boy were married to whom their fathers would, by a process of barter in which their own wishes were not for a moment considered. They submitted, or came to America. It was a patriarchal system of society.

It is not, then, difficult to see how it came about that Mr. Colum, who began to write so young, came to write so much about youth and the rebellion of youth, and to write about those other themes of his, themes all of them made more intense by the youth that is concerned with them — the land that obsesses the life of the man of the house all Ireland over, and through him obsesses the lives of his family; and love of woman.

Mr. Colum does not intrude his own personality into his plays, but it is felt, as it should be felt, in every one of his lyrics. Reading them one has a sense of a youth like the youth of some characters in his plays; a youth more manly than Cornelius's, less restless than Ellen's; a youth serious and troubled with thought; a youth in revolt against much in the old order, but tolerant of the passing generation that fears it "knocking at the door." It is a youth impassioned rather than passionate, more pronouncedly a youth of mind than a youth of heart. When I say youth of mind, I mean not immaturity of mind, but the outlook of the young mind; not radicalism, but a fixed determination to think things out afresh and not to accept them because of any convention.

Eloquence one always looks for in the writing of an Irishman, and humor and power over dialogue, but Mr. Colum is too serious with youth to care much for humor, and, like Mr. Martyn, though not to the same extent, he has trouble with his dialogue. The feeling for the situation, the understanding of what is in the characters' minds, is in Mr. Colum, but the dialogue does not always accommodate itself to situation and thought. What Mr. Colum makes his characters say has in it the thought and the sentiment of what they would say, but the words as often lack life as have it. It is this difficulty with dialogue that has prevented Mr. Colum, in his plays, true and finely planned as they are, from reaching great achievement. As dramatist he is still more full of promise than

of achievement, and to be a dramatist of promise after
ten years of playwriting is to be at a standstill. In lyric
poetry it is otherwise with Mr. Colum. There he has
attained. You will find his real value in "Wild Earth,"
slight though the book may seem. Here is reading of life,
here is imagination, here is lyric cry. Read these little
poems once and they will be your familiars forever.

## MR. WILLIAM BOYLE

One wonders if justice has been done Mr. William Boyle.
If it has not it is because he is a playwright of one play,
"The Building Fund" (1905). He has written three other
plays that count, "The Eloquent Dempsey" (1906), "The
Mineral Workers" (1906), and "Family Failings" (1912),
but "The Building Fund" is of a higher power than any
of these. "Family Failings," produced in the spring of
1912, I have not read, but according to all accounts it
does not mark any advance upon "The Mineral Workers" or "The Eloquent Dempsey." "The Mineral Workers," essentially a propagandist play, and "The Eloquent
Dempsey," essentially a satire, are hardly, even in intention, of the first order of seriousness in art. There are
characters in these two plays faithful to human nature,
and faithful to the ways of eastern Galway, where the
scenes of all of the plays of Mr. Boyle are laid. But there
are so many other characters in them that are either caricatures or "stock" that, funny as the plays seem upon the
stage, they do not impress the deliberate judgment as
real. The many characters of "The Mineral Workers"
and its several motives are too much for Mr. Boyle; he

loses his grip and the play falls to pieces. "The Eloquent Dempsey" suffers from the caricaturing of its characters, and its action degenerates into unbelievable farce almost on the curtain-rise. "The Building Fund," however, is serious and true, and at the same time just as full of wit and just as biting in satire and just as effective on the stage as "The Eloquent Dempsey." Its characterization is recognized as distinctive and authentic even on reading. Revealed through the almost perfect work of the players trusted with its presentation by the Abbey Theatre on their American tour of 1911–12, it seemed even more than distinctive and authentic, it seemed inspired by profound insight.

"The Building Fund" tells the story of the outgeneraling of grasping son and conniving daughter's daughter by a hard old woman of the strong farmer class in the west of Ireland. Mrs. Grogan is approached as the curtain rises by Michael O'Callaghan, an elderly farmer, and Dan MacSweeney, a young farmer, in the rôle of collectors for the fund for the new Catholic church. They are sent away by her and by her son Shan without any contribution, but their visit suggests to her a way by which she can disinherit her son and her granddaughter, wishful for her death, she thinks, in their eagerness for her fortune. Shan is open in his concern as to her disposal of her money; and although the girl hides her purpose under pretended solicitude for her grandmother's health and is a great help to the old woman, Mrs. Grogan believes her also to be plotting for the fortune and is equally resentful toward both. So when the collectors call again, Mrs. Grogan makes a will, in which we learn, on her death shortly after, she has left all her fortune away from her family to the church. For all their plotting, the audience feels that the old woman is more malevolent than either son or grand-daughter, and, after all, the son had worked hard on the home place and the granddaughter, slyboots as she was, undoubtedly was really kind. Both are of her blood, and it is human to feel that parents should leave their money to their children rather than to charity. There is some amelioration of the condition of Shan and Sheila in the thought that they may stay on, with Father Andrew's permission, as managers of the old farm, henceforth the church farm. But sympathize with them though you may, you feel it is only right that selfishness should over-reach itself.

The play is not any more complimentary to Catholic Galway than "The Drone" of Mr. Mayne is complimen-tary to Protestant Down, but it is seldom that comedy is complimentary to human nature, and "The Building Fund" is comedy. That is, it is comedy as Ibsen sees drama, or character farce as Coleridge defines it. It is, in the Greek sense, perhaps even tragedy; certainly, it is tragedy from the standpoint of Shan and Sheila, for cir-cumstances certainly get the better of them. From Mrs. Grogan's standpoint it is comedy, for she, through her will, even though she is now dead, has got the better of circumstances as represented by the plotting of her son and granddaughter. If we look at "The Building Fund" from the standpoint of Shan and Sheila, but without sympathy for them, it is only character farce, for although circumstances get the better of them, we do not then care for them, and a play in which characters are overwhelmed by fate, but in which our sympathy is not with them, is, if we follow Coleridge, really farce. Whatever "The Building Fund" is, its characterization is admirable. Some might say its men and women approximate to types, that Mrs. Grogan is the avaricious old woman, Shan the sanctimonious miser, Sheila the sly minx, Michael the benevolent old man, and Dan the gay blade. Types or not, you will find all of them in Ireland, and all of them wherever human nature is human nature. If they are types, however, each has a personality, but whether all of them would stand out with such individuality had one not seen them so fully realized on the stage, I cannot say. The tottering, bitter old woman of Miss Allgood and the miserly, fearful son of Mr. Sinclair are more memorable than the other impersonations only in that they are fatter parts than Sheila, Michael O'Callaghan, and Dan MacSweeney, played respectively by Miss McGee, Mr. O'Rourke, and Mr. O'Donovan.

Mother and son are, I am sure, just as complete in the writing of Mr. Boyle as in the acting of Miss Allgood and Mr. Sinclair. Both are, indeed, as finely imagined and as faithfully realized as any characters in modern English comedy. And you may have to go further afield than modern English comedy to find such a minute study of resentful and malevolent age as this portrait of Mrs. Grogan. We all know that perversity that will not allow its possessor to be satisfied with any effort to please. Here is an illustration of it as Mr. Boyle has seen it: —

*Sheila.* Will I boil an egg for your breakfast, granny?

*Mrs. Grogan (sarcastically).* Oh, to be sure! More extravagance. You know very well I could n't eat it, and you'll have it for yourself. Waste, waste; nothing but idleness and waste all round. God help me! (*Coughs.*)

*Sheila pours out a cup of tea and hands it to Mrs. Grogan.*

*Sheila.* Drink that drop of tea, granny — it's fresh made.

*Mrs. Grogan.* What did you do with the bottom of the pot? Threw it to the ducks, I suppose?

*Sheila (pointing to the table).* I have it here for myself, granny.

*Mrs. Grogan (sipping tea).* When I was a girl I never got a sup o' tea from year's end to year's end.

*Sheila.* It was very dear, then; was n't it?

*Mrs. Grogan.* It's dear enough still with everybody using it all day long. Did you feed the hens?

*Sheila.* Long ago, and let the ducks out, too.

*Mrs. Grogan.* I suppose it's in the oats they'll be by this time. What about the calves?  *Grogan goes out.*

*Sheila.* I gave them their milk and put them in the bawn.

*Mrs. Grogan.* With the linen on the hedge? Why, they'll chew it into rags, and, maybe, choke themselves.

*Sheila.* No, granny, dear; I spread the linen in the upper garden, where the sun comes the earliest.

*Mrs. Grogan.* I see it's stole ye want it. There's half a dozen tinkers squatted in the quarry.

*Sheila (wearily).* They went a week ago.

*Mrs. Grogan.* Ah, dear! There's what it is to be old! I never hear anything that's going on now till it's all over. Is that egg boiled?

*Sheila.* Granny, dear, I thought you could n't take one.

*Mrs. Grogan.* It's the little bit I eat that's grudged me now, I see.

Though there is little of it in this passage that I quote, the picturesque phrase that no Irish writer is without is Mr. Boyle's, as a matter of course, but there is no particular individuality in his handling of it. Style he has not, nor any background of romance, or beauty of that sort that illumines the grayness of the comedies of Ibsen, or of any other sort of beauty than that approach to beauty there is in skilled craftsmanship.

Admirably arranged, too, are the situations of "The Eloquent Dempsey," a satire on the man who straddles all questions, as at one time, at any rate, did so many Irish politicians. Dempsey might have continued his career of straddling indefinitely had he not a mania for speech-making that he could not control. In the end, however, he was undone by a well-intentioned conspiracy, arranged by his wife, to get him out of politics altogether and out of his liquor-selling and into farming far from town. I cannot identify Dempsey with any one prominent Irish statesman, but the lesser fry on both Nationalist and Unionist sides are as easy to identify as the men that suggested the characters of "A Tale of a Town." In "The Eloquent Dempsey" all the art of Mr. Boyle has been lavished on the central figure, which, when all is said, remains a caricature, and caricature uncompensated for by any great or noble characteristic of the play, whose primal quality is but cleverness. Effective as its satire is, and provocative of laughter as it always is' on the stage, it is altogether cheaper in its quality than "The Building Fund."

"The Mineral Workers," with its chief portrait that of a returned Irish-American mining engineer, takes us to certain phases of society not met among the publicans and politicians and peasants of Mr. Boyle's earlier plays.

Other than these are not only the hero, Stephen J. O'Reilly, but the aristocrat, Sir Thomas Musgrove, and his sister, Mrs. Walton, who is of the family connection of Sir Arthur Wing Pinero's Georgianna Tidman. Dan Fogarty, the holdback, unprogressive farmer, is the sharpest - cut and truest to life of all the characters, so clear - cut and true, in fact, that one thinks of him as almost a fellow of Shan Grogan in "The Building Fund." Uncle Bartle is sentimentalized, and Kitty Mulroy has no such personality as Sheila O'Dwyer. Contrast "The Mineral Workers" with a novel of the returned American, "Dan the Dollar" of Mr. Bullock, and the calibre of Mr. Boyle's play is quickly revealed.

What Mr. Boyle had been had he come into touch with the movement ten years earlier, it is of course beside the point to speculate. He was not a young man when he first became acquainted with the art of the Abbey Theatre in London and was impelled to write plays for it. He was, though, able to adapt the experience he had had as a story-writer to the stage in "The Building Fund." That being so, why is it that his later plays, successful though they have been as vehicles for the purveying of amusement on the stage, have not taken rank by their art or by their reading of life with "The Building Fund"? It may be that it was the one theme susceptible of dramatic presentation that he had brooded over long enough to transmute into terms of drama, and that the later plays, full of successful stage tricks though they are, did not come out of his knowledge of Irish life. Knowledge of Ireland he ought to have, for he is said to have lived for comparatively long periods in various places in the country as an excise officer. As such Mr. Boyle was himself one of the principal types, that of the official, that exist in Ireland, and in a position to learn much of many other types, surprisingly few of which he has realized with any depth of insight in his plays.

It would seem with his great success seven years back and his newer plays less effective, that we cannot look to Mr. Boyle with great hope for the future, as we can to Mr. Robinson or Mr. Murray. When we so say, however, let us remember that Lady Gregory did not attempt plays until she was close on fifty.

## MR. T. C. MURRAY

The North is generally held to be another country than the rest of Ireland. Ulster is alien alike in race and religion and economic conditions from Connacht and Leinster and Munster. It is Scotch Ireland, Protestant Ireland, industrial Ireland. It is, moreover, — many of its citizens say therefore, — prosperous Ireland. Certainly men would not divide all Irishmen into "Irishmen" and "Scotch Irishmen" were there not many grounds for such a distinction. All other of the immigrants into Ireland have, as a people, disappeared. The Norman has left his mark on the land in his castles and his names, but as a distinctive element of the population he no longer exists, any more than does Welshman or Englishman or Palatinate. Apart from distinctions of class the men of Ireland are "Irishmen" and "Scotch Irishmen," and until yesterday, therefore, Nationalists and Unionists.

And yet, definite as are these distinctions, life in the various parts of Ireland seems much alike, class for class, as it is represented by the many contemporaneous playwrights, whether the scenes of their plays are Down or Kerry, Galway or Wicklow. A tinker is a tinker wherever you find him, a strong farmer a strong farmer, a landlord a landlord. The same emotions dominate rival brothers in "The Turn of the Road" and in "Birthright," though the Orangeman turned actor wrote the one and the Cork schoolmaster the other. Mr. T. C. Murray is one of those to whom Mr. Yeats has given the name "Cork Realists." His first play, "The Wheel o' Fortune," was produced by the Cork Dramatic Society at the Dun, Cork, December 2, 1909. It has not been published, so far as I know, and all that I learn from the references to it in newspapers is that it is a one-act ironic comedy about matchmaking. Mr. Murray brought his next play, "Birthright," to the Abbey Theatre, where it was performed on October 27, 1910. If "Maurice Harte" (1912) stands the test of time and travel as has "Birthright," Mr. Murray has come to the Abbey Theatre to take a place of prominence among its playwrights. Some of the appeal of "Birthright" is in its story, the story of Cain and Abel, if you like, a story that is as lasting in its appeal as is "The Eternal Triangle," but there is as much appeal in the characterization, which you feel as you read almost as intimately as you come to know it on the stage. There are many plays that are altogether colorless in the reading unless you have unusual power of visualization and can see them as you sit in your study as if they were embodied before you

T. C. MURRAY

on the stage. Such plays, visualized or unvisualized in the study, are often real enough on the stage. "Birthright," as I have said, is not one of these. It visualizes itself for you, with no effort on your part, as you read it, though of course, as every real play will, it moves you more in the playing. It was admirably cast on its first production at the Abbey Theatre, and it was just as admirably cast on the American tour of 1911–12, Miss O'Doherty's Maura and Mr. Morgan's Bat Morrissey being wonderful pictures of a doting mother and a stern father troubled by their preferences, the one for the elder, the other for the younger son. The rival sons were done to the life by Mr. O'Donovan and Mr. Kerrigan, and the neighbor of Mr. O'Rourke was, too, a complete realization of the Irish peasant of the valley of the Lee. It is a stern and patient realism this of Mr. Murray in telling of how Hughie, the elder son, the apple of his mother's eye, the idol of the parish for his hurly playing, and his versemaking, and his free and pleasant ways, is disinherited and condemned to seek his fortune in America by his father because his younger son was the better man on the farm. There was back of Bat's decision, too, his feeling that his eldest-born was more of his mother, whose blood was part gentle, than of himself, the grubber of the earth. Shane, like his father, was the peasant plowman, Hughie something of the sporting gentleman. The end of it all is murder, the younger son killing the elder with the hurly when he is accused by his brother of plotting to grab the farm. Many who saw "Birthright" in America were moved by it more than by any other play in the repertoire of the company, and I have heard more than one whose supreme interest is the theatre say that it was the best play new to America presented in America during the winter of 1911–12. I do not so hold, for "The Well of the Saints" and "In the Shadow of the Glen" were new to America in the winter of 1911–12, and "The Playboy of the Western World" was new to every city in America save to Chicago, where Mr. Hart Conway presented it at his dramatic school in the spring of 1909. I can, however, understand why "Birthright" so appealed. It is because of the theme, because of the beautiful character of Maura Morrissey, because of the absolute faithfulness to life, as all the world knows it, of the play. I have traveled the road to Macroom that these farmers traveled, and so I know the externals of the life they lead: I have known intimately and I know intimately just such people as these, Irish peasants, some of whom spoiled their children, thinking the boy they loved must not be "crossed," and some of whom preferred one child to another even to the extent of reversing the custom of primogeniture that is as fixed a rule among them as if their property was entailed, and so I can vouch for the absolute fidelity of Mr. Murray's art. It is a realism little relieved by humor; unrelieved either by any background of romance, but gaining a dignity from its intensity of conception and its simplicity of unfolding that makes you feel, as you read, or as you watch and listen, that you are in the presence of nobility. Its style, maybe, is homespun, but it is none the worse for that, and it never approaches at all to the cheap or mean.

The appeal of this realism is as poignant in "Maurice Harte" (1912) as in "Birthright," though the story of the later play is not so universal as is that of the play that brought Mr. Murray his share of fame. "Maurice Harte" tells of the disaster that comes to a young divinity student of Maynooth whose parents drive him back to college to seek ordination even after he tells them that he has no vocation for the priesthood. The curtain rises on Maurice, a youth of twenty-two, trying to tell his mother, whose youngest he is, and the child of her middle age, that it would be sacrilege for him to take orders with no vocation. His courage fails him, as it had on previous occasions on which he tried to confess his agony because of his false position, and he finally begs the Parish Priest to break the desolating news to the family. They are only farmers in a small way, the Hartes: and the father and mother, the son at home, Owen, and the three older brothers in Boston, have all made sacrifices to give Maurice his education. When the priest tells of the boy's decision not to return to Maynooth, mother and father and brother all insist that he must stick to his earlier intention, vocation or no vocation.

They are in monetary difficulties because of him, and if the story went out that he was not back at Maynooth his mother declares it "would n't be east in Macroom when we'd have the bailiffs walking in that door." She tells him, too, his being a spoiled priest will cost his brother his bride and her fortune that would help them to pay off their debts. The boy cannot withstand their pleading, and the first act ends with his promise that he will go back to Maynooth, a promise wrung from him even though he knows at the time of its making that his return may bring him to madness in the end.

Act II, nine months later, shows us again the kitchen of the farmhouse of West Cork, with happiness in the hearts of all there, save some slight apprehension on the father's part over his new clothes and the terrors of a journey with Father Mangan to Maynooth. In this relaxing of the tension of the play humor is not out of place, and its attainment here by Mr. Murray shows that he could write comedy did he choose. We hear that the marriage settlement between Bride Burke and Owen has been made, and that Maurice is to marry them; and that he has bested all his classmates in his final examinations. Upon the pride and happiness in a son sure of a good match, and the glory of another son about to be "priested" and to say mass in the local church, breaks in word that he cannot be ordained because of illness. And close upon this bad news comes Maurice himself, broken down mentally from the strain of driving himself to do what he knows to be wrong, from the strain of committing, as he believes, sacrilege. Father and mother and brother realize that it is they who have driven him mad, but such is human nature that mother and brother, at least, have thoughts of themselves even at this moment, as well as thoughts for Maurice with "his mind that's gone." His brother fears that Bride will not come into a house so disgraced, and his mother, her years-long dream of her youngest a priest gone on the wind, is struck dumb with horror at the thought of what her life will be from this out.

The full significance of the tragedy of Maurice's fate can be realized only by those who know intimately the ambitions hugged close to heart by the Irish Catholic mother. It is more to her to have her boy a priest even than it was yesterday to the Scotch Presbyterian mother to have her boy a minister of the Kirk. It is the greatest glory that can come to such a peasant mother to give one of her sons to the priesthood.

There is, I think, no propaganda in the play, and no intentional satire, although in a way "Maurice Harte" affords a parallel to so definitely a propagandist satire as Mr. Robinson's "Harvest." It is not education that is the curse, however, in "Maurice Harte," but the belief that only priesthood in the end can justify the sacrifices without which a college education is almost impossible for an Irish peasant. Certain it is that it is only for the pride of having their boy a priest that the typical Irish Catholic peasant parents would make such sacrifices as the Hartes have made, sacrifices involving them in debt to the extent of a thousand dollars, to secure their son an education.

In a sense "Maurice Harte" is far other than the provincial study I have here outlined. Its theme is allied, unquestionably, to that theme so much larger in its relations than that of the spoiled priest, the theme of the rebellious son, the son who will live his own life no matter what may be his parents' will. It is only allied to it, however, not to be identified with it, because Maurice is too fearful of disappointing his parents, and too shrinking and ineffectual, to go against his parents' will. In Ireland, as I have said elsewhere, such parental will, by a survival of authority from the days of the clan system, was law until yesterday, and there will therefore be those, I have no doubt, who will find in the play a conflict of the old order and the new, but I do not believe such conflict was the author's intent. Indeed, the play is wholly of the old order. No love of man and woman figures as motive in it as none had figured in "Birthright." There is parental love, of course, in both plays, though in the case of both parents in "Maurice Harte" and in the father in "Birthright" parental pride is a stronger motive than parental love. Very true to Irish life is this absence of passion as a deciding factor in the fates of man and woman, this insistence upon the importance of the family, this subordination of the rights of the individual. Mr. Murray wished to write in "Maurice Harte" a play of the very heart of Irish Catholic life, and such a play he has written, a play that marks no decline, either in characterization or situation, from "Birthright," and to say that is to give "Maurice Harte" praise of the highest.

## MR. S. LENNOX ROBINSON

Mr. Lennox Robinson, like most of the Abbey Theatre dramatists, has chosen to write about the ground under his feet. The son of a clergyman whose charges have been in the southwest of Ireland, Mr. Robinson spent his boyhood and youth in the Bandon Valley. He had been trying his hand at writing from the time that he was ten years old, editing an amateur magazine as he grew older, feeling about for the thing that he could do. A visit of the Abbey Theatre Company to Cork was the awakening. He

LENNOX ROBINSON

saw a new acting, he saw a new art of the stage, and he knew as he saw that it was in drama his work lay. It was not, however, for the Cork Dramatic Society that he did his first play, but for the Abbey Theatre. "The Clancy Name" was put on on October 8, 1908, when its author was but four days past his twenty-second birthday. What this first version was like I do not know, but Mr. Robinson has reprinted the second version, put on with the full strength of the National Theatre Society at the Abbey Theatre on September 30, 1909. As printed, it is an ironic little play, recording the great day in the life of the Widow Clancy, the day on which she pays off a five years' loan and stands without a debt of any kind, her farm all her own, the Clancy name respected throughout her world. But on this day of her triumph, when she would add to her happiness by making a match for her son, John cannot rejoice with her, and on her questioning him as to his moodiness he blurts out that he is the man who killed James Power, a quiet man whose unexplained disappearance is the mystery of the countryside. Worse yet, John insists that he will give himself up to the authorities. It is terrible to know one's son a murderer; it is intolerable to think of a Clancy being hanged and of the glory of the name forever departed. She persuades him finally not to tell, but he fears he will, so, when the chance comes, he finds the only way out, the way of peace for his mother and peace for himself. A car driven by a drunken neighbor is threatening the life of a little child playing in the middle of the road. John Clancy pushes him out of the way and allows himself to be driven down. They bring him to his mother's house still alive and raving incoherently of the murder, but he dies before he tells his secret and the Clancy name is saved. It is not a very gripping theme, but the play brings to us an acute character study of the typical managing woman of the small farmer class. We feel her tireless energy, her drive, her high pride, assets of worth in the fight to live. There is a little humor, natural and unforced, some picturesqueness of phrase, a revelation of knowledge of life in one corner of Ireland. There is nothing, however, in the play to make it comparable with the three that followed it on the stage of the Abbey Theatre, "The Crossroads" (1909); "Harvest" (1910); and "Patriots" (1912). "The Lesson of Life," a little one-act comedy, presented at the Dun Theatre, Cork, December 2, 1909, Mr. Robinson has disowned. Why I do not know, though the fact that it was not produced at the Abbey may indicate that even at the time of its production he felt that it was not up to the level of his work. Mr. Robinson has not republished "The Lesson of Life," but the reviews state that it was an amusing little play, though in no way a serious reading of life.

"The Clancy Name," "The Crossroads," "Harvest," and "Patriots" are all on themes that hit home at Irish institutions, and yet it would be wrong to say any one of them is basically either satirical or propagandist. All are primarily readings of life. "The Crossroads" alone, perhaps, is more than a reading of life. Certainly, after its needless prologue, it is fine art through to the end. This scene, with its satire of Irish debating societies, is now, wisely, dropped when the play is produced. We can learn enough of Ellen in the play itself to understand why she does as she does without this picture of her in Dublin. Her story is that of a woman who hates the much talk of patriotism in Dublin and the lack of doing anything tangible for Ireland. In Dublin she has worked her way up from servant to assistant in a bookshop, but she goes back happily to the country to give her sister a chance in town such as she has had, thinking that perhaps she herself can lead her people into better ways of farming and of ordering their lives generally through the knowledge she has got in town. It is through such as Ellen that the Irish Industries Organization Society in actual life accomplishes an important part of its work.

In the first act of "The Crossroads" we find Ellen at home, in her old peasant dress, having made the hens lay so well in winter as to arouse wonder in a neighbor as to whether, "Is it right for hens to be laying that way so early in the year?" A match is being made for her by her mother with a man that has a good farm. Ellen desires the match very much, for this is just the farm on which to try the new methods that shall bring prosperity to the people of the valley and so stem the emigration to America. She does not love Tom Dempsey, this strong farmer, and she does half-love Brian Connor, whom she had known in Dublin, but now that he has come down to ask her to marry him she chooses the farmer, brutal though she knows him, because as his wife she can do the work for Ireland that she has imagined for herself. The loveless marriage, so universal an institution all over Ireland, made it nothing out of the way for Ellen to act as she did,

even though at the time of the action of the play a higher
ideal of marriage than that of the old matchmaking had
come in. It is this institution that Mr. Robinson, from
one point of view, might be thought to be attacking in the
play; it is this institution, certainly, that is the theme of
the play. Is it a tribute to Irishmen and Irishwomen to
acknowledge that this loveless marriage has worked on
the whole as well as the marriage of sentiment, or as the
marriage of sexual infatuation, or as the marriage of com-
rade hearts that we believe we have in America? As a
matter of fact there were not as many loveless marriages
as might seem at first thought. The match made up between the father of the girl and the father of the boy was
the usual sort of marriage among the stay-at-home Irish
girls and boys up to 1880, but how many girls and boys
for the past one hundred and fifty years have come to
America to escape it? Look up your family traditions,
you who have Irish ancestors, and find is it not true that
these ancestors, whether Reeds of Down or Nolans of
Meath, fled to America because they would wed the mate
of their choice. Even to-day boys and girls come here
from the same motive, though of course it would be pre-
posterous to deny that to many it is rather Eldorado than
the land of freedom.

Act II reveals poor Ellen seven years later. She has lost
her two boys by fever; she has failed in her work on her
own farm, though she has brought untold blessings of
progressiveness to the other farms around Ballygurteen;
she has lost the appreciation of her husband. She whom
we loved for a personality as winning as that of an Emma

or a Tess is now a drudge, almost a slattern, gray-haired, hopeless, almost hated by a brutal husband. The loveless marriage has proved a curse. Upon the woman of his dreams so dethroned comes Brian Connor, now a successful novelist, and, finding how things are, falls, for all his intended restraint, into a fight with Tom, whom but for Ellen he would have choked to death. Brian urges Ellen to go away with him, but, after a moment's faltering, she refuses to go. This is the last scene. Tom, who has heard Brian's proposal and his wife's rejection of it, comes slowly down the room.

*Tom.* Was it me you saved or was it the young man? When you pulled him off me, did you save me, or was it him you saved from being hung? Tell me that, Ellen McCarthy.

[*Silence.*

Ah! 't is aisy seen.

[*Puts his hat on, and goes to the door, and takes the key out of the lock.*

*Ellen* (*looking round*). What are you doing? (*Frightened.*) What are you doing?

*Tom.* I 'll tell you what I'm doing. I'm locking the door the way you won't go after that young man; an' I'm going to step down to the village now for a sup of drink. An' then — I'm coming back; an', by God, I'll make you pay for this night's work, Ellen McCarthy, till you'd wish you were dead — for the black curse you brought on this farm, an' for the liking you have to the young man.

[*Goes out. Ellen remains sitting at the table, staring in front of her with sad, hopeless eyes.*

The turning of the key in the lock ends the play, leaving brutality unimaginable as the fate of Ellen.

It is a severe reading of the Irish peasant, this of Tom

Dempsey. Murder may come of his blackness of heart. He is a far worse man, of course, than poor John Clancy, who killed a man in an unpremeditated fight, sure murderer though Clancy be. Yet despite such heroes or at least such characters in his plays, no one would say that in either "The Clancy Name" or "The Crossroads" Mr. Robinson held a brief against the Irish peasant. He most certainly does not. He likes the Irish peasant. His plays are "stories of mine own people" faithfully told. He does not spare the Cork farmer, but he does not distort him. Why, however, his "Harvest" was allowed to be played unmolested in New York, after the "The Playboy of the Western World" met with organized opposition, can be explained only by recognition of the fact that the Irishmen of the patriotic societies are slaves of precedent. "The Playboy of the Western World" had always met with opposition, so it should meet with opposition in New York. "Harvest" escaped in New York because its uncomplimentary personages were unheralded. Not that there is anything in "Harvest," any more than in "The Playboy of the Western World," that any self-respecting Irishman need object to. "Harvest" shows the disastrous effects the wrong sort of primary education, as taught by the country schoolmaster of the old type, the type that was prevalent before the present type, brought about, The present-day schoolmaster is in sympathy with a system of education that will keep the children on the land or in an industry near the home place; the older type would give them an education that would send them to the cities to be priests and lawyers and secretaries and typists and chemists and what-nots. Old William Lordan, the schoolmaster, had, evidently, in the opinion of the playwright, the sins of many on his shoulders, and yet one, knowing that it is the system and not the man that is at fault, cannot help feeling that Mr. Robinson is rather severe on what is in life a really lovable though mistaken sort of man.

"Harvest" shows that of the six children of Tim Hurley, but the three that come into the play are loyal to their father: Maurice, who works the home farm; Jack, the apothecary's clerk from Dublin, who tries to help with the farmwork, but is too much of a weakling to be anything of a help; and Mary, who from typist has turned mistress, now to this man, now to that. Mary, come home to get away from her wrong life, is called back to London by the excitement of its life, which has become a necessity to her. Jack, the chemist, in the end deserts the home; and is off at the end of the play, with his upper-class wife, for America or the colonies. Only Maurice is more than half-entitled to our respect. The son who is the priest is in America to collect for the Church at the time of his family's need, and so is not helpful to his family; the solicitor son is climbing socially, and, needing a motor-car to help him to position, prefers to spend his money on himself rather than on the home place that was robbed to pay for his education; and the secretary son is so ashamed of "the ditch out of which he was digged" that he has changed both his name and his religion.

All five of the children who went out from the home educated, as the schoolmaster wished them to go, have been educated at the expense of those that remained on the farm, Maurice the hard-working farmer and old Timothy the father. But the father, too, is far from what he should be, as one must suspect, not believing that education alone can account for so many gone wrong. Timothy burns down some unimportant farm buildings for the insurance upon them. This practice is so common in all parts of the world civilized sufficiently to have insurance that I wonder insurance companies take risks on backwoods farms anywhere. An old man with whom I have talked often in the mountains of northeastern Pennsylvania answered me one day, when I asked him how it was his barn caught fire, "The insurance got too hot." He was a German, a man in his prime a good worker and not a bad representative of the mountaineer of his state. One must not, then, fasten on old Timothy as a character distinctively Irish, at least in this phase of his character. He surely is universal, a representative of one type of disingenuous countryman.

The characterization in "Harvest" falls short of that of "The Crossroads," but perhaps it had to be if Mr. Robinson was to make his point. As one realizes that perhaps these people are but pawns with which to win the game that Mr. Robinson has set out, one remembers that their creator spent some weeks with Mr. Shaw and Mr. Barker in London, and one understands, too, many other of the failings of "Harvest." It is but another of many illustrations of the blight that Mr. Shaw has brought upon the modern English stage.

It is a two-edged satire that Mr. Robinson employs in

his "Patriots" (1912), a satire that cuts into the sham agitation of some political leagues, an agitation that is talk only, and at the same time cuts with almost equal sharpness into the physical force party. It is true that it is not the motives but the wisdom of these latter men that Mr. Robinson satirizes in the failure of James Nugent, the returned political prisoner, to stir his townsmen with the kind of talk that set them to arming in 1893. That their propaganda is no longer possible, if it was ever possible, is a corollary to the play, even if it could overcome the inertia that has come to Irishmen with their greater prosperity since the Land Purchase Act went into force.

The revolt of the patriot who hates talk and is willing to sacrifice personal happiness for country is recorded here as it was in "The Crossroads," and the uselessness of the sacrifice made only too plain. To one not an Irishman it would perhaps seem that the real drama there is in the play is smothered by the political satire and that the politics satirized are of too local an interest for it to have so universal an appeal as "The Crossroads" or "Harvest." There is an universal story in "Patriots" that is but slightly developed — the story of the prisoner's wife, Ann; her love for her daughter, who is a cripple because of her mother's being dragged here and there by James Nugent in his campaigning just before her birth; Ann Nugent's turning against her husband, on his liberation from an eighteen years' imprisonment for political murder, because of the wrong done her so long ago and because of the danger to Rose's health that cam-

paigning with her father would entail. The turning of
Ann Nugent from her husband is the really significant
part of the play, — and in thoughts of that we pay scant
heed to the political satire and even to the pathos of the
desertion of a leader by almost all he expected to follow
him, and the reduction of his life, as he puts it bitterly,
"to an anecdote — a thing to be told stories about." And
in the end that is the fate he will meet. Time and a wife
that he wronged have broken him. As he staggers off at
the end of the play, a stricken man and older than his
forty-five years, this is his cry : —

> I've killed a man, I've crippled a child, I've got myself shut
> up for eighteen years — God knows what good came of it all —
> but — Peter — I meant — I tried . . . I know I meant right
> — and in prison my cell used to be filled with the sad faces of
> men like me who had given everything for Ireland — they
> wouldn't have come to me, would they? if I hadn't been of their
> company. They are here now — I see them all around me —
> there is Wolfe Tone, and there is . . . oh, quiet watching faces,
> I have tried — tried as you tried — and been broken. . . .

With this ability of his to pick out a theme that is basic
in Irish life, and with the years bringing him an experience
of life that will dominate any propagandist purpose, Mr.
Robinson should grow in seriousness of intention and
accomplishment. He hates sham, he has sane and cleans-
ing satire of pretension, he writes good dialogue, his experience as stage manager of the Abbey Theatre is teaching him the stage; he is only twenty-five. Do not these
things augur a future?

## MR. RUTHERFORD MAYNE

It so happened that the last time I was reading the plays of Mr. Rutherford Mayne, I was also reading the plays of Sir Arthur Wing Pinero. All the world has heard of the one; only the little band scattered here and there through the English-speaking countries to whom letters are a real part of life has heard of the other. I laughed over "Dandy Dick"; I thought of Miss Rehan playing Georgianna Tidman with all that gush of spirits that was hers; I thought of Miss Nethersole in her wonderful youth playing Paula Tanqueray; and as I thought of these two, each in her way inimitable in her part, thoughts of past moments with the characters of Mr. Mayne's plays, plays I have never seen on the stage, came back to me. Had I seen them on the stage would my thoughts of them have been thoughts of the theatre, as were all my thoughts of Sir Arthur's plays? It may be, but I think not. I think the great strength of Mr. Mayne is that he takes you to life; I think the great weakness of the wide-heard author is that he takes you immediately, in almost all of his plays, to the theatre, and only secondarily, if at all, after the memory of his artificiality has died away, to life itself.

William John Granahan and John Smith the Tory, — will you forget them, or Robbie John whom the fiddle called away, or Ebenezer McKie and Francey Moore, Protestant and Catholic, who together lay in wait for the hated landlord and shot him as he passed through the glen; or John Murray, good man, and his bauchle of a brother?

You will not forget them, for they are from life; you have known them, all save Francey, if you have known Scotchmen who are Lowlanders and Presbyterians, or such North of Ireland men as are unalterably opposed to Home Rule. They are very like the Orangemen of the novels of Mr. Shan Bullock, very like the peasants the English-speaking world outside of Scotland first met in the verse of Burns; harsher than the Baillie Nicol Jarvies and Dugald Dalgettys of the kindly Sir Walter, but akin to them and to his Davie Deans and Dumbiedikeses.

We are in a more familiar world in the plays of Mr. Mayne than in those of most of the other writers in the movement — that is, I mean most American readers are — simply because of Burns and Scott. Had Ireland had a peer of either in his generation as satirist or romancer the Irish - Irish would to - day be as familiar to us as are the Scotch - Irish, who are, of course, transplanted Scotch. The women of this world are not, however, of types so well known to us as are the men, because the chivalry of Sir Walter prevented him from giving us his peasant Scotswomen in as full detail as he gave us his men; but it is not difficult for us to appreciate Mrs. Granahan and her daughter; Mrs. McKie, a "woman with a dead soul"; Mary Murray with her daftness over the boys; and even Sarah McMinn, so true in her managing and meanness, qualities necessary to the prosperity of her folk. Puritan America can understand these women and men because they are Puritan, too, with the ignoble that is in the Puritan as well as with the noble that is just as surely there.

It is in the first three plays of Mr. Mayne that we meet
these people I have named, County Down folk all of
them, and all Protestant but Francey Moore. They are
the leading characters in "The Turn of the Road" (1906),
"The Drone" (1908), and "The Troth" (1908). The
motive of Mr. Mayne's first play is the old call to wander,
the unrest of the vagrant heart, here the heart of the
musician. It is the story of Robbie John Granahan, who,
after burning his fiddle at the desire of a strong farmer
whose daughter he wished to marry, is driven out into the
world to try his fortune with another through her determination that her lover should follow his star. There is
more beauty in "The Turn of the Road" than in either of
the other plays of the North of Ireland, more beauty of
theme, more beauty of thought, more beauty of expression. Its themes are not new, *Wanderlust* and the Puri-
tans' hatred of art; its thoughts are not new, but they are
beautiful, and the words themselves are freshly used. Its
phrases that hold in memory are given to Robbie John
and to his father and to his grandfather, most of them to
the grandfather. This is the grandfather's lament for the
boy gone on the roads with his fiddle and his father's
curse: —

It's the wee things you think nothing of, but that make your
home a joy to come back till, after a hard day's work. And
you've sent out into the could and wet the one that was making
your home something more than the common. D'ye think
them proud city folk will listen to his poor ould ballads with the
heart of the boy singing through them? It's only us — it's only
us, I say, as knows the long wild nights, and the wet and the
rain and the mist of nights on the boglands — it's only us, I say,

could listen him in the right way. And ye knowed, right well ye knowed, that every string of his fiddle was keyed to the crying of your own heart.

There is no beauty at all in "The Drone." There is little beauty possible to such a subject realistically treated as that of the exposure of the utter sham that is the pretended inventor of a bellows, a man who has for years fattened on a brother's tolerance and family pride. There might have been beauty of construction, but dramatic construction is not Mr. Mayne's strongest quality. Let that not be held too much against him, for many an English dramatist, like almost every English novelist, is weak in the architectonic qualities of his work. Yet such is the hardness of the people that exposed Daniel Murray that you rejoice in his duping of them at the end through his sale to them of his pretended invention, especially as that frees his brother John, and John's daughter, artful coax that she is, from Sarah McMinn, who is determined to marry the one and manage the two. The ideals of the people of the play and the grim humor of Mr. Mayne are well illustrated by this declaration of John Murray, the best of them all, anent the suit for breach of promise with which Sarah threatens him: "I would as soon do without the marrying if I could. I don't want the woman at all, but I'll marry her before she gets a ha'penny off me."

The people here are the people of "The Squireen" of Mr. Bullock, — hard, grasping, resentful, passionate, brutal even, but doers of the world's work. All that differentiates them from the Fermanagh Protestants is the different conditions of County Down and a slightly lower social position.

In "The Troth" the theme is the shooting of a landlord by two peasants whom his agents are to evict on the morrow. To the cottage of the Protestant McKie comes his Catholic neighbor, Francey Moore, whose wife is dying. Here there is no turf for the fire, and no hope in the heart of father or mother, for the child of the house has died, and, they think, because of the landlord's hardness to them. The two men swear a troth that they shall lie in wait for Colonel Fotheringham, and that if but one escapes, as is likely, the one arrested shall hold his tongue as to his companion. You do not see the murder on the stage, but you hear the shot and see McKie return to his home, and you know it was he killed the landlord. The tension of the last scene is almost unendurable. His wife's providential lie for McKie, her agony in her knowledge of his guilt when she sees his face on his return, the man's terror, are handled with masterly firmness and sureness. To see this scene on the stage in the hands of actors worthy of it must be to know real tragedy. In this play, too, brief as is the glimpse we have into these four lives of small farmer and his wife, his farmhand and his neighbor, a neighbor of alien race and hated faith, you get to know them as if they were friends of long standing. Character creation and character presentation in pithy, tense dialogue are the great gifts of Mr. Mayne. Francey Moore, the "dark man," with his sensibility, his eloquence, and his flaming rage, is not of the characteristic men of Mr. Mayne. They are men of slow ways all un-Celtic and with smouldering hearts like those of the Northmen we read about in the tales of "Origines Islandicæ."

In "Red Turf" (1911) Mr. Mayne turns away from County Down to the Galway bogs, admirably symboliz- ing the hot land feud between neighbors in his title. There are but five characters in the play, Martin Burke, farmer, and his spitfire of a wife; and his neighbors the Flanagans, father and son, who have won away from the Burkes, by the surveyor's decision, their bank of stone turf that had come to Mary Burke from her father; and an old fellow little better than a beggar. Mary taunts her hus- band until he shoots the elder Flanagan as he is working away on the "great stone bank." It was not his own gun Burke had, but, ironically, it was one just brought to his house by the poor old man whom they had often be- friended, John Heffernan, brought that it might not be found in his house by the gauger, and he unable to pay the license. It is not made clear that there was malevo- lence in the leaving of the gun at the Burkes by the old fellow, malevolent as are some of his remarks. Akin to him, not in his malevolence but in that each is in a way a bit of a prophet, is the grandfather in "The Turn of the Road," but more nearly akin to old Granahan is Uncle Bartle of "The Mineral Workers" of Mr. Boyle. Synge records old men of prophecy and tales in his travel sketches, but he put none such who were gentle in his plays, or I would say that Grandfather Granahan, like the old gaffer in Mr. Masefield's "Nan," was a part of the influence of Synge that is felt by both Mr. Masefield and

Mr. Mayne. Their styles, respectively, in "Nan" and "Red Turf," have in them more than echoes of the style of Synge. The "wambling" old men of Mr. Hardy come also to mind as one thinks of these old men of Mr. Masefield and Mr. Mayne and Mr. Boyle. All in a sense play "chorus" to the action of the play, but there is no one of them that is in the story or play in which he appears on such grounds only. There are, of course, old men everywhere, in all life they are an integral part, and everywhere they are commentators on life once they feel that their day is done, spectators of a pageant from the forefront of which they have dropped to watch the following troupe pass by.

There is little mating in these plays of Mr. Mayne, and love of woman worthy of the name of love only in "The Turn of the Road"; there is parental love, too, but perhaps more of parental tyranny. Such parental love as there is, however, actually expressed, makes one of the memorable passages of Mr. Mayne. Mary Burke, after taunting her husband to madness, tries to turn him from murder when she sees him, gun in hand, by crying: "For the love of God, would you leave it down. Leave it down and go in and look at the child sleeping. It would take the badness from your mind the same as it did with me."

Though Mr. Mayne is a writer for the Ulster Literary Theatre of Belfast, his allegiance to the Abbey group is clearly indicated in "Red Turf," which is the result of a study of Synge. I do not mean to say that Mr. Mayne is not familiar with the speech of Connacht, but that it is Synge who has taught him how to listen to it. There is little of the influence of Synge in his three plays of the Black North, but when he turns to Galway in "Red Turf," it is but natural that, writing of other than his own people, he should write in a speech that has in it an echo of that of him who has transmuted this speech into prose of the most beautiful rhythm that English dramatic prose has known. The Bible is the book of books in Ulster, and there is no page of Mr. Mayne's Ulster plays but shows him acquainted with its great rhythms. Mr. Boyle, skillful artificer of situation, and truthful depicter of character that he is, and Mr. Colum, too, for all his closeness to the earth, are now and then betrayed, Mr. Boyle more often than now and then, into the English of the newspaper or of the public speaker; but the English of Mr. Mayne is all but always an unworn English, an English used freshly, or if with reminiscences in it, reminiscences of the seventeenth-century English that has survived in the Bible or in the memory of the folk from the time of King James.

Mr. Mayne has, then, style, and his dialogue is living speech; he has knowledge of the people of North Ireland, earnestness and sincerity; and having these qualities, he has more that is precious to art than have most of the dramatists his countrymen. There is no consistent reading of life in his plays, no great power over the unrolling of plot, but perhaps these will come with the years. An actor himself, he knows the stage; and this knowledge has given him power over situation. Once he learns to lead situation into situation, once he ripens into fuller knowledge of life, Mr. Mayne will be a dramatist to reckon with, indeed.

## "NORREYS CONNELL"

There have been many other dramatists than these I have mentioned who have had one or more plays produced at the Abbey Theatre. Some of these, like Mr. Bernard Shaw, are Irishmen abroad that have gained the ear of the world and do a play for Dublin out of a sense of duty. It was thus that "John Bull's Other Island" came into being, but that play, being considered "beyond the scope" of the National Theatre Society, was not produced at the Abbey, but at the Court Theatre, London, November 1, 1904. When "The Showing-up of Blanco Posnet" was "censored" in London, however, the Abbey opened its doors to it, the "crude melodrama" receiving its premier in late August, 1909. Little as "John Bull's Other Island" was in the Abbey tradition, with moral purpose and unhumanity of its very essence, it was at least a newspaper leader on an Irish subject, but "The Showing-up of Blanco Posnet," a sort of sentimentalized travesty of Bret Harte preaching the usual Shavian evangel, has no more relation to Irish life than it has to literature. It marred the repertoire the Abbey Company brought to America, as would a camp-meeting hymn the music of the pipes.

Out of the Abbey tradition, too, are the plays of "Norreys Connell" (Mr. Conal O'Riordan), whose "Piper" had its day of lesser notoriety of Playboy-like quality on its presentation on February 13, 1908. It is a very obvious allegory, outlining under guise of an incident of '98 the weaknesses of contemporaneous Ireland, its love of talk; its lack of hold-together; its refusal to see things as they are; its incapacity in practical matters; the reckless temper of this faction of its people, the subjection to clerical influence of that, the suicidal patriotism of a third; in short, the Celts' willful rebellion against the despotism of fact. It was not pleasant listening to, or seeing, "The Piper," to many groups of Irishmen, for it cut alike at the Parliamentary Nationalists, the Sein Feiner, and the shoneen. Even though one admires the courage of the Piper and Black Mike, one realizes the futility of both, and of Larry the Talker, Tim the Trimmer, and Pat Dennehy, all typical of too many men in Ireland to be endurable to the usual theatre audience. There is a white heat of feeling, however, under the play that to some degree makes one forget its rather indifferent writing, its failure to attain true dramatic speech, its obviousness as of a morality play.

Another little drama of Mr. O'Riordan, "Time," is almost a morality play. It was produced shortly after its author became director of the Abbey Theatre, succeeding Mr. Synge in the spring of 1909. Mr. O'Riordan does not include "Time" among the plays of his volume of 1912, "Shakespeare's End, and Other Irish Plays," but one cannot but feel there was room for it there, if there was room for the play that gives title to the volume. "Shakespeare's End," however, was doubtless included because it gives its author's ideas as to the mission of Ireland in the world. "An Imaginary Conversation," the second play of the volume, was performed at the Abbey Theatre May 13, 1909, following shortly after "Time": a discussion of art and patriotism and love among Tom

Moore and his sister Kate and Robert Emmet, with a little, a very little, of the intensity that made "The Piper" something more than second-rate.

## MR. ST. JOHN G. ERVINE

Mr. St. John G. Ervine I know through two plays, "Mixed Marriage," produced at the Abbey Theatre on March 30, 1911, and "The Magnanimous Lover," produced in the same playhouse on October 17, 1912. Like his fellow from County Down, the master dramatist of the Ulster Literary Theatre, Mr. Mayne, Mr. Ervine excels in characterization. You remember his people, even after one reading of the plays, so clearly are they distinguished, so definite are their personalities. With the five men and women of "The Magnanimous Lover," you pass but a few minutes, as it is only a one-act play, but you remember them as well as you do the six of "Mixed Marriage," though you follow their fortunes through four acts. All these characters are typical of the artisan class of the North of Ireland, the five Protestants of "The Magnanimous Lover" and the four Protestants and two Catholics of "Mixed Marriage." It is the troubles that arise from the difference in religion of the Protestant Raineys, mother, father, and the two young men; the Catholic betrothed, Nora, of the elder son Hugh; and their common friend the Catholic labor agitator, O'Hara, that are the motive forces of the latter play. Faintest etched is Tom, the younger son, and most like a stock character. Nora and O'Hara are well done, but one

remembers both as stage parts rather than as characterizations. Hugh is still better done, but the two absolute
creations are the father and mother. Tom Rainey, the
Orangeman, forgets his bitterness against "Cathliks" for
a moment to help win the strike in which his fellow work-
men of Belfast, "Cathlik an' Prodesans," both are fighting side by side. He is all the more bitter, however, when
he learns that his eldest son is going to marry out of his
faith, and his speeches, hitherto devoted to smoothing out
the troubles between the men of different faith, turn to
bitter denunciations of the strike as "a Popish Plot." In
the end Tom Rainey is responsible for riots his wild words
have stirred up, the calling-out of the soldiery, and the
death of Nora, who is shot down by a volley as she runs
out of the Rainey house into the rioting street. On the
stage, of course, Mrs. Rainey is the more sympathetic
character, her tolerance, her tact, her humor, her infinite
kindliness winning an audience as it is given to few characters to win it. She is less like a type, too, than her husband, but for all, I cannot but think he is better drawn.

Mr. Ervine has not a style like Mr. Mayne, nor such
a rhythm to his prose, but he has more humor, and it is a
natural humor, a humor that arises out of the situation
and is not simply dragged in for the purposes of comic
relief. Mr. Ervine evidently knows the life he depicts in
and out. He ought to know it, for he was born to it, being
the son of a workingman in the shipyards of Belfast. And
knowing it well he finds it far from hopeless. It is a pleasure to come upon a play of the North written in a spirit
other than that of revolt against its Puritanism. There

are "kindly Irish of the Irish" in the Black North as well as in the three other provinces, but most of the authors of the North are content to picture its hardness, its hypocrisy, its bigotry, its love of wife and child remorselessly concealed as a weakness of the flesh.

It is to this darker picturing of the North, however, that Mr. Ervine turns in "The Magnanimous Lover," which indicts the self-righteousness of the Ulster Protestant with a severity such as is possible only to a man bitter against a weakness of his own people. It is an old theme Mr. Ervine has to handle, the refusal of the wronged woman to wed her betrayer, when, after years of disloyalty, he is willing, by marrying her, to make her again an "honest woman." To speak only of recent plays of similar plot, there is "The Last of the De Mullens" of St. John Hankin, and "A Woman of No Importance" of Wilde. Mr. Ervine, it is true, handles the theme freshly, but the real power of the play is in his creation of the heroine, Maggie Cather. The danger with such a character is that it will be only a mouthpiece for woman's demand for a common moral standard for men and women; but Maggie is not a mouthpiece but a real woman, triumphantly alive, with hot anger in her heart at the injustice of the world, and at the "unco guidness" of her old-time lover, Henry Hinde. Ten years before the time of the action of the play Henry Hinde had fled, just as her child was to be born, to Liverpool, and there he has prospered, and so risen in the world that it is possible for him to wed a minister's daughter. Fear of God's wrath has now driven him home to make such amends as he can, but there is in him no pity for the woman or love for his child. Maggie has faced it out alone all these years in the seaside village of Down as Hester faced it out in the seaside village of Massachusetts, while Henry forgot it all until he was "saved" and "convicted of sin." If no more cowardly than Dimmesdale, Henry is more heartless, utterly callous, indeed, — as he confesses, in "the devil's grip." And yet Mr. Ervine is so true to the life that he is depicting, a life at once passionate and prosaic, that he makes anger for the past and fear of a nagged future with Henry as effective agents in her rejection of him as are self-respect and right feeling. It is a "big" part that Mr. Ervine has created for the leading actress, and though the story is unequivocally "unpleasant" and may prevent "The Magnanimous Lover" from being a favorite play, there can be no two minds as to its success as drama. It is very real drama, of elemental human emotion all unveiled. With such a play as this, and with "Mixed Marriage" to his credit, I look forward eagerly to the promised production and publication of "The Eviction."

### MR. JOSEPH CAMPBELL

Another dramatist from the North and of promise is Mr. Joseph Campbell. His "Judgment" is of the northwest, however, the whole breadth of Ulster between its Donegal mountains and the Belfast of "Mixed Marriage"; and it is of the country, not of the city; and of an Ireland wholly Catholic, not of an Ireland of Protestant and Catholic at war over religion. There are moments of real drama in "Judgment," but no such inevitable rise to climax as in "Mixed Marriage." Its undoubted power is in the feeling underlying it, in its characterization, and in its style. Mr. Campbell was already known when his play was put on at the Abbey Theatre, April 15, 1912, as the author of "The Mountainy Singer" (1909), a volume of freshly felt and singing verse; and of "Mearing Stones" (1911), little prose records of things seen and of moods felt in a corner of Donegal. Many a striking phrase of "Judgment," indeed, is already written down in the paragraphs of "Mearing Stones" as actual talk heard in the roads, and several of the situations of the plays are workings-up of situations of which its author found himself a spectator on the streets of Andara or on the highway between Slieve a-Tooey and the sea.

I first came upon his verses, if I remember rightly, in "The United Irishmen," but I was first impressed by him as an illustrator, his name being always signed in those days after the Irish fashion, Seosamh MacCathmhaoil. A Dublin friend sent me at Christmas in 1907 a "Calendar of the Saints," for which Mr. Campbell did the illustrations, illustrations akin to those of Miss Althea Gyles, which so surely take one back to Ireland's heroic age, instinct as they are with the primitive aloofness of antiquity.

It is not antiquity, however, that Mr. Campbell has chosen for his play. Indeed, he rejects antiquity, deliberately "using peasants as . . . protagonists instead of kings — who, like Pharaoh, are 'but a cry in Egypt,' outworn figures in these days with no beauty and no significance." "Judgment" is made out of the story of the countryside concerning "a tinker's woman," Peg Straw, and we may well believe Mr. Campbell has changed it but little, as he says, for the purposes of his play. It had been a better play, perhaps, had he changed more the facts of the story. As it stands, the first act of the play is adequate dramatically, and beautiful with that sort of wild and outworld beauty Synge brought into English literature in Ireland; and the second act beautiful with that beauty, and inadequate dramatically.

Peg Straw is an old, worn woman of the roads whom the people hold little better than a witch, even attributing to her the power fabled of the witches in folk-tales of turning themselves into hares. Her nickname "Straw" indicates the nature of the mild dementia that sets the children and the idlers at her heels. She goes about picking up "straws" until "she'd have a bunch in her hand . . . every little stalk bit off as neat as neat, and it like a scrubber or dandy brush you'd put to a horse."

Peg speaks no word at all in the play, coming into sight in it only to die, but always she is in the background. Talk of her comes up early in the first act, and we learn that Nabla, the woman whose cabin is the play's first scene, has turned Peg away from the door only that morning; and from the moment we first hear of her most of the talk is of her, and the action because of her. Toward this first act's end you hear her cries as the tinkers beat her, and at its end she crawls into the cabin to die, and in dying to shock the woman of the house so that her child comes before its time. All the second act Peg lies in sight in the room just off the stage with candles stuck around her, bringing the horror and dignity of death into the wild scenes of her wake. These are wild not because of drinking, for no one is drunk and only one "had drink taken," but because of the wildness of nature of these men of westernmost Europe, and because of the wildness of the roads that a "traveling man" brings with him out of the night. There is no action in this second and last act save that sprung of this stranger's entrance and quarrelsomeness, and his interruptions of an old, old man's story of what he knows of Peg's life. The stranger listens while Parry Cam tells of the cause of her madness, but when he repeats what for years has been the gossip of the countryside about her supposed killing of her babe, the "traveling man" interrupts and declares he is the son whom it was rumored she had drowned. In the end he is turned out of the house, not altogether unkindly, but as much for decency's sake as for his own. That the son, for any motive at all, should be turned out of the house where his mother lies dead, even though he had not stood by her living, is hard enough in the estimation of any people, but in the estimation of the Irish peasant it is intolerably tragic. If we realize this, the ending of the play will be on a note deeper and more significant than if we fail to realize it, but not even the utmost sympathy with the intention of the author and a full realization of the significance to Donegal peasants of the action can bring this act to an intensity comparable to that of the end of Act i, where two mysteries confront one another — "the passing of a life from this world, the coming of a life into it."

All the characters in "Judgment" are "created." The personality of each colors his words and puts him before you distinct from every other.  Owen Ban the weaver, who takes in Peg when his wife Nabla, heavy with her first child, and nervous because of her condition and fearful of the birth, would keep out the outcast; old Parry Cam; John Gilla Carr; Colum Johnston and Father John; Nabla herself; and Kate Kinsella the midwife — each is himself or herself, each remains as distinct in your mind as the unforgettable scenes of the play.  Somehow or other, too, the country is suggested; you are aware that you are on a wild hillside above a glen, — you are aware of this not because the author tells us at the outset that the scene of the play is in the mountains of western Donegal, south of Lochros Beg Bay, but through the dialogue of the play itself.  Both scenes of the play are indoors, and on dark nights of midwinter, but so instinct with many phases of the life of the people is it that its background of landscape rises before you only less distinctly than the visualization of its characters.  Atmosphere the play has, and quality, both sprung of the sincerity of its feeling and imagination.  So true are these, and so keen the author's reading of human nature, and so sure his character drawing, that for all his weakness of construction we may speak of his play alongside of the best Irish plays.  The future promises finer things: meanwhile we are thankful for what is, for "Judgment," — especially for its far-offness, its desolateness as of the world's end and the wind crying.

WILLIAM SHARP

# CHAPTER IX

## WILLIAM SHARP ("FIONA MACLEOD")

THERE were relations other than that of a common purpose between William Sharp and the Irish writers of the Celtic Renaissance. He was a friend of Mr. Yeats, a correspondent of Mr. Russell, and the chief commentator in the English reviews on the work of the Irish group of its writers. At one time, after 1897, the relationship promised to be very close, indeed. William Sharp, experimenting in psychics with Mr. Yeats, found occasion to interest him in "Fiona Macleod," and as a result of that interest Mr. Yeats came to think the new writer might write Celtic plays for performances he intended to arrange for Irish literary organizations. Thus it is that Mrs. Sharp has to include in her memoir of her husband a long letter to "Fiona Macleod" from Mr. Yeats, in which he suggests: "The plays might be almost in some cases modern mystery plays. Your 'Last Supper,' for instance, would make such a play." Mr. Sharp, apparently, did not follow up this suggestion, but shortly after the first performances of "The Irish Literary Theatre" in 1899 he wrote the two plays that, together with "Vistas," comprise all the dramatic writing that he has to his name. That "The Immortal Hour" and "The House of Usna" were intended for "The Irish Literary Theatre," I think there is little doubt, and it was only, I take it, when circumstances dictated that only plays by Irish writers should be put on by that theatre that Mr. Sharp looked elsewhere for their presentation. Only "The House of Usna" was, however, placed, — in the spring performances in London of The Stage Society, on April 29, 1900. Two months later "The House of Usna" was published in the July number of "The National Review." It pleased more, if we are to judge by the reviews, in the pages of the magazine than on the stage, but I hardly know why. "The House of Usna" is profoundly moving read in the study, surely, and if acted in such simplicity and enthusiasm as is that of the Abbey Theatre Players, I should think it would appeal as do the verse plays of Mr. Yeats. No play I have read carries me further into antiquity than this, none preserves more of what imagination tells us must have been the wilder beauty of what still are places of wild beauty, of the savagery of that old life of the hero tales of Ireland. Mr. Yeats's plays do not so recapture the past, they take us rather to places out of time, where all things are possible, because the world we know is put aside and all but forgot. Even on the stage, however, the new beauty of "The House of Usna" was recognized, a beauty as distinctive as that of the two plays of M. Maeterlinck that were produced with it, "Interior" and "The Death of Tintagiles," but it was adjudged not to be drama in the accepted sense of the word. "The House of Usna" is written in a prose that has many of the effects of verse, but that is less luxuriant than the prose of "Vistas." "The Immortal Hour," published shortly afterwards in the "Fortnightly Review" (1900), is written in blank verse that shows its author has been carefully attentive to the free rhythms of the blank verse of Mr. Yeats, but it is neither so poetic nor so dramatic as "The House of Usna." Both plays are written out of the old legends that are the common property of Irish and Scottish Gael, and in both Sharp has treated his material with his wonted freedom of adaptation, a freedom that is generally justified by his results, his instinctive surety of reconstruction of myths being such as to make one wonder, with Mr. Russell, if Sharp is not, in some fashion, a reincarnation of a shanachie that sang as contemporary in the wars of Gael and Gall.

A common preoccupation with the plays of M. Maeterlinck is another bond between the founder of the Abbey Theatre and Sharp, a preoccupation passing rather quickly from Mr. Yeats, but long retaining its hold on the changing selves of Sharp. For all his early interest in "spiritual things," an interest very definitely expressed in "Romantic Ballads" (1888), Sharp would not have come to "Vistas" (1894) without the guidance of M. Maeterlinck, and he admits as much in his preface to these "psychic episodes." "Vistas" he often referred to as heralding a "great dramatic epoch," and he evidently regarded them as, in a way, drama, but it is hardly likely that he dreamed of their enactment on the stage. Many of them are essentially dramatic, but their method of presentation is almost always lyric or narrative rather than dramatic, even in the Maeterlinckian sense of the word.

It is possible, however, that Sharp might have written

other of his projected plays, "The Enchanted Valleys," "The King of Ys," "Drosdan and Yssul," and their many fellows he had projected by title, and others, too, had not developments in Dublin, as I have said, carried Mr. Yeats away from him during 1899 and 1900, and had Sharp himself not during this drifting written that article "Celtic" which so aroused many in Ireland on its appearance in "The Contemporary Review." In this essay, basically a literary protest, "Fiona Macleod" declared "herself" against Separatist politics and affirmed "her" belief, as "she" had in "The House of Usna," that the future greatness of Ireland was to come, not through independence, but through the rebirth of her ancient spirituality in other nations to whom she had given her children.

The Celtic element in our national life [wrote "Fiona Macleod"] has a vital and great part to play. We have a most noble ideal if we will but accept it. And that is, not to perpetuate feuds, not to try to win back what is gone away upon the wind, not to repay ignorance with scorn, or dullness with contempt, or past wrongs with present hatred, but so to live, so to pray, so to hope, so to work, so to achieve, that we, what is left of the Celtic races, of the Celtic genius, may permeate the greater race of which we are a vital part, so that, with this Celtic emotion, Celtic love of beauty, and Celtic spirituality, a nation greater than any the world has seen may issue, a nation refined and strengthened by the wise relinquishings and steadfast ideals of Celt and Saxon, united in a common fatherland, and in singleness of pride and faith.

There was, however, if less intimacy with the Irish writers in these later years, no less admiration of their art, an admiration that led not only to praise of them in crit-

ical articles, but to a greater praise of imitation of their
art. So possessed, indeed, was Sharp by the verse of the
younger Irish poets as he read them to write of them, that
when he turned to verse as "Fiona Macleod," he fell into
their rhythms and reproduced the colors of their styles.
Writing in prose as a critic of Mr. Yeats, Sharp came to
write in verse as Mr. Yeats wrote, as in "The Dirge of the
Four Cities": writing of "A. E." in prose as critic, Sharp
came to write in verse as "A. E." wrote, as in "Flame on
the Wind": writing of "Moira O'Neill," in prose as critic,
Sharp came to write in verse as "Moira O'Neill" wrote,
as in "I — Brasil": writing in prose as critic, of "Ethna
Carberry," Sharp came to write in verse as "Ethna Carberry" wrote, as in "The Exile." So it was, also, that,
coming to write of Celtic literature after study of Renan
and Arnold, Sharp attained to something of their large
utterance.

Sharp sees the Celtic Renaissance, however, always in
relation to English literature, and always, it should be
added, with French literature and Greek literature in the
background. In this wide outlook, in his freedom from
political prejudice, in his sympathy with Celtic literature
and his knowledge of it, is his greatest strength as a critic
of the Celtic Renaissance. His greatest weakness is his
willingness in this writing, as elsewhere in his writing, to
abide by first impressions, to abide also by the first-come
phrase or epithet, banes of the ready writer. But read his
essay "Celtic" after you have read the great essays of
Renan and Arnold, and read it alongside of what Mr.
Yeats has to say of that literature, and you will find it, as

I said, of the stature of these. You will at the same time find in this writing the answer to the contention that there were really two personalities in William Sharp. Even Mrs. Sharp, who writes so restrainedly about this question of dual personality, believes the analytical faculty belonged to William Sharp, the imaginative to "Fiona Macleod." But in this criticism of the Celtic Renaissance which is signed "Fiona Macleod," there is as much analysis as is to be found anywhere in his work as William Sharp. So obviously was he identifying "F. M." with "W. S." in this critical writing that Mrs. Janvier, of those in the secret, wrote to him to take warning lest he betray himself. She pointed out to him that such a display of learning as he was making in the later "Fiona Macleod" work would surely lead to discovery. But he did not heed. The truth probably was that he wrote about Celtic things as "Fiona Macleod" because he perhaps felt about them, as "Fiona Macleod," as one who is bilingual thinks about work he is doing, say in German, in German, and about work he is doing in English, in English; but just as surely I believe, because what "Fiona Macleod" wrote commanded more respect than what William Sharp wrote, a readier entrance into the magazines, and better pay. If there are those to whom such an explanation seems belittling to William Sharp, I can only say that they cannot have realized that he was a driven man earning his living by his pen. I am not, I confess, a sentimentalist in such matters, and while I do not wholly like his procedure in maintaining the fiction of "Fiona Macleod," it does not seem to me a very heinous sin.

He who would write of the work of William Sharp, indeed, must be resolute to remember that it is to be considered as an essay in the art of letters. There are so many temptations toward writing of it as a scientific problem, — for who is not interested in "dual personality"? — or as a "psychic revelation," if one is bitten — and who is not? — by curiosity about hidden "things"; or as an irritating hoax, if one has been befooled — and who, for one moment or another has not been? — into believing that this writing under the pseudonym of "Fiona Macleod" was the confession of a woman. The romance of it remains, no matter from what point of view you consider it, and, despite your preoccupation with this or that phase of it, the beauty of literary art of parts of it. Parts of it, I say, for to me no writer of our time was more uneven in his work. My point of view, indicated perhaps brutally, and with a firstly and secondly is: —

Firstly, that until he was nearly forty, William Sharp was no more than a skillful literary practitioner, a higher sort of hack, who had done some better writing of a tenuous kind of beauty but imitative in substance and art, in "Sospiri di Roma" and "Vistas," and that after forty, when he was developing one undeveloped side of himself as "Fiona Macleod," he developed another undeveloped side of himself in "Silence Farm." That he attained in a sort of writing, and greatly, that he had not attained in before, in "Silence Farm," has not been acknowledged, so easy has it been to those interested in his work to lose sight of all else in their pursuit of the "Fiona Macleod" side of his nature. It is true of "Silence Farm," as of almost all his other work done under the name of William Sharp, that it is imitative; but it is equally true that a large part of the "Fiona Macleod" work is imitative, too. "Silence Farm" is done under [the influence of the later work of Mr. Hardy, but the material of "Silence Farm" is its author's own, and the color of the writing is as distinctly of the Lowlands as the color of "Tess" is of Wessex. That "Silence Farm" is better work in its kind, though that kind is less original than some of his writing as "Fiona Macleod," I have been forced against my prejudices to believe. If I did not so believe I would not have spoken of it side by side with "Tess."

Secondly, that as "Fiona Macleod," William Sharp did much good writing in almost everything published under the pseudonym, achieving wholeness of good tissue in certain sketches and tales and verses on rather varying kinds of subjects, but that his work as "Fiona Macleod" that is really distinguished is in stories of prehistoric Scotland and Ireland, and of Scotland and Ireland in the earliest historic time. In these tales of the Gaels of old time he for the first time breaks ground for others. Before he wrote "Silk o' the Kine," and "The Harping of Cravetheen," "The Annir Choile," and "Enya of the Dark Eyes," there were no short tales of like temper and content and style in literature.

To me little is significant in the early verse of "Fiona Macleod," as little was significant in all the verse of William Sharp until the time of "Sospiri di Roma." And for all the beauty of these pictures in words of the Campagna it is but a transient beauty. It was not until he was mastered by the new beauty that Mr. Yeats brought into English poetry that the verse of William Sharp won to itself abiding beauty and glamour and inevitable phrase. "The House of Usna" (1900) brought to me "Dim face of beauty haunting all the world," and the 1901 edition of "From the Hills of Dream," "The Enchanted Valleys"; but it was not until after his death that I came upon his best verse of all, the verse of his last five years, which was gathered together posthumously in the 1907 edition of "From the Hills of Dream," and included as "The House of Beauty" in "The Poems and Dramas" of 1911. Who does not know these sets of verses and "The Dirge of the Four Cities," does not know the ultimate accomplishment of William Sharp in poetry.

That the "'Fiona Macleod' mystery" ended with the death of William Sharp is, then, my belief, as it is that it began before he conceived of exploiting a feminine subself he had long been aware of in himself. The beginnings of that sort of writing that made "Fiona Macleod" a reputation are to be found very early in his writing, in "The Son of Allan" of 1881, in the "Record" of 1884, in the preface to the "Romantic Ballads" of 1888, in the "Vistas" of 1894. That these earlier expressions of "spiritual" states and guesses at mysteries are not, except for certain parts of "Vistas," so well written as the best writing of similar kind by "Fiona Macleod," is true, and perhaps, at first glance, a matter of wonder. It is, however, I think, not difficult to find an explanation of the better quality of the later work, and that explanation is afforded, firstly and most largely, by the Celtic Renaissance. A man of thirty-five, to all who know him a very vital force, a very original personality, who has all his life wanted to make beautiful things in words out of his dream of life, has disappointed himself and his friends. He is suddenly afforded the opportunity, by the interest in Gaelic subjects that the Celtic Renaissance has awakened, to gain a hearing for work of a kind he has long wanted to do. He had not done such work previously, because he had to live by his pen and could work consistently only at the sort of thing that would sell. He was well known as a journeyman of letters, so well known for bookmaking, and the ways of getting commissions from London editors and publishers, that his knowledge of Highland life would be questioned. All in London knew him as a Londoner. It would be useless for him to say that the Celtic Renaissance had brought back his childhood to him, a childhood as definitely dominated by a Highland nurse as Stevenson's was by the Lowland Alison Cunningham. It would be useless to tell of his summers in Argyllshire and among the inner isles, his intimacy with fishermen who were as elemental as his own dreams of old time. It would have been cast up to him that the editor of "The Canterbury Poets" could not be an original writer, and the very nine days' wonder of "Vistas" would have been pointed to to prove that he might now do well enough, as an imitator, perhaps of Mr. Yeats, as he was in "Vistas" successful as an imitator of M. Maeterlinck, but that an original Highland writer could not come out of Hampstead. There is no doubt in my mind that it was the part of wisdom for Sharp to put out the new work under a pseudonym, worldly wise if you will, but wise, too, with a higher wisdom. If he could keep the side of him he had never yet exhausted through hackwork apart from his other work, it would grow as it could not if it were a part of his daily stint.

Why Sharp chose a woman's name for his pseudonym has troubled many, but this choice was, I think, as was the assumption of a pseudonym, the part of wisdom. I do not believe, as he at times liked to believe, that he attained a woman's standpoint. He had been complimented on all sides for his composition of the wife's letters in "A Fellowe and his Wife" (1892), in which Mrs. von Teuffel wrote the husband's. Sharp enjoyed their writing as a *tour de force* and he probably believed they were very womanly. I should say that they showed insight into womanly ways of looking at things rather than a dramatic identification of himself with woman such as is George Meredith's. Sharp had already been experimenting with pseudonyms, that of "H. P. Siwaarmill," an anagram on his own name, being that he recurred to most often. He had written the whole of "The Pagan Review" in 1892 under eight different pseudonyms, and though, in the estimation of those to whom "Fiona Macleod" is all but a sacred name, it be sacrilegious to say it, William Sharp loved all sorts of fantastic tricks, hoaxes, mystifications, though in almost all his writing save in "Wives in Exile" he was seriousness itself. But the chiefest reason of all, in my estimation, for his assumption of a woman's name as his pseudonym was that it afforded greater protection against discovery. There are those who believe that he chose it because he wanted a chance to express that womanly element of human nature there is in all men, and there are others who believe that he was the possessor of a real dual personality in which the "Fiona Macleod's self" was a woman's consciousness; but he very infrequently, after "The Mountain Lovers" (1895), kept in mind in the writings he published as "Fiona Macleod's" that their author was supposed to be a woman, and it is wonderful, indeed, that he was able to preserve the secret until the end. In the earlier "Fiona Macleod" writing there is no revelation of the wide acquaintance with literature that was Sharp's, but despite his harassment by the constant identification of himself with "Fiona Macleod," he gradually allowed to creep into that writing more and more of what was known to be the knowledge of William Sharp, a knowledge unlikely to be also that of a Highland lady who lived apart from the world. His friends pointed out to him the danger he was running in writing from what was obviously a man's standpoint, as in his tales of the wars of Gael and Gall, and of revealing several sorts of interest that were known to be his, but their warnings were in vain. He was apparently unable to limit himself to the restrictions of the part of himself he had essayed to restrict himself to.

For my own part I was now sure the writing must be Sharp's and now sure it could not be his. I did not know of his intimate concern with questions of feminism until I read Mrs. Sharp's "Memoir," so that outspoken chant, the "Prayer of Women" in "Pharais," "Fiona Macleod's" first book, colored my outlook on all the writing that followed. I had no doubt at all but that "Pharais" was written by a woman, but "The Dan-nan-Ron" and "Silk o' the Kine" in "The Sin-Eater" (1895) seemed to me hardly a woman's. "The Washer of the Ford" (1896) was written from the man's point of view, too, but "Green Fire" (1896) seemed feminine again. So I wobbled in my opinion until "The Divine Adventure" (1900) and the critical writings of the volume that story gives title to, and the critical writing in "The Winged Destiny" (1905), made me believe again that "Fiona Macleod" was surely Sharp. I did not come upon the articles that now make up "Where the Forest Murmurs" (1907) until after the death of Sharp and the disclosure of the secret. Had his death not divulged the secret of the identity of "Fiona Macleod," it seems to me that collection must have disclosed it. Had Sharp lived after this there would not have been possible for him much further work from the seclusion his pseudonym gave him, and I doubt, once the secret was out, it would have been possible for him to write of things Celtic with the old gusto.

After all has been said it must be confessed, I think, that Sharp did not know the Highlander, either of the mainland or of the islands, very intimately. He wrote much better of his dream of life on the west coast in prehistoric times — out of his imagination of what that life must have been, an imagination founded on the reading of the old legends and modern collections of folk-lore, such as the "Carmina Gadelica" of Mr. Carmichael — than he did out of his knowledge of Highland life of today. The Achannas are in many of his tales of modern times, and wherever they are there is unreality, if not melo-drama. Unreality, too, there is, in many phases, in the modern tales, and "highfalutinness" everywhere in them. And both unreality and "highfalutinness" offend in these modern tales as they would not in the tales of far times, though in these, as a matter of fact, they are not so much in evidence.

It would almost seem that the approach to reality drove Highland atmosphere from the stories. In "The Sin-Eater," one of the best of his writings that might be classed as a short story, the sin-eater and his confidant are Highlanders, but the description of the scene of his mis-fortune, the steading of the Blairs, might well have been that nearest to "Silence Farm." It is faithfully described, the scenes about the little home, whose owner lies dead, having the very smack of realism. In the latter part of the story the scene shifts to the coast and the tang of the story turns Gaelic and unreal. Was it thus, I wonder, al-ways to the imagination of William Sharp, Lowland life real, Highland life mystical?

Sharp was handicapped, of course, in coming to the sub-ject material he could best handle late in life, "Pharais" (1894) and "The Mountain Lovers" (1895), the first books published as by "F. M.," being just as definitely 'pren-ticework in their kind as was "Children of To-morrow" (1890) in its kind. Of the long stories other than "Child-ren of To-morrow" published in his own name, "A Fellowe and his Wife" (1892) and "Wives in Exile" (1896) have no very serious intention, though both are well done after their kind, records of imaginings, respectively, of experiences of art life in Rome, and of yachting experiences in the Irish Sea. It was not until "Silence Farm" (1899), as I have said, that, as William Sharp, he found himself.

"The Gypsy Christ" (1896), which might well have been developed into a full-fledged romance, is less original than any of his longer writings. It is, like "The Weird of Michael Scott" and "A Northern Night," closely allied to essays of his other rôle, that of "F. M.," to catch and express "the tempestuous loveliness of terror," such as the catastrophe of "The Mountain Lovers," "The Barbaric Tales," and those short stories in which Gloom Achanna is hero-villain. It is in such work that Sharp shows his affinities to Poe, affinities which are not elsewhere as obvious as his affinities to De Quincey. Narrative was not native to De Quincey any more than it was to Sharp, though Sharp was led toward it by his interest in character, an interest that was not in any large measure given to De Quincey, who, when he turned to narrative other than that which relates what had happened to him or what he had dreamed had happened to him, makes the reader feel he did so as a concession to the public. Another interest that was Sharp's, an interest amounting to a passion, — out-of-doors, — De Quincey had not at all, for all his devotion to Wordsworth and to Wordsworth's interests. Like De Quincey, on the other hand, Sharp delights in "fine writing," in both senses of the phrase, in the "highfalutin" that is objectionable, and in the ornately beautiful that is one fitting expression of romantic thought. Both men preferred the mouth-

filling word to the simple one, the Latinical adjective to the
Saxon; both had rather see visions and dream dreams than
write about the "common light of common hours"; both
goad their imaginations until they run riot and so confuse their possessors, who should control them, that they
are unable to distinguish between what is fact and what is
fancy. You could carry the analogy further, to events of
their lives — the runnings-away in boyhood; the devoted
friendships to poets in youth; the incredible amount of
hard work achieved in manhood despite of often recurring
illnesses.

Of the long stories published as by "F. M.," Sharp re-
pudiated "Flora MacDonald" because it was too much
in the way of "ordinary romance," and "Green Fire" for
the same reason and because it was largely about Brittany, a country with which, by some strange chance, he
did not make himself familiar, though he had visited and
learned to know well at least parts of all the other Celtic
countries. It is to my mind, however, if not so definitely
of a wholeness of texture as "Pharais" or "The Mountain
Lovers," or so singular, less monotonous than either.
All three of these stories disappoint my memory of them
when I again read them. This is, I believe, because all
three of them — and for that matter many of the short
stories as well — are incompletely realized, or because
— in the case of two of them, "The Mountain Lovers"
and "Green Fire" — they are unevenly written. Their
high intention and atmosphere remain with you after you
have put the books aside, and in the course of time you
forget their hurried writing, their inconsistencies, and

their qualities of the "Shilling Shocker," the result of their author's failure to attain "the tempestuous loveliness of terror" that are in so many of them, long or short. As aids to this effacement of the cheapening elements are the very materials of the tales, their characters, now elemental, now other-worldly, and their background of mountains that uplift the spirit, and of menacing sea.

That Sharp wrote less exactly of the present-day people of the Highlands than of the background of their lives was largely because he had few opportunities to learn to know them intimately. There was a basis for such intimacy laid in his childhood, in the fact that his nurse was a Highland woman; there was something built on this basis by his boyhood's vacations in many parts of Argyllshire and voyages elsewhere along the west coast. Youth spent in Arran and Skye would have counted for much more, for the boy, once he is no longer child and before he has reached his youth and is awakening man, is not much more interested in people in real life for what they are than he is in minute description of their characters in books. He likes men for the sportsmanlike and adventurous things they can do, and he likes to read records of things sportsmanlike and adventurous, but men as men, unless they are eccentric to grotesqueness, do not arrest his attention. Even the dreamy boys, the artistic boys, are not likely to learn much of others, so preoccupied are they with themselves.

It was thus, I think, that Sharp's childhood was not what he would in later years have had it, not what in "The Laughter of Peterkin" he alleges the childhood of

"Fiona Macleod" to have been. For all the influence of
"Barabal," his nurse, it seems from his writing that her
stories remain with him more as suggestions to imagination than as definite memories, and that the fisherman
referred to in "Sheumas" left with him little more than
"Barabal." How fresh and wonderful to him was actual
contact with Highland life is almost pathetically revealed
in a letter he wrote to Mrs. Sharp from Kilcreggan in the
summer of 1894. In this letter he is all but exultant in the
recording of the securing of "Celtic" material from a
"Celtic Islesman from Iona." Of the actual life of the
Islesmen and Glensmen he could have known but little,
for long living among them is necessary to their understanding, — they are, as he wrote in this same letter,
"passionately reticent." It was not the way of Sharp to
fall back, in this deficiency of experience, on old legends
and folk-tales collected in his own day, but to trust to
his imagination as that was quickened by what knowledge
he had of life in the inner isles and in Argyllshire, and by
the very atmosphere of known places there that seemed
to demand, as Stevenson put it, to have stories invented
to fit them.

It is said, too, — Mrs. Sharp gives her authority to the
story, — that friendship with the woman to whom he
dedicated "Pharais," "E. W. R.," stimulated him to the
work. "Because of her beauty, her strong sense of life, and
of her joy of life," writes Mrs. Sharp in her memoir of her
husband, "because of her keen intuitions and mental alert-
ness, her personality stood for him as a symbol of the
heroic women of Greek and Celtic days, a symbol that,

as he expressed it, unlocked new doors in his mind and put him in touch with the ancestral memories of his race." And Mrs. Sharp quotes him further as declaring "without her there would have been no 'Fiona Macleod.'" Perhaps; but I doubt if, after the Celtic Renaissance had won a hearing, anything could have prevented Sharp from following what was, after all, a natural bent. I am not going to argue the matter out, but he himself admitted that his development as "Fiona Macleod" began "while I was still a child," and there is proof in almost every volume he published, even before he knew Mrs. Rinder ("E. W. R." must of course be the author of "The Shadow of Arvor"), that his tendency was toward what became characteristic of "Fiona Macleod."

It was the love that Sharp had for all sorts of "psychic things," the mysterious, the unaccountable, the hidden, that led him to believe that "without her there would have been no 'Fiona Macleod.'" Sharp himself, when his "other self," with sense of humor alert, was more than willing to admit that it is easy to believe what one wishes to believe; and he delighted to tell a story at the expense of Mr. Yeats illustrative of the trite fact. Sharp went one day, in London, to call on Mr. Yeats. When lunch-time came, they set about cooking eggs. Mr. Yeats held them in a frying-pan over the little fire in the grate. As they slipped about, Mr. Yeats, all the while looking back in the room away from the fire as he talked to Sharp, allowed the pan to tip too far and the eggs fell out into the fire. So absorbed was he in the topic of conversation, most appropriately the disappearance of material things, that he did not notice the catastrophe or the quick disappearance of the eggs among the coals. When his perfervidness subsided for a moment, he turned to see if they were done. "There, what did I tell you!" said he; "our talk of these things has conjured up the powers and the eggs are gone." Sharp did not tell him of the accident. And there were no more eggs in the room to have for lunch.

One of the reasons that led William Sharp to write "Silence Farm" (1899) was to have something under his own name that might be very different from the stories of "Fiona Macleod." And "Silence Farm" is very different, a story without the distinguishing qualities of "Pharais" or "The Divine Adventure," and suggesting kinship to the work of his other self only through certain likenesses of domestic irregularity in the family of Archibald Ruthven to other domestic irregularity in the family of Torcall Cameron of "The Mountain Lovers." Though not of so original a kind, perhaps, as the best of the "Fiona Macleod" work, "Silence Farm" has to it a "wholeness of good tissue" that belongs to little work of this most uneven writer. "Silence Farm," I would emphasize again as I emphasized at the opening of this paper, is better written, both as regards style and architectonic quality, and it is a truer reading of life, than any of the Highland stories. Though it is a story of to-day, and about a life much like that made familiar by the writers of the Kailyard school, it is not to them, but to such kindred unsentimentalized work as Mr. Shan Bullock's, that you instinctively compare it. The people, indeed, are the same dour Presbyterians, though the one writes of Scotland and the other of the North of Ireland. And as you compare the material of "Silence Farm" with that of "The Squireen," for instance, you note, too, that the art of both is the art of Mr. Hardy.

There is little modern writing with which to compare the Highland stories of Sharp. It is not that the Highlands have not been much written about, but that they have been written about intimately by but few. No part of the world so out of the world as their outlying islands, the Hebrides, has been so bewritten by travelers from Martin's time to our own; but comparatively few have known either islands or mainland well enough to dare novels of their life, and of those who have so dared no one up to the time of Sharp had written a great realistic story of the Highlands, and but one or two great romances. Now we have Mr. Neil Munro, like Sharp a very uneven writer, whose "Children of Tempest" — to take one of his best stories — now delights and now tortures you; and yesterday we had William Black, famous for sunsets. Black knew the Hebrides well, very well for a Lowlandman turned Londoner, and he labored hard to make his books true and beautiful. Unfortunately it was not in him to do fine work, not even the best sort of the second order of novelists, — such work as Trollope's, for instance, which by dint of faithfulness and humanity almost persuades you now and then that it is of higher than second order. Black was faithful to what he saw and broadly sympathetic, but his writing not only lacks distinction, but, even at its best, as in "The Princess of Thule," home thrust to one's interest. Yet, such as it is, it is all but all that we have which attempts to put before us any broad view of Highland life. The one man of the generation older than the generation of Mr. Sharp who might have drawn Highland life greatly, Robert Buchanan, was diverted all his life, as Sharp was in the twenties and thirties, from doing what he would to what would boil the pot, but he left at least one story, a story of Sutherland, "A Child of Nature," to prove to us what his reading of Highland life might have been. Had Stevenson been born a Highlander, he might have given us both novels of the Highlands of the order of "Weir of Hermiston," and romances really Highland in quality, as "Kidnapped" and "Catriona" are not.

I suppose that, back of all the failure to deal realistically with Highland life, this rare attainment of a romance of Highland life at all faithful to it, is the making of the Highlander into a stage hero by Scott. There are those to-day who fail to find any glamour in "Waverley" or "Rob Roy" or "The Legend of Montrose," but it is still there to me, investing the figures of Fergus MacIvor and the MacGregor and the Children of the Mist as it did in childhood, when I was so fascinated that I prized my Campbell plaided paper soldiers next to my Continentals in blue and buff. In going through an old trunkful of school-books only the other day, I came upon one of these bonneted fellows, still wonderfully preserved, in an old atlas of the heavens, and then I knew all of a flash why it was that the poor boy soldiers that I saw in Highland accoutrement in the yard of Edinburgh Castle during the Boer War so disappointed me by their appearance and bearing. They were not half so brave as the piper who used to make the rounds of my boyhood's town and bring tears to my eyes with his "Campbells are Comin'." I write this that my quarrel with much of what Sharp has written of the Highlands, that portion that seems to me sentimentalized or one-sided, may not be put down to lack of appreciation of the romance, the eeriness, and other-worldliness that there unquestionably are in that life.

It is their aloofness from the everyday story, their unusual use of the supernatural that has given the longer stories written out of the "Fiona mood," as Mr. Sharp once spoke of his possession, their appeal to most readers, but there is here in America a class who put the highest valuation on the shorter stories Mr. Sharp called "spiritual tales." To those who hold this view "The Divine Adventure" is of the nature of revelation. To me it is hardly this, but very interesting, not so much for its putting of the relations of Body, Will, and Spirit to one another in life and at death, as for its beautiful writing, and for its definite betrayal, when its author is writing most intimately, of a man's attitude, though he published the story as the work of "Fiona Macleod." These "spiritual tales" do not belong, all of them, to his "Fiona Macleod" period, for "Vistas" (1894) contains many of them, though they are cast here in dialogue form, and there are others among the work published under his own name. In fact, the writing under the two names never becomes liker in quality and intention than when it is "spiritual." The sketch from Part II of "The Dominion of Dreams" (1899), entitled "The Book of the Opal," for instance, is written on the very key of "Fragments of the Lost Journals of Piero di Cosimo" (1896), far apart as is their subject material, and "The Hill-Wind" by "W. S.," dedicated as it is to "F. M.," might well be a rejected passage from "The Mountain Lovers." There is the color of the Highlands and Islands about many of these mystical stories, about "The Hill-Wind," by "W. S." and "The Wind, the Shadow, and the Soul," the epilogue "F. M." wrote to the "Dominion of Dreams"; but most of these shorter mystical tales have not the tang and savor of farm - home on lonely moors, or fisher's hut on the lonelier machar, that is characteristic of most of the tales, long and short, that deal with modern days.

Nor are the meanings of these "spiritual tales" consistently indicated in symbols taken from Scottish life, nor is their supernaturalism native to it. Mrs. Spoer (Ada Goodrich-Freer), in her "Outer Isles" (1902), tells us "The Celtic Gloom" amuses the Hebridean. If so, what effect would such discussion as that of "The Lynn of Dreams" and "Maya" have upon him? But if such essays are not written out of Highland life, they are none the less interesting, and in the case of "Maya," with its consideration of waking dream, beautiful as art, and valuable, too, as a contribution to science.

So far does Sharp go in his belief as to the apprehension of thought through powers other than those of the senses, that in "The Winged Destiny" he can look forward to a time "when the imagination shall lay aside words and pigments and clay, as raiment needless during the festivals of the spirit, and express itself in the thoughts which inhabit words — as light inhabits water or as greenness inhabits grass." Not only does he foresee such a time, but he foreshadows it, heralds it in some of his sketches, "Aileen" for one, by attempting it. Perhaps he has succeeded, perhaps not. To me the attempt is a failure, not, I think, because he is writing for to-morrow, for that age when the spiritual awakening he so often prophesied shall have come, but because he is attempting what cannot be done in any age. If he were seeking only suggestion, well and good. But he seeks more, and fails, I think, to attain more. It seems to me impossible that the suggestions he creates can ever be more than suggestions. They cannot become definite concepts that will mean the same thing to all men. Suggestion, the opening-up of vistas, is a high attribute of the art he follows; but he is not content with suggestion, he would seek more definite expression of what, after all, is not thought but mood. So it is that he is most successful when conveying mood and less successful when conveying esoteric thought. As a critic, of course, on a plane easier for the conveyance of thought, Sharp is definite enough, completely successful in conveying the ideas that he intends to convey.

Often, I fear, when Sharp intends "spiritual history," either in a tale wholly devoted to this purpose, as "The Divine Adventure," or as explanatory to the incidents of some more tangible tale, he is really only playing with words, beautiful words, words sometimes so beautiful that we are apt to forget that words are to be used not alone for beauty's sake. Often, again, I fear, he will introduce beautiful symbols simply for their beauty and not because they have a real purpose, not because they will more intimately convey, even to the initiated, the intent of his writing. That these practices are the result of carelessness, sometimes, as well as of his subservience to beauty, the fascination that words merely as words or visions merely as visions exert upon him, is, I think, true. It is but seldom, I believe, that the underlying thought is incoherent. In almost all of his earlier writing, however, even in the earlier "Fiona" writing, he is very careless. He contradicts himself in his short stories as to facts, he gets his family relationships tangled in a way that cannot be explained by any process of nature, and so, too, I think, he gets his symbols mixed, or deludes himself into the belief that something that was hastily written "came to him" that way and so should be preserved in that exact expression, even though to him at the second reading it meant nothing definite. He jumps to conclusions again and again in what he writes about birds, where I can follow him on a certain footing of knowledge. If he is so careless about facts, if he can, even though it is a slip, confuse Mary Magdalene and the Virgin Mary, if he can mention birds in a description of Highland landscape that is characteristic of a certain time of year when birds of that species would be in the Highlands only by accident at that time of year, it is more than likely, slips though these may be, that there will be similar slips in all he writes, no fewer, it is likely, in his writings of psychic things than elsewhere.

There is possible, of course, no hard-and-fast classification of his writings. Class shades into class almost imperceptibly. It is particularly difficult to draw the line between the several kinds of stories and sketches he writes that involve supernaturalism of one kind and another. There is possible, however, a rough-and-ready distinction between those stories of his which are esoterically mystical and those which, while concerned with the supernatural, are concerned with it in the way familiar in old romance. Of this "usual supernatural" are those in which "second sight" is the motive, second sight which is always to be looked for as the commonest supernatural motive in the writing of all Gaels, either Alban or Irish. Sharp introduced "second sight" into "The Son of Allan" (1881); it is in "Pharais" (1894), the first of his "F. M." work; it is developed at some length in "Iona" (1900), which is a microcosm of all his writing. In "Iona," Sharp puts himself on record as holding stoutly belief in the reality of the power: —

The faculty itself is so apt to the spiritual law that one wonders why it is so set apart in doubt. It would, I think, be far stranger if there were no such faculties. That I believe, it were needless to say, were it not that these words may be read by many to whom this quickened inward vision is a superstition, or a fantastic glorification of insight.

The Achannas, in the uncanny stories in which they are heroes and villains, are all possessed by the power of the second sight, but second sight is not the most remarkable of their supernatural powers. Hypnotic suggestion Gloom uses as an everyday agent in his affairs. It is through hypnotic suggestion that he puts madness upon Alasdair M'Ian, playing to him the Pibroch of the Mad,

Alasdair M'Ian, in telling whose story "Fiona Macleod" revealed — I suppose, by chance — something of the struggle of William Sharp to succeed in letters. Much more frequently, however, he uses a supernatural power that is further removed from those in which modern science is interested, such as the machination of fairies that made Allison Achanna the "Anointed Man" — that, in plain speech, had driven him fey; or such as the lure of the serpent goddess that drove to his death the piper hero of "By the Yellow Moon Rock," or the exchanging of human child for fairy child that is the burden of "Faraghaol."

It is much more likely that William Sharp would have made more of this changeling motive had it not come so near to the question of dual personality, which it would be dangerous to him to discuss, as would that question so closely akin, the question of people who are "away," — that is, with the fairies, — a kindly explanation of insanity, chronic or recurrent. As William Sharp he has touched on the question of dual personality several times in his verses, and very definitely in "A Fellowe and his Wife." In this last-named book he says, in a letter that the Countess Ilse writes to her husband in Rügen: "This duality is so bewildering. I to be myself, whom you know, and whom I know — and then that other I, whom you do not know at all and whom I only catch glimpses of as in a mirror, or hear whispering for a moment in the twilight." That he could not take up the topic so definitely in his later writings must have, indeed, been a cross to him, for there was hardly any other question, unless perhaps that of "ancestral memory," which interested him more deeply. It might be argued, I suppose, that he did discuss it in "The Divine Adventure," in considering the relations of Spirit, Will, and Body. Mrs. Sharp, I take it, so holds when she says in her "Memoir" that the William Sharp work was that of the Will and the "Fiona Macleod" work beyond the control of the Will. And it is true that these three, the Spirit, Will, and Body, though each is given a distinctive personality, each a memory distinct from the memory of the others, are all but the component parts of one man. Mrs. Sharp does not, however, anywhere avow directly a belief in the possession of a real dual personality by her husband, and she definitely contradicts Mr. Yeats for his expression of belief that "William Sharp could not remember what as 'Fiona Macleod' he had said to you in conversation."

Very different from these short stories I have been discussing are three of the four contained in the volume entitled "Madge o' the Pool" (1896), published as by William Sharp. Of the one that is somewhat in the manner of certain of the "F. M." stories, the "Gypsy Christ," I have spoken. Two, "The Coward" and "The Lady in Hosea," are but "the usual thing." "Madge o' the Pool" is the one really worth while. In this story, with such river pirates as we have met, sentimentalized, in "Our Mutual Friend," as material, Sharp writes as realistically as he does in "Silence Farm," and with a sympathy and pathos that his objective method cannot exclude.

There are episodes or sketches, some of them what Sharp calls "prose imaginings," throughout his many books, that one may hardly call short stories, or myths, or studies in folk-lore, or criticism, or any of the other many kinds of writing that he essayed. Perhaps "memories" would be the proper general term for writing of this kind. In almost every one of these episodes or sketches there is a germ of a story, and some, I suppose, regard them as but unrealized art. But I for one am glad Mr. Sharp did not "work them up." In them are some of his best writing and some of that most personal and intimate. I have spoken of "Aileen" and "Barabal"; "Sheumas, a Memory," is another that is memorable, and memorable, too, are "The Sea Madness" and "The Triad." "The Triad" is almost his *credo*, certainly a statement of the things he holds "most excellent" — "primitive genius, primitive love, primitive memory." Here Sharp recurs, as so often in his writing, to "ancestral memory," that possession of men by which they are aware of what was in the world before they were, through oneness with the universal memory into which they are absorbed in dream or vision or of which they become aware by what we call intuition. If such a power be restricted so that its possessor recalls only certain parts of antiquity, he is virtually in the state of him who believes he remembers what he remembers because of previous incarnations. I have no personal opinion to express on the subject, but if such memories exist in us because of our participation in a universal memory or because of reincarnation, it is easy to explain why Sharp is best in his writing of myths, his pictures of the wild beauties of love and war and dream in barbaric Erin and Alba. It is because he is the reincarnation of the shanachie of the Dark Ages. When he thought of reincarnation, however, in relation to himself, he thought, I have no doubt, of himself as the reincarnation of a druid, one who had been aware of mysteries; but what he really was, in life, with his magnificent enthusiasm and bravado, — picturesque raiment after all and no more for the high-hearted and inherently ailing body of him, — was this reincarnation of the shanachie, such an one as his own Oran the Monk turned tale-teller. If you doubt that he was shanachie, not druid, compare the two legends in "Beyond the Blue Septentrions." The ordered beauty of the legend that tells of the derivation of the name of Arthur from Arcturus falls familiarly on our ears. It is evidently made under a lamp by one who has read many old legends. It is no druidic revelation. The other, that which ends with the three great hero-leaps of Fionn from the Arctic Floes to the Pole, from the Pole up to Arcturus, from Arcturus to the Hill of Heaven itself, is fantastic, bizarre, extravagant to grotesqueness, with the very flamboyance of old Irish legend and modern Irish folk-tale. In other words, it is in the very manner of the shanachie of the Dark Ages, whether his work was re-corded then as court poem or has been handed down by word of mouth among the folk. Nor is there anything inconsistent in this wild imagining with a very different power displayed in "moralities" like his "Last Supper." I have heard stories as incongruous, one uproarious, another of cloistral quiet and piety, from the old Irish gardener with whom I spent a large part of my happier days, the days from seven to seventeen. Lawrence lost his life doing a "retreat" morning after morning on the cold stone floor of a Vincentian church, not in any sudden repentance at fourscore and three for the sins of his youth, for they had been fewer than those of almost all I know, but in the usual way of his austere life. Yet Lawrence was just as much himself when he was telling me stories of Dean Swift that were full of malice and brutality and orgiac ecstasy.

The range of the shanachie is wide, and wide, too, the range of Sharp in the rôle of shanachie of barbaric life on both sides of the Moyle. Among such writings there are few tellings of the order of the folk-tale, more of the order of the hero saga, many — perhaps the best of them — of an order all his own that has developed, it is likely, from the old "Saints' Lives," but to which he has given a ring of authenticity that makes them seem descended from an antiquity as remote as that of folk-tale or hero-tale. "The Flight of the Culdees" brings before you with vividness what must have been the life of the Celtic missionaries in the days when the men out of Lochlin began to seek the Summer Isles; and "The Annir Choile" and "The Woman with the Net," what was the fate they meted out to those among themselves who slipped back into the pleasant old ways of paganism. These are written out of his own revisualization of the past. More immediately sprung of the old legends are "The Three Marvels of Hy," which tells of the inner life of Columba and his brethren on Iona, and "Muime Chriosd," which utilizes folk-lore as old or older than the legends collected by Mr. Alexander Carmichael in his pursuit of the stories of St. Bride among the peasantry of the Outer Isles. "The Song of the Sword" and "Mircath" have in them the battle-madness of the Viking, whetted to its keenest intensity as he meets the hard resistance of the Hebrideans; and "The Laughter of Scathach" and "The Sad Queen," that more terrible fury of the Amazon who ruled in Skye. Than this last-named story Sharp has done no starker writing, but it is so evidently from a man's point of view that it confirmed many in the belief that "Fiona Macleod" could not be a woman.

"The Washer of the Ford" has its roots in folk-lore, but it is so remoulded in the mind of the writer that it is rather a re-creation of the old belief than a restoration of it. There are those who would rather have had Sharp follow the tales as they are told by Campbell of Islay, Cameron of Brodick, and Carmichael of South Uist, but to me, unless the tale is one familiar to many readers, such a remoulding, if done with power, is surely a pre-rogative of the artist. But when he takes a well-known legendary character, as well known among the Gaels as Achilles among English school-boys, and changes his hair from black to golden and his stature from short to tall, utterly transforming not only our picture of him, but the significance of his deeds, then I object, as I would object if he had made the fair-haired and great-statured Achilles into such "a little dark man" as the Red Branch legends record Cuchullin to have been. Nor would I quarrel even with his changing of the spirit of the old tales if he had always, as he has almost always, substituted a new beauty for the old beauty of the legend in its bardic or folk form. It is in the few instances in which his dream of the old tale does not lift to so great a power in its way as the old tale possessed in its way that I protest. Of such a nature are some of the changes Sharp made in his retelling of the "Three Sorrows of Story-Telling" in "The Laughter of Peterkin," which, it must be remembered, however, was hurried work, almost hackwork.

Sharp was particularly successful, I think, in his handling, in the three tales — he calls them "legendary moralities" — in which he brings Christ to the straths of Argyll. These three are "The Last Supper," "The Fisher of Men," and "The Wayfarer." The last is the least successful of the three, but significant in its attack on certain forms of Presbyterianism for their attempts to kill out, as un-Christian, the old ways of life among the Highlanders. This charge was made fifty years ago by Campbell of Islay, and it had been repeated only yesterday by Mr. Carmichael. William Black and Mr. Munro confirm it, too, in their novels, and, in fact, it is only what one expects of Puritanism, whether in its dominating of the Scotch Presbyterian minister or of the Irish Catholic priest. The latter is to-day doing as much to kill the joy of life in Connacht as did even the minister of the Free Kirk yesterday on the Lews. It may have been partly to hide his identity that Sharp assumed what some thought an anti-Presbyterian attitude in his "Fiona Macleod" writing; it may have been the sympathy of the artist toward a church that has conserved art that led him to what some thought a pro-Catholic attitude; but scratch this gypsy artist and you find, surprising as it may be, a moral prejudice for Protestantism. Does he not admire

Torcall Cameron and Archibald Ruthven, stern Calvinists both? "The Fisher of Men," and "The Last Supper" have in them the austere beauty of the old morality plays, a beauty that is akin to the beauty of the Puritan imagination of Bunyan, and a tenderness that we may in vain look for there. They are written in all reverence and simplicity, and it is no wonder we find Mr. Yeats suggesting that "Fiona Macleod" turn them into plays for the Irish Theatre.

I do not care so much for "The Birds of Emar," myths he has rewoven from the "Mabinogion" into Gaelic texture, or the series that purport to be collected among the Isles and are found to be very like certain well-known Greek legends. These, too, seem to me reweavings, and the "Treud-nan-Ron" and "The Woman at the Crossways"; and "The Man on the Moor," though its origin is far from their origins, is also a reweaving. In certain of his writing of this time Sharp passes over virtually into criticism or comparative mythology, as in "Queens of Beauty" and "Orpheus and Oisin," and in many of the papers of "Where the Forest Murmurs." These all have interest; but some smell much of the lamp; and none of them are to be compared to the best of his "Seanchas," to "The Harping of Cravetheen," or "Enya of the Dark Eyes," or "Silk o' the Kine," or "Ula and Urla"; or to his plays "The House of Usna" and "The Immortal Hour," in which, for all the savagery, there is nobility, the nobility that was in the old legends themselves, that nobility that withstood even the hand of Macpherson, that nobility that has been reproduced most nobly of all in the "Deirdre" of Synge.

I am not so sure that the tone of these old myths is always distinctively Celtic, as it is undoubtedly in "The Annir Choile," and in other "Seanchas" that reveal him at his best. There was viking blood in Sharp, and it comes out, I think, in such tales as "The Song of the Sword." How he came to write these barbaric tales I do not know, though I have sometimes thought that the "Dhoya" (1891) of Mr. Yeats may have suggested them, as the Hanrahan stories may have suggested certain of the more modern tales. But whatever their genesis, the heroes and heroines of the "Seanchas" seem to him like the heroes and heroines of Homer and the Greek tragedians; and his friend whom he thought inspired him to much of the "F. M." work stood, we must remember, as symbolical to him of the women of Greek as well as of Celtic legend.

There are many indications, in his last writing, not only in that unpublished book on "Greek Backgrounds" and in his articles in the magazines on Sicily, all by William Sharp, but in the "Fiona Macleod" work, that he would have come to write of Greek antiquity with an enthusiasm very like that with which he wrote of Gaelic antiquity. "W. S." is speaking with the voice of "F. M." when he says in a letter to Mrs. Sharp, dated Athens, January 29, 1904: "It is a marvelous homecoming feeling I have here. And I know a strange stirring, a kind of spiritual rebirth."

One reason, perhaps, that the best work of Sharp has come out of his consideration of the Celts of antiquity is that the stark stories he has to tell of them restrain his style, a style too flamboyant when there is in what he is writing a large opportunity for description of landscape or exhibition of great emotion in his characters. Another reason is, perhaps, that his tendency to introduce the supernatural is more in harmony with the subject material got out of antiquity than of the subject material got out of to-day. We can accept magic in these old tales, even to the incantations of Bobaran the White that swayed the waves of the sea so that Gaer, the son of Deirdre, was saved from the men of Lochlin. That is as it should be in druidic times. It is impossible, of course, that Bobaran had power over the waves, but in such a story such an episode seems more probable than the possible hypnotic suggestion of Gloom Achanna's pipe-playing that sent Manus MacOdrum to his death among the fighting seals, because to-day we do not often come upon such things. It is even less easy to accept the piping to madness of Alasdair in "Alasdair the Proud." Hypnotic suggestion may drive to death in the sea a man half fey because of sorrow long endured and the superstition that he is descended from seals, but pipe-playing cannot believably in modern tales drive a man insane, whatever it may do in the famous old "Pied Piper of Hamelin" or other folk-tale.

So, too, in the verse of Sharp, whether lyric or dramatic, it is the Celt that inspires him to his best work. Nowhere does his verse win so much of beauty and glamour as when his thought turns to the four cities of Murias and Finias and Falias and Glorias, or when it breaks into a chant on the lips of Etain, in "The Immortal Hour."

Though there is less unevenness of technique, both in the style and in the unfolding of the story, in these "Seanchas" than elsewhere in his writing, the technique breaks down at times here, too, more usually through sins of omission than through sins of commission. Sharp realized the something wanting that so many find in much of his writing, even in much that is most beautiful, realized it so keenly that he felt called upon to explain. He explained not directly, it is true, as if in answer to criticism, but none the less definitely in thus affirming his attitude toward legends in the "Sunset of Old Tales": "We owe a debt, indeed, to the few who are truly fit for the task [the collecting of tales from oral tradition], but there are some minds which care very little to hear about things when they can have the things themselves." This statement explains in part why it is that the life of the people, even that part of their life that fronts the past, has escaped him. He prefers his dream, thinking that it is their dream, or the dream of their ancestors. He has, indeed, the thing itself, the Highlander's dream, and when it is given to him to impart that dream fully we forgive him the proud words I have just quoted. The pity of it is he has not always so succeeded through the way he has chosen, and then it is, of course, that we condemn him for the lack of that humility the great dramatic artist must have whereby he must forget himself and so subordinate himself that tradition or life speaks through him.

It is not to be wondered, then, that there is little direct record of folk-lore of his own collecting in his writing,

even when he is writing of folk-topics. There are borrowings in plenty, especially in "Where the Forest Murmurs,"
and even when the collecting seems his own, as it does
in "Earth, Fire, and Water," "Children of Water," and
"Cuilidh Mhoire," it is diamond dust, not diamonds, to
which he gives so beautiful setting.

Just as appealing to Sharp as the old myths themselves
are the localities that tradition or the stories themselves
assign as background to them. He loves Iona not only
for its gray and barren beauty, but because it was here
Columba wrought his wonders. "Iona," which fills the
major part of the volume "The Divine Adventure" gives
title to, is the finest in quality as well as the longest of his
writings that may be called, prosaically, topographical.
They, in their varying ways, are much more than merely
topographical, whether done in the way of "F. M.," as
"Iona" is, and as "From the Hebrid Isles" is, and several
papers from "Where the Forest Murmurs"; or in the way
of "W. S.," as "Literary Geography" is. In this last-
named book, Scott and Stevenson, among others, are put
against the background that inspired their work, as in
"Iona" certain stories are imagined so as to fit their
surroundings and certain legendary history narrated that
is fitting to these surroundings with an appropriateness
almost too exact to be believable. In "Iona," because he
loved the island that inspired its writing beyond any
other of the places he loved greatly, is to be found some
of his very best work, and examples of all kinds of his
writing, as I have said; and even when this "topographical writing," as in some of his magazine articles, is evi-

dently of the sort initially intended to "float cuts," it is very well done, done most often with distinction. At times, of course, it suffers from over-emphasis, as do the descriptive portions of his long stories, but generally he attunes his writing to the genius of the place. This is as true of his letters as of what he wrote for the public, especially true of that series on Algiers from which Mrs. Sharp quotes in her "Memoir." Papers of this sort, papers giving the genius of place, Sharp was happier in, I think, than in those which are more definitely the out-of-door essay. Sharp knew much of birds and small mammals, of trees and plants, with a knowledge that evidently began in childhood, but, as with so much else in his life, this knowledge he never had time to fill out and deepen through patient observation. You must not, then, turn to "Where the Forest Murmurs" to find writing of a kind with that in which Thoreau and Jefferies so finely attained, much less that loving intimacy with the personal side of birds and animals that so humanly tempers the scientific spirit in White of Selborne. Nor is there in them the racy earthiness of Mr. Burroughs. Their greatest asset is their enthusiasm over the beauty of the world they are written to praise; the next greatest their power of catching in words the mood of a landscape; their next greatest their distinction of style, though there are several in which the style is wholly without distinction. Now and then, too, they are valuable for their guesses at the whys and wherefores of things. There are to-day many explanations of what is commonly called "The Lure of the Wild." Is not this as revelatory as any? —

Is this because, in the wilderness, we recover something of what we have lost? . . . Because we newly find ourselves as though surprised into an intimate relationship of which we have been unaware or have indifferently ignored? What a long way the ancestral memory has to go, seeking, like a pale sleuth-hound, among obscure dusks and forgotten nocturnal silences, for the lost trails of the soul! It is not we only, you and I, who look into the still waters of the wilderness and lonely places, and are often dimly perplext, are often troubled we know not how or why: some forgotten reminiscence in us is aroused, some memory, not our own, but yet our heritage is perturbed, footsteps that have immemorially sunk in ancient dusk move furtively along obscure corridors in our brain, the ancestral hunter or fisher awakes, the primitive hillman or woodlander communicates again with old forgotten intimacies and the secret oracular things of lost wisdoms. This is no fanciful challenge of speculation. In the order of psychology it is as logical as in the order of biology is the tracing of our upright posture or the deft and illimitable use of our hands, from unrealizably remote periods wherein the pioneers of man reach slowly forward to inconceivable arrivals.

The weakness of these essays that are like out-of-door essays, but are not out-of-door essays, is their dearth of freshly observed fact. This dearth would not matter so much if there were not so many of them, but a book full of such essays with little original observation will pall, no matter how well written, no matter how interesting the personality of the writer. Thus it is that some of the essays of Jefferies pall, some of those written in his last days, of Jefferies who had in his earlier writing been so objective. In Thoreau there is a happy combination of freshly observed fact with personal comment, and in Mr.

Burroughs a personal element greatly subdued, and presented in most of the essays only through the selective art that has preserved the incidents he relates out of many of a vast store of their kind.

In these "nature studies" of Sharp, as in so much of his writing, there is a great deal of generalization from phenomena superficially observed. He is not so often inaccurate, but he is very often merely repetitive, giving us in beautiful and oftentimes distinguished phrase what others have given us before. Sharp wrote sometimes, I have no doubt, with the thing he describes before him, but oftener, it would seem, from notes, and oftenest, I take it, from memory. Sometimes it is best to write thus from memory. The unessential will fade out, the essential remain; but with Sharp the trouble is that the first observation has often been hurried. He was content with the beauty that he saw when he first noticed the incident; he did not wait to observe what in the further actions of the life observed would make that beautiful incident more significant. It may, of course, be said that all he was after was the impression that the passing incident made upon him. Perhaps so, and if so, more is the pity, because, while, as I have said, one out-of-door essay with little or even with nothing but the personality of the writer may interest, or perhaps two such, or even ten, a book full will be monotonous. At its best, however, his writing of "natural romance" is of great beauty. "Still Waters," for one, is almost perfect, as perfect as this sort of thing may be. It is wrought of his own experiences with just enough of mythological data to give it the texture of old and lasting things.

"The Rainy Hyades," on the other hand, is largely a rehash of folk-lore notes, second-hand work with very little added from experience and very little finely imagined or recaptured by way of ancestral memory. At times it would seem that, poor, tired man, he had to feed his flagging invention from a dictionary of quotations. So, it appears, he has done in his "Winter Stars" as well as in "The Rainy Hyades." As I think over the unevenness of these essays, the beauty of "Still Waters," and the obviousness of these others, I am brought back again to wondering what Sharp would have done had all his time been his to do as he would with. Such wonderment is, of course, idle, idle as that as to what Keats would have done had he lived, for a man's art is judged by what it is, with no tempering of the appraisement by what the man's life has been. Fortunately there is inspiring work in plenty in Sharp, in this, as in other phases of his work, to make readers turn to him when interest in him as a phenomenon of current literature has passed away. It is hard to think of the time when writing so beautiful as that of "Still Waters" will not be sought by lovers of beauty in words and by lovers of beauty in landscape, and when the opening of "The Coming of Dusk" will not be turned to, as the opening of Emerson's "Nature" is turned to to-day.

Were I to attempt to enumerate the critical writings of Sharp, from the "Rossetti" of 1882 to "The Winged Destiny" of 1904, I should run up a catalogue that would exceed any even of Walt Whitman's. For years Sharp lived by criticism, as editor of "The Canterbury Poets" and as reviewer for many of the London journals. To me none of this critical work is significant until he came to write of the movement that carried him to fame, — to fame, I say, because "Fiona Macleod" was famous for a decade, and not only as a mystery, but as a revealer of a new beauty in words, and as a widener of horizons.

I have, I think, by this time made clear what to me is the great strength of William Sharp — his power to revisualize the Celtic past of Scotland and to imagine stories of that past that are as native to it as those handed down in Bardic legend or folk-lore. I have emphasized my belief that in other kinds of writing his attainment is less original, though often beautiful in its imitativeness, and this imitativeness I will explain as being due partly to that quality of the play-actor that was in him as in so many of Celtic blood, partly to his lack of time to hew out for himself a way of his own, and partly to his quick responsiveness to any new beauty pointed out by work that he admired. It was not altogether, however, lack of time that prevented his attainment of a larger originality, an originality in other sorts of writing than the "Sean-chas." Sharp had an unfortunate disbelief in early life in the value of technique. In the preface to the "Romantic Ballads" (1888), for instance, he expressed the belief that "the supreme merit of a poem is not perfection of art, but the quality of the imagination which is the source of such real or approximate perfection." This, as I interpret it, means that a poem, when of perfect art, has back of that perfect art a high imaginative quality; but by his own practice Sharp knows that he thought the quality would suffice without the highest art in its expression. It was this belief that made him leave his work incomplete; he read his verses, no doubt, with the glow in which he wrote them recalled to memory, and without the realization that he had not got down on paper for others half of the creative force that was in him as he wrote.

I have found a reason for a lesser success than the early work of "Fiona Macleod" promised to him in his imitativeness, but in some ways he was handicapped, too, by lack of models to follow. Granted he could have blazed other ways for himself than that of the "Seanchas," he lessened the originality of his attainment by imitation, but if he could not have so blazed other ways he just as surely could have gone further had he had models, or rather good models, to follow, models, for instance, in novels of Highland life. The very fact of there being great realistic stories of Highland life might have made it possible for him to have written a Highland "Silence Farm."

But enough of what might have been: what is is good enough, good enough at its best to treasure among those things that are a lasting part of our lives. However great may be the reaction against his work because of the nine days' wonder about the identity of its creator, certain parts of it, certain tales and certain verses and a play, will hold their own against the years. Through such tales as "The Sad Queen," and such verses as "The Dirge of the Four Cities," and "The House of Usna" even eyes of little vision may see "eternal beauty wandering on her way," leaving about them a glamour as recurrent to the mind as sunset to the skies.

THE END

# APPENDIX

# APPENDIX

PLAYS PRODUCED, IN DUBLIN, BY THE ABBEY
THEATRE COMPANY AND ITS PREDECESSORS,
WITH DATES OF FIRST PERFORMANCES

### IRISH LITERARY THEATRE AT ANTIENT CONCERT ROOMS

May  8, 1899. "The Countess Cathleen."     W. B. Yeats.
May  9, 1899. "The Heather Field."     Edward Martyn.

### IRISH LITERARY THEATRE AT THE GAIETY THEATRE

Feb. 19, 1900. "The Bending of the Bough."  George Moore.
Feb. 19, 1900. "The Last Feast of the Fi-
anna."     Alice Milligan.
Feb. 20, 1900. "Maeve."     Edward Martyn.
Oct. 21, 1901. "Diarmuid and Grania."     W. B. Yeats and
George Moore.
Oct. 21, 1901. "The Twisting of the Rope."  Douglas Hyde.
(The first Gaelic play produced in any theatre.)

### MR. W. G. FAY'S IRISH NATIONAL DRAMATIC COMPANY AT ST. TERESA'S HALL, CLARENDON STREET

Apr.  2, 1902. "Deirdre."     "A. E."
Apr.  2, 1902. "Kathleen ni Houlihan."     W. B. Yeats.

### IRISH NATIONAL DRAMATIC COMPANY AT ANTIENT CONCERT ROOMS

Oct. 29, 1902. "The Sleep of the King."     Seumas O'Cuisin.
Oct. 29, 1902. "The Laying of the Founda-
tions."     Fred Ryan.
Oct. 30, 1902. "A Pot of Broth."     W. B. Yeats.
Oct. 31, 1902. "The Racing Lug."     Seumas O'Cuisin.

### IRISH NATIONAL THEATRE SOCIETY, MOLESWORTH HALL

| | |
|---|---|
| Mar. 14, 1903. "The Hour-Glass." | W. B. Yeats. |
| Mar. 14, 1903. "Twenty-Five." | Lady Gregory. |
| Oct. 8, 1903. "The King's Threshold." | W. B. Yeats. |
| Oct. 8, 1903. "In the Shadow of the Glen." | J. M. Synge. |
| Dec. 3, 1903. "Broken Soil." | Padraic Colum. |
| Jan. 14, 1904. "The Shadowy Waters." | W. B. Yeats. |
| Jan. 14, 1904. "The Townland of Tamney." | Seumas McManus. |
| Feb. 25, 1904. "Riders to the Sea." | J. M. Synge. |

### IRISH NATIONAL THEATRE SOCIETY AT THE ABBEY THEATRE

| | |
|---|---|
| Dec. 27, 1904. "On Baile's Strand." | W. B. Yeats. |
| Dec. 27, 1904. "Spreading the News." | Lady Gregory. |
| Feb. 4, 1905. "The Well of the Saints." | J. M. Synge. |
| Mar. 25, 1905. "Kincora." | Lady Gregory. |
| Apr. 25, 1905. "The Building Fund." | William Boyle. |
| June 9, 1905. "The Land." | Padraic Colum. |

### NATIONAL THEATRE SOCIETY, LTD. (ABBEY COMPANY)

| | |
|---|---|
| Dec. 9, 1905. "The White Cockade." | Lady Gregory. |
| Jan. 20, 1906. "The Eloquent Dempsey." | William Boyle. |
| Feb. 19, 1906. "Hyacinth Halvey." | Lady Gregory. |
| Oct. 20, 1906. "The Gaol Gate." | Lady Gregory. |
| Oct. 20, 1906. "The Mineral Workers." | William Boyle. |
| Nov. 24, 1906. "Deirdre." | W. B. Yeats. |
| Dec. 8, 1906. "The Canavans." | Lady Gregory. |
| Dec. 8, 1906. New Version of "The Shadowy Waters." | W. B. Yeats. |
| Jan. 26, 1907. "The Playboy of the Western World." | J. M. Synge. |
| Feb. 23, 1907. "The Jackdaw." | Lady Gregory. |
| Mar. 9, 1907. "The Rising of the Moon." | Lady Gregory. |
| Apr. 1, 1907. "The Eyes of the Blind." | Miss W. M. Letts. |
| Apr. 3, 1907. "The Poorhouse." | Douglas Hyde and Lady Gregory. |
| Apr. 27, 1907. "Fand." | Wilfred Scawen Blunt |

| | | |
|---|---|---|
| Oct. 3, 1907. | "The Country Dressmaker." | George Fitzmaurice. |
| Oct. 31, 1907. | "Devorgilla." | Lady Gregory. |
| Nov. 21, 1907. | "The Unicorn from the Stars." | W. B. Yeats and Lady Gregory. |
| Feb. 13, 1908. | "The Man who missed the Tide." | W. F. Casey. |
| Feb. 13, 1908. | "The Piper." | "Norreys Connell." |
| Mar. 10, 1908. | "The Piedish." | George Fitzmaurice. |
| Mar. 19, 1908. | "The Golden Helmet." | W. B. Yeats. |
| Apr. 20, 1908. | "The Workhouse Ward." | Lady Gregory. |
| Oct. 1, 1908. | "The Suburban Groove." | W. F. Casey. |
| Oct. 8, 1908. | "The Clancy Name." | Lennox Robinson. |
| Oct. 15, 1908. | "When the Dawn is come." | Thomas MacDonogh. |
| Oct. 21, 1908. | New Version of "The Man who missed the Tide." | W. F. Casey. |
| Feb. 11, 1909. | Revised Version of "Kincora." | Lady Gregory. |
| Mar. 11, 1909. | "Stephen Grey." | D. L. Kelleher. |
| Apr. 1, 1909. | "The Crossroads." | Lennox Robinson. |
| Apr. 1, 1909. | "Time." | "Norreys Connell." |
| Apr. 29, 1909. | "The Glittering Gate." | Lord Dunsany. |
| May 27, 1909. | "An Imaginary Conversation." | "Norreys Connell." |
| Aug. 25, 1909. | "The Showing-up of Blanco Posnet." | Bernard Shaw. |
| Sept. 16, 1909. | "The White Feather." | R. J. Ray. |
| Oct. 14, 1909. | "The Challenge." | Miss W. M. Letts. |
| Nov. 11, 1909. | "The Image." | Lady Gregory. |
| Jan. 13, 1910. | "Deirdre of the Sorrows." | J. M. Synge. |
| Feb. 10, 1910. | "The Green Helmet." | W. B. Yeats. |
| Mar. 2, 1910. | "The Travelling Man." | Lady Gregory. |
| May 12, 1910. | "Thomas Muskerry." | Padraic Colum. |
| May 26, 1910. | "Harvest." | Lennox Robinson. |
| Sept. 28, 1910. | "The Casting-out of Martin Whelan." | R. J. Ray. |
| Oct. 27, 1910. | "Birthright." | T. C. Murray. |
| Nov. 10, 1910. | "The Full Moon." | Lady Gregory. |
| Nov. 24, 1910. | "The Shuiler's Child." [1] | Seumas O'Kelly. |
| Dec. 1, 1910. | "Coats." | Lady Gregory. |

[1] First produced by an amateur company at the Molesworth Hall in 1909.

Jan. 12, 1911. "The Deliverer."     Lady Gregory.

Jan. 26, 1911. "King Argimenes and the Unknown Warrior."     Lord Dunsany.

Feb. 16, 1911. "The Land of Heart's Desire." [1]     W. B. Yeats.

Mar. 30, 1911. "Mixed Marriage."     St. John G. Ervine.

Nov. 23, 1911. "The Interlude of Youth."     Anon., first printed
1554.

Nov. 23, 1911. "The Second Shepherds' Play."     Anon., *circa* 1400.

Nov. 30, 1911. "The Marriage."     Douglas Hyde.

Dec. 7, 1911. "Red Turf."     Rutherford Mayne.

Dec. 16, 1911. Revival of "The Countess
Cathleen."     W. B. Yeats.

Jan. 4, 1912. "The Annunciation."     *circa* 1400.

Jan. 4, 1912. "The Flight into Egypt."     *circa* 1400.

Jan. 11, 1912. "MacDarragh's Wife."     Lady Gregory.

Feb. 1, 1912. Revival of "The Country
Dressmaker."     George Fitzmaurice.

Feb. 16, 1912. "The Tinker and the Fairy."     Douglas Hyde.
(Played in Gaelic.)

Feb. 29, 1912. "The Worlde and the Chylde."     15th century.

Mar. 28, 1912. "Family Failings."     William Boyle.

Apr. 11, 1912. "Patriots."     Lennox Robinson.

June 20, 1912. "Maurice Harte."     T. C. Murray.

July 4, 1912. "The Bogie Men."     Lady Gregory.

Oct. 17, 1912. "The Magnanimous Lover."     St. John G. Ervine.

Nov. 21, 1912. "Damer's Gold."     Lady Gregory.

### TRANSLATIONS OF THE FOLLOWING HAVE BEEN PRODUCED

Apr. 16, 1906. "The Doctor in spite of Himself."     (Molière.) Translated
by Lady Gregory.

Mar. 16, 1907. "Interior."     (Maeterlinck.)

Mar. 19, 1908. "Teja."     (Sudermann.) Translated by Lady Greg-
ory.

Apr. 4, 1909. "The Rogueries of Scapin."     (Molière.) Translated
by Lady Gregory.

[1] First produced at the Avenue Theatre, London, in 1894.

| | | |
|---|---|---|
| Jan. 21, 1909. | "The Miser." | (Molière.) Translated by Lady Gregory. |
| Feb. 24, 1910. | "Mirandolina." | (Goldini.) Translated by Lady Gregory. |
| Jan. 5, 1911. | "Nativity Play." | (Douglas Hyde.) Translated by Lady Gregory. |

# INDEX

Abbey Theatre, organization of company, 13–36.
*All Ireland Review*, 86.
*All on the Irish Shore*, 6.
Allgood, Sara, 19, 22, 23, 24, 26, 27, 28, 211.
Allingham, William, 39.
*Ancient Legends of Ireland*, 51.
Antient Concert Rooms, the, 18, 78, 86, 106, 200.
*Apostle, The*, 111.
*Aran Islands, The*, 168, 187, 188, 191.
Aran Islands, the, 147, 162, 166, 170, 171, 177, 178, 179, 181, 187, 188, 190, 191, 192.
Argyll, 4, 267, 268.
Arnold, Matthew, 3, 59, 255.
Arran, 267.
Arthurian stories, 3, 48.
Austen, Jane, 155, 156.
*Ave*, 73, 76, 94, 99, 108, 109.
Avenue Theatre, London, 25, 50.

*Bards and Saints*, 8.
Barker, Granville, 230.
Barlow, Jane, 1, 7, 148.
Beerbohm, Max, 81.
Belfast, 47.
*Beltaine*, 75, 85.
*Bending of the Bough, The*, 76, 88, 95, 98, 105.
Benson, Sir Frank, 18.
Benson Company, the, 106.
Beowulf, 142.
Berkeley, George, 135.
Bernhardt, Sara, 16.
Bhagavad-Gîta, 117.
Birmingham, George A. (The Rev. Dr. James O. Hannay), 8.
*Birthright*, 216, 217, 218, 219, 222.
Björnson, Björnstjerne, 36.

Black, William, 271, 284.
Blake, William, 38.
Bodley Head, the, 2.
*Book of Saints and Wonders*, 138, 142.
Borrow, George, 161, 165, 173, 179.
Boucicault, Dion, 168.
Boyle, William, 15, 33, 208–215, 238, 239, 240.
  *Building Fund, The*, 209–213; *Eloquent Dempsey, The*, 208, 209, 213; *Family Failings*, 208; *Mineral Workers, The*, 208, 213–214, 238.
Brigit, St., 142, 147, 282.
Brittany, 3, 266.
*Broken Soil*, 32, 202.
Brown, T. E., 4, 5.
Browning, Robert, 50.
Buchanan, Robert, 272.
Buckley, William, 7, 8.
*Building Fund, The*, 208, 209–213, 214.
Bullock, Shan, 7, 214, 234, 236, 270.
Bunyan, John, 285.
Burns, Robert, "Jolly Beggars," 177, 234.
Burroughs, John, 290, 292.
*Bursting of the Bubble, The*, 9.
*By Thrasna River*, 7.

*Calendar of the Saints*, 247.
Cameron, Dr., of Brodick, 283.
Campbell, John F., of Islay, 283, 284.
Campbell, Joseph (Seosamh Mac-Cathmhaoil), 246–250.
  *Judgment*, 247–250; *Mearing Stones*, 247; *The Mountainy Singer*, 247.

# 306 INDEX

𝔒𝔥𝔢 𝔕𝔦𝔳𝔢𝔯𝔰𝔦𝔡𝔢 𝔓𝔯𝔢𝔰𝔰

CAMBRIDGE . MASSACHUSETTS

U . S . A

WITHDRAWN

# THIS BOOK MAY BE KEPT
# FOURTEEN DAYS

and may be renewed once for the same time.
The term expires on the date last stamped
below. The fine for keeping it overtime is
**Two Cents a Day,** Sundays and holidays included.

JAN 1 1927
APR 2 1927
FEB 23 1929
DEC 20 1929
N 8 '46
JUN 29 '52
MAR 24 '56
DEC 4 1964
DEC 17 1966
NOV 6 1970
MAR 19 1975
APR 1973
NOV 27 1979
MAR 11 1981
MAR 31 1991

Irish plays and playwrights, b

3    00063326 1
GOSHEN COLLEGE-GOOD LIBRARY